WHETHER A CHRISTIAN WOMAN
SHOULD BE EDUCATED
AND OTHER WRITINGS FROM
HER INTELLECTUAL CIRCLE

THE
OTHER VOICE
IN
EARLY MODERN
EUROPE

A Series Edited by
Margaret L. King and
Albert Rabil, Jr.

OTHER BOOKS IN THE SERIES

HENRICUS CORNELIUS AGRIPPA
Declamation on the Nobility and Preeminence of the Female Sex
EDITED BY ALBERT RABIL, JR.

LAURA CERETA
Collected Letters
EDITED BY DIANA ROBIN

TULLIA D'ARAGONA
Dialogue on the Infinity of Love
EDITED BY RINALDINA RUSSELL AND BRUCE MERRY

CECILIA FERRAZZI
Autobiography of an Aspiring Saint
EDITED BY ANNE JACOBSON SCHUTTE

MODERATA FONTE
The Worth of Women
EDITED BY VIRGINIA COX

ANTONIA PULCI
Florentine Drama for Convent and Festival
EDITED BY JAMES WYATT COOK

Anna Maria van Schurman

WHETHER A CHRISTIAN WOMAN SHOULD BE EDUCATED AND OTHER WRITINGS FROM HER INTELLECTUAL CIRCLE

Edited and Translated by
Joyce L. Irwin

THE UNIVERSITY OF CHICAGO PRESS
Chicago & London

Joyce L. Irwin is an independent scholar and research associate in the department of philosophy and religion at Colgate University.

The University of Chicago Press, Chicago 60637
The University of Chicago Press, Ltd., London
© 1998 by The University of Chicago
All rights reserved. Published 1998
08 07 06 05 04 03 02 01 00 99   1 2 3 4 5

ISBN: 0-226-84998-8 (cloth)
ISBN: 0-226-84999-6 (paper)

This translation was supported by a generous grant from the
National Endowment for the Humanities.

Library of Congress Cataloging-in-Publication Data

Schurman, Anna Maria van, 1607–1678.
       [Selections. English. 1998]
       Whether a Christian woman should be educated and other writings from her
intellectual circle / Anna Maria van Schurman ; edited and translated by Joyce L.
Irwin.
       p.   cm. — (The other voice in early modern Europe)
       Includes translated selections from the writings of Gijsbert Voet.
       Includes bibliographical references and index.
       ISBN 0-226-84998-8 (hardcover : alk. paper). — ISBN 0-226-84999-6 (pbk. : alk.
paper)
       1. Woman (Christian theology) 2. Woman (Christian theology)—History of
doctrines—17th century—Sources. 3. Women in Christianity. 4. Women in the
Reformed Church—Europe—History—17th century—Sources. 5. Christian women—
Education. 6. Reformed Church—Doctrines. 7. Reformed Church—Doctrines—
History—17th century—Sources. I. Irwin, Joyce L. II. Voet, Gijsbert, 1589–1676.
Selections. English. 1998. III. Title. IV. Series.
BT704.S38   1998
305.42—dc21   98-5295
                                                                                            CIP

CONTENTS

Introduction to the Series *vii*

Introduction: Anna Maria van Schurman and Her Intellectual Circle *1*

Selections from the Writings of Anna Maria van Schurman 23

A Practical Problem:
Whether the Study of Letters Is Fitting for a Christian Woman 25

Correspondence with André Rivet on this Question 39

Correspondence with Other Women 57

Eukleria, chapters 1 and 2 73

Concerning Women, by Gisbertus Voetius 95

Chapter I:
The Natural Status and Condition of Women 97

Chapter II:
The Secular and Political Status of Women 117

Chapter III:
The Spiritual and Ecclesiastical Status of Women 130

Bibliography 139

Index 145

THE OTHER VOICE IN
EARLY MODERN EUROPE:
INTRODUCTION TO THE SERIES

Margaret L. King and Albert Rabil, Jr.

THE OLD VOICE AND THE OTHER VOICE

In western Europe and the United States women are nearing equality in the professions, in business, and in politics. Most enjoy access to education, reproductive rights, and autonomy in financial affairs. Issues vital to women are on the public agenda: equal pay, child care, domestic abuse, breast cancer research, and curricular revision with an eye to the inclusion of women.

These recent achievements have their origins in things women (and some male supporters) said for the first time about six hundred years ago. Theirs is the "other voice," in contradistinction to the "first voice," the voice of the educated men who created Western culture. Coincident with a general reshaping of European culture in the period 1300 to 1700 (called the Renaissance or early modern period), questions of female equality and opportunity were raised that still resound and are still unresolved.

The "other voice" emerged against the backdrop of a three-thousand-year history of misogyny—the hatred of women—rooted in the civilizations related to Western culture: Hebrew, Greek, Roman, and Christian. Misogyny inherited from these traditions pervaded the intellectual, medical, legal, religious, and social systems that developed during the European Middle Ages.

The following pages describe the misogynistic tradition inherited by early modern Europeans, and the new tradition which the "other voice" called into being to challenge reigning assumptions. This review should serve as a framework for the understanding of the texts published in the series "The Other Voice in Early Modern Europe." Introductions specific to each text and author follow this essay in all the volumes of the series. *vii*

THE MISOGYNIST TRADITION, 500 B.C.E.–1500 C.E.

Embedded in the philosophical and medical theories of the ancient Greeks were perceptions of the female as inferior to the male in both mind and body. Similarly, the structure of civil legislation inherited from the ancient Romans was biased against women, and the views on women developed by Christian thinkers out of the Hebrew Bible and the Christian New Testament were negative and disabling. Literary works composed in the vernacular language of ordinary people, and widely recited or read, conveyed these negative assumptions. The social networks within which most women lived—those of the family and the institutions of the Roman Catholic church—were shaped by this misogynist tradition and sharply limited the areas in which women might act in and upon the world.

GREEK PHILOSOPHY AND FEMALE NATURE. Greek biology assumed that women were inferior to men and defined them merely as childbearers and housekeepers. This view was authoritatively expressed in the works of the philosopher Aristotle.

Aristotle thought in dualities. He considered action superior to inaction, form (the inner design or structure of any object) superior to matter, completion to incompletion, possession to deprivation. In each of these dualities, he associated the male principle with the superior quality and the female with the inferior. "The male principle in nature," he argued, "is associated with active, formative and perfected characteristics, while the female is passive, material and deprived, desiring the male in order to become complete.[1] Men are always identified with virile qualities, such as judgment, courage, and stamina; women with their opposites—irrationality, cowardice, and weakness.

The masculine principle was considered to be superior even in the womb. Man's semen, Aristotle believed, created the form of a new human creature, while the female body contributed only matter. (The existence of the ovum, and the other facts of human embryology, were not established until the seventeenth century.) Although the later Greek physician Galen believed that there was a female component in generation, contributed by "female semen," the followers of both Aristotle and Galen saw the male role in human generation as more active and more important.

In the Aristotelian view, the male principle sought always to reproduce itself. The creation of a female was always a mistake, therefore, resulting from an imperfect act of generation. Every female born was consid-

---

1. Aristotle, *Physics*, 1.9 192a20–24, in *The Complete Works of Aristotle*, ed. Jonathan Barnes, rev. Oxford translation, 2 vols. (Princeton, 1984), 1:328.

ered a "defective" or "mutilated" male (as Aristotle's terminology has variously been translated), a "monstrosity" of nature.[2]

For Greek theorists, the biology of males and females was the key to their psychology. The female was softer and more docile, more apt to be despondent, querulous, and deceitful. Being incomplete, moreover, she craved sexual fulfillment in intercourse with a male. The male was intellectual, active, and in control of his passions.

These psychological polarities derived from the theory that the universe consisted of four elements (earth, fire, air, and water), expressed in human bodies as four "humors" (black bile, yellow bile, blood, and phlegm) considered respectively dry, hot, damp, and cold, and corresponding to mental states ("melancholic," "choleric," "sanguine," "phlegmatic"). In this schematization, the male, sharing the principles of earth and fire, was dry and hot; the female, sharing the principles of air and water, was cold and damp.

Female psychology was further affected by her dominant organ, the uterus (womb), *hystera* in Greek. The passions generated by the womb made women lustful, deceitful, talkative, irrational, indeed—when these affects were in excess—"hysterical."

Aristotle's biology also had social and political consequences. If the male principle was superior and the female inferior, then in the household, as in the state, men should rule and women must be subordinate. That hierarchy did not rule out the companionship of husband and wife, whose cooperation was necessary for the welfare of children and the preservation of property. Such mutuality supported male preeminence.

Aristotle's teacher, Plato, suggested a different possibility: that men and women might possess the same virtues. The setting for this proposal is the imaginary and ideal Republic that Plato sketches in his dialogue of that name. Here, for a privileged elite capable of leading wisely, all distinctions of class and wealth dissolve, as do consequently those of gender. Without households or property, as Plato constructs his ideal society, there is no need for the subordination of women. Women may, therefore, be educated to the same level as men to assume leadership responsibilities. Plato's Republic remained imaginary, however. In real societies, the subordination of women remained the norm and the prescription.

The views of women inherited from the Greek philosophical tradition became the basis for medieval thought. In the thirteenth century, the supreme scholastic philosopher Thomas Aquinas, among others, still echoed

---

2. Aristotle, *Generation of Animals*, 2.3 737a27–28 (Barnes, 1:1144).

Aristotle's views of human reproduction, of male and female personalities, and of the preeminent male role in the social hierarchy.

ROMAN LAW AND THE FEMALE CONDITION. Roman law, like Greek philosophy, underlay medieval thought and shaped medieval society. The ancient belief that adult, property-owning men should administer households and make decisions affecting the community at large is the very fulcrum of Roman law.

Around 450 B.C.E., during Rome's Republican era, the community's customary law was recorded (legendarily) on the Twelve Tables, erected in the city's central forum. It was later elaborated by professional jurists whose activity increased in the imperial era, when much new legislation, especially on issues affecting family and inheritance, was passed. This growing, changing body of laws was eventually codified in the *Corpus of Civil Law* under the direction of the emperor Justinian, generations after the empire ceased to be ruled from Rome. That *Corpus*, read and commented upon by medieval scholars from the eleventh century on, inspired the legal systems of most of the cities and kingdoms of Europe.

Laws regarding dowries, divorce, and inheritance most pertain to women. Since those laws aimed to maintain and preserve property, the women concerned were those from the property-owning minority. Their subordination to male family members points to the even greater subordination of lower-class and slave women, about whom the laws speak little.

In the early Republic, the *paterfamilias*, "father of the family," possessed *patria potestas*, "paternal power." The term *pater*, "father," in both these cases does not necessarily mean biological father, but householder. The father was the person who owned the household's property and, indeed, its human members. The *paterfamilias* had absolute power—including the power, rarely exercised, of life or death—over his wife, his children, and his slaves, as much as over his cattle.

Male children could be "emancipated," an act that granted legal autonomy and the right to own property. Males over the age of fourteen could be emancipated by a special grant from the father, or automatically by their father's death. But females never could be emancipated; instead, they passed from the authority of their father to a husband or, if widowed or orphaned while still unmarried, to a guardian or tutor.

Marriage under its traditional form placed the woman under her husband's authority, or *manus*. He could divorce her on grounds of adultery, drinking wine, or stealing from the household, but she could not divorce him. She could possess no property in her own right, nor bequeath any to her children upon her death. When her husband died, the household property passed not to her but to his male heirs. And when her father died, she had no claim to any family inheritance, which was directed to her brothers or more remote male relatives. The effect of these laws was to exclude women from civil society, itself based on property ownership.

In the later Republican and Imperial periods, these rules were significantly modified. Women rarely married according to the traditional form, but according to the form of "free" marriage. That practice allowed a woman to remain under her father's authority, to possess property given her by her father (most frequently the "dowry," recoverable from the husband's household in the event of his death), and to inherit from her father. She could also bequeath property to her own children and divorce her husband, just as he could divorce her.

Despite this greater freedom, women still suffered enormous disability under Roman law. Heirs could belong only to the father's side, never the mother's. Moreover, although she could bequeath her property to her children, she could not establish a line of succession in doing so. A woman was "the beginning and end of her own family," growled the jurist Ulpian. Moreover, women could play no public role. They could not hold public office, represent anyone in a legal case, or even witness a will. Women had only a private existence, and no public personality.

The dowry system, the guardian, women's limited ability to transmit wealth, and their total political disability are all features of Roman law adopted, although modified according to local customary laws, by the medieval communities of western Europe.

CHRISTIAN DOCTRINE AND WOMEN'S PLACE. The Hebrew Bible and the Christian New Testament authorized later writers to limit women to the realm of the family and to burden them with the guilt of original sin. The passages most fruitful for this purpose were the creation narratives in Genesis and sentences from the Epistles defining women's role within the Christian family and community.

Each of the first two chapters of Genesis contains a creation narrative. In the first "God created humankind in his image, in the image of God he created them; male and female he created them" (NRSV, Genesis 1:27). In the second, God created Eve from Adam's rib (2:21–23). Christian theologians relied principally on Genesis 2 for their understanding of the relation between man and woman, interpreting the creation of Eve from Adam as proof of her subordination to him.

The creation story in Genesis 2 leads to that of the temptations in

Genesis 3: of Eve by the wily serpent, and of Adam by Eve. As read by Christian theologians from Tertullian to Thomas Aquinas, the narrative made Eve responsible for the Fall and its consequences. She instigated the act; she deceived her husband; she suffered the greater punishment. Her disobedience made it necessary for Jesus to be incarnated and to die on the cross. From the pulpit, moralists and preachers for centuries conveyed to women the guilt that they bore for original sin.

The Epistles offered advice to early Christians on building communities of the faithful. Among the matters to be regulated was the place of women. Paul offered views favorable to women in Galatians 3:28: "There is neither Jew nor Greek, there is neither slave nor free, there is neither male nor female; for you are all one in Christ Jesus." Paul also referred to women as his coworkers and placed them on a par with himself and his male co-workers (Philippians 4:2–3; Romans 16:1–3; 1 Corinthians 16:19). Elsewhere Paul limited women's possibilities: "But I want you to understand that the head of every man is Christ, the head of a woman is her husband, and the head of Christ is God" (1 Corinthians 11:3).

Biblical passages by later writers (though attributed to Paul) enjoined women to forego jewels, expensive clothes, and elaborate coiffures; and they forbade women to "teach or have authority over men," telling them to "learn in silence with all submissiveness" as is proper for one responsible for sin, consoling them however with the thought that they would be saved through childbearing (1 Timothy 2:9–15). Other texts among the later Epistles defined women as the weaker sex, and emphasized their subordination to their husbands (1 Peter 3:7; Colossians 3:18; Ephesians 5:22–23).

These passages from the New Testament became the arsenal employed by theologians of the early church to transmit negative attitudes toward women to medieval Christian culture—above all, Tertullian ("On the Apparel of Women"), Jerome (*Against Jovinian*), and Augustine (*The Literal Meaning of Genesis*).

THE IMAGE OF WOMEN IN MEDIEVAL LITERATURE. The philosophical, legal, and religious traditions born in antiquity formed the basis of the medieval intellectual synthesis wrought by trained thinkers, mostly clerics, writing in Latin and based largely in universities. The vernacular literary tradition that developed alongside the learned tradition also spoke about female nature and women's roles. Medieval stories, poems, and epics were infused with misogyny. They portrayed most women as lustful and deceitful, while praising good housekeepers and loyal wives, or replicas of the Virgin Mary, or the female saints and martyrs.

There is an exception in the movement of "courtly love" that evolved in southern France from the twelfth century. Courtly love was the erotic love between a nobleman and noblewoman, the latter usually superior in social rank. It was always adulterous. From the conventions of courtly love derive modern Western notions of romantic love. The phenomenon has had an impact disproportionate to its size, for it affected only a tiny elite, and very few women. The exaltation of the female lover probably does not reflect a higher evaluation of women, or a step toward their sexual liberation. More likely it gives expression to the social and sexual tensions besetting the knightly class at a specific historical juncture.

The literary fashion of courtly love was on the wane by the thirteenth century, when the widely read *Romance of the Rose* was composed in French by two authors of significantly different dispositions. Guillaume de Lorris composed the initial four thousand verses around 1235, and Jean de Meun added about seventeen thousand verses—more than four times the original—around 1265.

The fragment composed by Guillaume de Lorris stands squarely in the courtly love tradition. Here the poet, in a dream, is admitted into a walled garden where he finds a magic fountain in which a rosebush is reflected. He longs to pick one rose but the thorns around it prevent his doing so, even as he is wounded by arrows from the God of Love, whose commands he agrees to obey. The remainder of this part of the poem recounts the poet's unsuccessful efforts to pluck the rose.

The longer part of the *Romance* by Jean de Meun also describes a dream. But here allegorical characters give long didactic speeches, providing a social satire on a variety of themes, including those pertaining to women. Love is an anxious and tormented state, the poem explains, women are greedy and manipulative, marriage is miserable, beautiful women are lustful, ugly ones cease to please, and a chaste woman is as rare as a black swan.

Shortly after Jean de Meun completed *The Romance of the Rose*, Mathéolus penned his *Lamentations*, a long Latin diatribe against marriage translated into French about a century later. The *Lamentations* sum up medieval attitudes toward women, and they provoked the important response by Christine de Pizan in her *Book of the City of Ladies*.

In 1355, Giovanni Boccaccio wrote *Il Corbaccio*, another antifeminist manifesto, though ironically by an author whose other works pioneered new directions in Renaissance thought. The former husband of his lover appears to Boccaccio, condemning his unmoderated lust and detailing the defects of women. Boccaccio concedes at the end "how much men naturally surpass women in nobility"[3] and is cured of his desires.

WOMEN'S ROLES: THE FAMILY. The negative perceptions of women expressed in the intellectual tradition are also implicit in the actual roles that women played in European society. Assigned to subordinate positions in the household and the church, they were barred from significant participation in public life.

Medieval European households, like those in antiquity and in non-Western civilizations, were headed by males. It was the male serf, or peasant, feudal lord, town merchant, or citizen who was polled or taxed or who succeeded to an inheritance or had any acknowledged public role, although his wife or widow could stand on a temporary basis as a surrogate for him. From about 1100, the position of property-holding males was enhanced further. Inheritance was confined to the male, or agnate, line—with depressing consequences for women.

A wife never fully belonged to her husband's family or a daughter to her father's family. She left her father's house young to marry whomever her parents chose. Her dowry was managed by her husband and normally passed to her children by him at her death.

A married woman's life was occupied nearly constantly with cycles of pregnancy, childbearing, and lactation. Women bore children through all the years of their fertility, and many died in childbirth before the end of that term. They also bore responsibility for raising young children up to six or seven. That responsibility was shared in the propertied classes, since it was common for a wet nurse to take over the job of breastfeeding, and servants took over other chores.

Women trained their daughters in the household responsibilities appropriate to their status, nearly always in tasks associated with textiles: spinning, weaving, sewing, embroidering. Their sons were sent out of the house as apprentices or students, or their training was assumed by fathers in later childhood and adolescence. On the death of her husband, a woman's children became the responsibility of his family. She generally did not take "his" children with her to a new marriage or back to her father's house, except sometimes in artisan classes.

Women also worked. Rural peasants performed farm chores, merchant wives often practiced their husbands' trades, the unmarried daughters of the urban poor worked as servants or prostitutes. All wives produced or embellished textiles and did the housekeeping, while wealthy ones man-

---

3. Giovanni Boccaccio, *The Corbaccio or The Labyrinth of Love,* trans. and ed. Anthony K. Cassell (Binghamton, N.Y.; rev. paper ed., 1993), 71.

aged servants. These labors were unpaid or poorly paid, but often contributed substantially to family wealth.

WOMEN'S ROLES: THE CHURCH. Membership in a household, whether a father's or a husband's, meant for women a lifelong subordination to others. In western Europe, the Roman Catholic church offered an alternative to the career of wife and mother. A woman could enter a convent parallel in function to the monasteries for men that evolved in the early Christian centuries.

In the convent, a woman pledged herself to a celibate life, lived according to strict community rules, and worshiped daily. Often the convent offered training in Latin, allowing some women to become considerable scholars and authors, as well as scribes, artists, and musicians. For women who chose the conventual life, the benefits could be enormous, but for numerous others placed in convents by paternal choice, the life could be restrictive and burdensome.

The conventual life declined as an alternative for women as the modern age approached. Reformed monastic institutions resisted responsibility for related female orders. The church increasingly restricted female institutional life by insisting on closer male supervision.

Women often sought other options. Some joined the communities of laywomen that sprang up spontaneously in the thirteenth century in the urban zones of western Europe, especially in Flanders and Italy. Some joined the heretical movements flourishing in late medieval Christendom, whose anticlerical and often antifamily positions particularly appealed to women. In these communities, some women were acclaimed as "holy women" or "saints," while others often were condemned as frauds or heretics.

Though the options offered to women by the church were sometimes less than satisfactory, sometimes they were richly rewarding. After 1520, the convent remained an option only in Roman Catholic territories. Protestantism engendered an ideal of marriage as a heroic endeavor, and appeared to place husband and wife on a more equal footing. Sermons and treatises, however, still called for female subordination and obedience.

THE OTHER VOICE, 1300–1700

Misogyny was so long established in European culture when the modern era opened that to dismantle it was a monumental labor. The process began as part of a larger cultural movement that entailed the critical reexamination of ideas inherited from the ancient and medieval past. The humanists launched that critical reexamination.

THE HUMANIST FOUNDATION. Originating in Italy in the fourteenth century, humanism quickly became the dominant intellectual movement in Europe. Spreading in the sixteenth century from Italy to the rest of Europe, it fueled the literary, scientific, and philosophical movements of the era, and laid the basis for the eighteenth-century Enlightenment.

Humanists regarded the scholastic philosophy of medieval universities as out of touch with the realities of urban life. They found in the rhetorical discourse of classical Rome a language adapted to civic life and public speech. They learned to read, speak, and write classical Latin, and eventually classical Greek. They founded schools to teach others to do so, establishing the pattern for elementary and secondary education for the next three hundred years.

In the service of complex government bureaucracies, humanists employed their skills to write eloquent letters, deliver public orations, and formulate public policy. They developed new scripts for copying manuscripts and used the new printing press for the dissemination of texts, for which they created methods of critical editing.

Humanism was a movement led by men who accepted the evaluation of women in ancient texts and generally shared the misogynist perceptions of their culture. (Female humanists, as will be seen, did not.) Yet humanism also opened the door to the critique of the misogynist tradition. By calling authors, texts, and ideas into question, it made possible the fundamental rereading of the whole intellectual tradition that was required in order to free women from cultural prejudice and social subordination.

A DIFFERENT CITY. The other voice first appeared when, after so many centuries, the accumulation of misogynist concepts evoked a response from a capable female defender, Christine de Pizan. Introducing her *Book of the City of Ladies* (1405), she described how she was affected by reading Mathéolus's *Lamentations:* "Just the sight of this book . . . made me wonder how it happened that so many different men . . . are so inclined to express both in speaking and in their treatises and writings so many wicked insults about women and their behavior."[4] These statements impelled her to detest herself "and the entire feminine sex, as though we were monstrosities in nature."[5]

The remainder of the *Book of the City of Ladies* presents a justification of the female sex and a vision of an ideal community of women. A pioneer,

---

4. Christine de Pizan, *The Book of the City of Ladies,* trans. Earl Jeffrey Richards; foreword by Marina Warner (New York, 1982), 1.1.1., pp. 3–4.

5. Ibid., 1.1.1–2, p. 5.

she has not only received the misogynist message, but she rejects it. From the fourteenth to seventeenth century, a huge body of literature accumulated that responded to the dominant tradition.

The result was a literary explosion consisting of works by both men and women, in Latin and in vernacular languages: works enumerating the achievements of notable women; works rebutting the main accusations made against women; works arguing for the equal education of men and women; works defining and redefining women's proper role in the family, at court, and in public; and works describing women's lives and experiences. Recent monographs and articles have begun to hint at the great range of this phenomenon, involving probably several thousand titles. The protofeminism of these "other voices" constitute a significant fraction of the literary product of the early modern era.

THE CATALOGUES. Around 1365, the same Boccaccio whose *Corbaccio* rehearses the usual charges against female nature wrote another work, *Concerning Famous Women*. A humanist treatise drawing on classical texts, it praised 106 notable women—100 of them from pagan Greek and Roman antiquity, and 6 from the religious and cultural tradition since antiquity—and helped make all readers aware of a sex normally condemned or forgotten. Boccaccio's outlook, nevertheless, was misogynist, for it singled out for praise those women who possessed the traditional virtues of chastity, silence, and obedience. Women who were active in the public realm, for example, rulers and warriors, were depicted as suffering terrible punishments for entering into the masculine sphere. Women were his subject, but Boccaccio's standard remained male.

Christine de Pizan's *Book of the City of Ladies* contains a second catalogue, one responding specifically to Boccaccio's. Where Boccaccio portrays female virtue as exceptional, she depicts it as universal. Many women in history were leaders, or remained chaste despite the lascivious approaches of men, or were visionaries and brave martyrs.

The work of Boccaccio inspired a series of catalogues of illustrious women of the biblical, classical, Christian, and local past: works by Alvaro de Luna, Jacopo Filippo Foresti (1497), Brantôme, Pierre Le Moyne, Pietro Paolo de Ribera (who listed 845 figures), and many others. Whatever their embedded prejudices, these catalogues of illustrious women drove home to the public the possibility of female excellence.

THE DEBATE. At the same time, many questions remained: Could a woman be virtuous? Could she perform noteworthy deeds? Was she even, strictly speaking, of the same human species as men? These questions were debated over four centuries, in French, German, Italian, Spanish, and English, by authors male and female, among Catholics, Protestants, and Jews, in ponderous volumes and breezy pamphlets. The whole literary phenomenon has been called the *querelle des femmes*, the "woman question."

The opening volley of this battle occurred in the first years of the fifteenth century, in a literary debate sparked by Christine de Pizan. She exchanged letters critical of Jean de Meun's contribution to the *Romance of the Rose* with two French humanists and royal secretaries, Jean de Montreuil and Gontier Col. When the matter became public, Jean Gerson, one of Europe's leading theologians, supported de Pizan's arguments against de Meun, for the moment silencing the opposition.

The debate resurfaced repeatedly over the next two hundred years. *The Triumph of Women* (1438) by Juan Rodríguez de la Camara (or Juan Rodríguez del Padron) struck a new note by presenting arguments for the superiority of women to men. *The Champion of Women* (1440–42) by Martin Le Franc addresses once again the misogynist claims of *The Romance of the Rose*, and offers counterevidence of female virtue and achievement.

A cameo of the debate on women is included in *The Courtier*, one of the most read books of the era, published by the Italian Baldassare Castiglione in 1528 and immediately translated into other European vernaculars. *The Courtier* depicts a series of evenings at the court of the Duke of Urbino in which many men and some women of the highest social stratum amuse themselves by discussing a range of literary and social issues. The "woman question" is a pervasive theme throughout, and the third of its four books is devoted entirely to that issue.

In a verbal duel, Gasparo Pallavicino and Giuliano de' Medici present the main claims of the two traditions—the prevailing misogynist one, and the newly emerging alternative one. Gasparo argues the innate inferiority of women and their inclination to vice. Only in bearing children do they profit the world. Giuliano counters that women share the same spiritual and mental capacities as men and may excel in wisdom and action. Men and women are of the same essence: just as no stone can be more perfectly a stone than another, so no human being can be more perfectly human than others, whether male or female. It was an astonishing assertion, boldly made to an audience as large as all Europe.

THE TREATISES. Humanism provided the materials for a positive counterconcept to the misogyny embedded in scholastic philosophy and law, and inherited from the Greek, Roman, and Christian pasts. A series of humanist treatises on marriage and family, on education and deportment, and on the nature of women helped construct these new perspectives.

The works by Francesco Barbaro and Leon Battista Alberti, respectively *On Marriage* (1415) and *On the Family* (1434–37), far from defending female equality, reasserted women's responsibilities for rearing children and managing the housekeeping while being obedient, chaste, and silent. Nevertheless, they served the cause of reexamining the issue of women's nature by placing domestic issues at the center of scholarly concern and reopening the pertinent classical texts. In addition, Barbaro emphasized the companionate nature of marriage and the importance of a wife's spiritual and mental qualities for the well-being of the family.

These themes reappear in later humanist works on marriage and the education of women by Juan Luis Vives and Erasmus. Both were moderately sympathetic to the condition of women, without reaching beyond the usual masculine prescriptions for female behavior.

An outlook more favorable to women characterizes the nearly unknown work *In Praise of Women* (ca. 1487) by the Italian humanist Bartolommeo Goggio. In addition to providing a catalogue of illustrious women, Goggio argued that male and female are the same in essence, but that women (reworking from quite a new angle the Adam and Eve narrative) are actually superior. In the same vein, the Italian humanist Mario Equicola asserted the spiritual equality of men and women in *On Women* (1501). In 1525, Galeazzo Flavio Capra (or Capella) published his work *On the Excellence and Dignity of Women*. This humanist tradition of treatises defending the worthiness of women culminates in the work of Henricus Cornelius Agrippa, *On the Nobility and Preeminence of the Female Sex*. No work by a male humanist more succinctly or explicitly presents the case for female dignity.

THE WITCH BOOKS. While humanists grappled with the issues pertaining to women and family, other learned men turned their attention to what they perceived as a very great problem: witches. Witch-hunting manuals, explorations of the witch phenomenon, and even defenses of witches are not at first glance pertinent to the tradition of the other voice. But they do relate in this way: most accused witches were women. The hostility aroused by supposed witch activity is comparable to the hostility aroused by women. The evil deeds the victims of the hunt were charged with were exaggerations of the vices to which, many believed, all women were prone.

The connection between the witch accusation and the hatred of women is explicit in the notorious witch-hunting manual, *The Hammer of Witches* (1486), by two Dominican inquisitors, Heinrich Krämer and Jacob Sprenger. Here the inconstancy, deceitfulness, and lustfulness traditionally associated with women are depicted in exaggerated form as the core features of witch behavior. These inclined women to make a bargain with the devil—sealed by sexual intercourse—by which they acquired unholy powers. Such bizarre claims, far from being rejected by rational men, were broadcast by intellectuals. The German Ulrich Molitur, the Frenchman Nicolas Rémy, the Italian Stefano Guazzo coolly informed the public of sinister orgies and midnight pacts with the devil. The celebrated French jurist, historian, and political philosopher Jean Bodin argued that, because women were especially prone to diabolism, regular legal procedures could properly be suspended in order to try those accused of this "exceptional crime."

A few experts, such as the physician Johann Weyer, a student of Agrippa's, raised their voices in protest. In 1563, Weyer explained the witch phenomenon thus, without discarding belief in diabolism: the devil deluded foolish old women afflicted by melancholia, causing them to believe that they had magical powers. His rational skepticism, which had good credibility in the community of the learned, worked to revise the conventional views of women and witchcraft.

WOMEN'S WORKS. To the many categories of works produced on the question of women's worth must be added nearly all works written by women. A woman writing was in herself a statement of women's claim to dignity.

Only a few women wrote anything prior to the dawn of the modern era, for three reasons. First, they rarely received the education that would enable them to write. Second, they were not admitted to the public roles—as administrator, bureaucrat, lawyer or notary, university professor—in which they might gain knowledge of the kinds of things the literate public thought worth writing about. Third, the culture imposed silence upon women, considering speaking out a form of unchastity. Given these conditions, it is remarkable that any women wrote. Those who did before the fourteenth century were almost always nuns or religious women whose isolation made their pronouncements more acceptable.

From the fourteenth century on, the volume of women's writings increased. Women continued to write devotional literature, although not always as cloistered nuns. They also wrote diaries, often intended as keepsakes for their children; books of advice to their sons and daughters; letters to family members and friends; and family memoirs, in a few cases elaborate enough to be considered histories.

A few women wrote works directly concerning the "woman question," and some of these, such as the humanists Isotta Nogarola, Cassandra

Fedele, Laura Cereta, and Olympia Morata, were highly trained. A few were professional writers, living by the income of their pen: the very first among them Christine de Pizan, noteworthy in this context as in so many others. In addition to *The Book of the City of Ladies* and her critiques of *The Romance of the Rose*, she wrote *The Treasure of the City of Ladies* (a guide to social decorum for women), an advice book for her son, much courtly verse, and a full-scale history of the reign of King Charles V of France.

WOMEN PATRONS. Women who did not themselves write but encouraged others to do so boosted the development of an alternative tradition. Highly placed women patrons supported authors, artists, musicians, poets, and learned men. Such patrons, drawn mostly from the Italian elites and the courts of northern Europe, figure disproportionately as the dedicatees of the important works of early feminism.

For a start, it might be noted that the catalogues of Boccaccio and Alvaro de Luna were dedicated to the Florentine noblewoman Andrea Acciaiuoli and to Doña María, first wife of King Juan II of Castile, while the French translation of Boccaccio's work was commissioned by Anne of Brittany, wife of King Charles VIII of France. The humanist treatises of Goggio, Equicola, Vives, and Agrippa were dedicated, respectively, to Eleanora of Aragon, wife of Ercole I d'Este, duke of Ferrara; to Margherita Cantelma of Mantua; to Catherine of Aragon, wife of King Henry VIII of England; and to Margaret, duchess of Austria and regent of the Netherlands. As late as 1696, Mary Astell's *Serious Proposal to the Ladies, for the Advancement of Their True and Greatest Interest* was dedicated to Princess Ann of Denmark.

These authors presumed that their efforts would be welcome to female patrons, or they may have written at the bidding of those patrons. Silent themselves, perhaps even unresponsive, these loftily placed women helped shape the tradition of the other voice.

THE ISSUES. The literary forms and patterns in which the tradition of the other voice presented itself have now been sketched. It remains to highlight the major issues about which this tradition crystallizes. In brief, there are four problems to which our authors return again and again, in plays and catalogues, in verse and in letters, in treatises and dialogues, in every language: the problem of chastity, the problem of power, the problem of speech, and the problem of knowledge. Of these the greatest, preconditioning the others, is the problem of chastity.

THE PROBLEM OF CHASTITY. In traditional European culture, as in those of antiquity and others around the globe, chastity was perceived as woman's quintessential virtue—in contrast to courage, or generosity, or leadership, or rationality, seen as virtues characteristic of men. Opponents of women charged them with insatiable lust. Women themselves and their defenders—without disputing the validity of the standard—responded that women were capable of chastity.

The requirement of chastity kept women at home, silenced them, isolated them, left them in ignorance. It was the source of all other impediments. Why was it so important to the society of men, of whom chastity was not required, and who, more often than not, considered it their right to violate the chastity of any woman they encountered?

Female chastity ensured the continuity of the male-headed household. If a man's wife was not chaste, he could not be sure of the legitimacy of his offspring. If they were not his, and they acquired his property, it was not his household, but some other man's, that had endured. If his daughter was not chaste, she could not be transferred to another man's household as his wife, and he was dishonored.

The whole system of the integrity of the household and the transmission of property was bound up in female chastity. Such a requirement pertained only to property-owning classes, of course. Poor women could not expect to maintain their chastity, least of all if they were in contact with high-status men to whom all women but those of their own household were prey.

In Catholic Europe, the requirement of chastity was further buttressed by moral and religious imperatives. Original sin was inextricably linked with the sexual act. Virginity was seen as heroic virtue, far more impressive than, say, the avoidance of idleness or greed. Monasticism, the cultural institution that dominated medieval Europe for centuries, was grounded in the renunciation of the flesh. The Catholic reform of the eleventh century imposed a similar standard on all the clergy, and a heightened awareness of sexual requirements on all the laity. Although men were asked to be chaste, female unchastity was much worse: it led to the devil, as Eve had led mankind to sin.

To such requirements, women and their defenders protested their innocence. Following the example of holy women who had escaped the requirements of family and sought the religious life, some women began to conceive of female communities as alternatives both to family and to the cloister. Christine de Pizan's city of ladies was such a community. Moderata Fonte and Mary Astell envisioned others. The luxurious salons of the French *précieuses* of the seventeenth century, or the comfortable English drawing rooms of the next, may have been born of the same impulse. Here women might not only escape, if briefly, the subordinate position that life in the family entailed, but they might make claims to power, exercise their capacity for speech, and display their knowledge.

THE PROBLEM OF POWER. Women were excluded from power: the whole cultural tradition insisted upon it. Only men were citizens, only men bore arms, only men could be chiefs or lords or kings. There were exceptions that did not disprove the rule, when wives or widows or mothers took the place of men, awaiting their return or the maturation of a male heir. A woman who attempted to rule in her own right was perceived as an anomaly, a monster, at once a deformed woman and an insufficient male, sexually confused and, consequently, unsafe.

The association of such images with women who held or sought power explains some otherwise odd features of early modern culture. Queen Elizabeth I of England, one of the few women to hold full regal authority in European history, played with such male/female images—positive ones, of course—in representing herself to her subjects. She was a prince, and manly, even though she was female. She was also (she claimed) virginal, a condition absolutely essential if she was to avoid the attacks of her opponents. Catherine de' Medici, who ruled France as widow and regent for her sons, also adopted such imagery in defining her position. She chose as one symbol the figure of Artemisia, an androgynous ancient warrior-heroine, who combined a female persona with masculine powers.

Power in a woman, without such sexual imagery, seems to have been indigestible by the culture. A rare note was struck by the Englishman Sir Thomas Elyot in his *Defence of Good Women* (1540), justifying both women's participation in civic life and their prowess in arms. The old tune was sung by the Scots reformer John Knox in his *First Blast of the Trumpet against the Monstrous Regiment of Women* (1558), for whom rule by women, defects in nature, was a hideous contradiction in terms.

The confused sexuality of the imagery of female potency was not reserved for rulers. Any woman who excelled was likely to be called an Amazon, recalling the self-mutilated warrior women of antiquity who repudiated all men, gave up their sons, and raised only their daughters. She was often said to have "exceeded her sex," or to have possessed "masculine virtue"—as the very fact of conspicuous excellence conferred masculinity, even on the female subject. The catalogues of notable women often showed those female heroes dressed in armor, armed to the teeth, like men. Amazonian heroines romp through the epics of the age—Ariosto's

Orlando Furioso (1532), Spenser's *Faerie Queene* (1590–1609). Excellence in a woman was perceived as a claim for power, and power was reserved for the masculine realm. A woman who possessed either was masculinized, and lost title to her own female identity.

THE PROBLEM OF SPEECH. Just as power had a sexual dimension when it was claimed by women, so did speech. A good woman spoke little. Excessive speech was an indication of unchastity. By speech women seduced men. Eve had lured Adam into sin by her speech. Accused witches were commonly accused of having spoken abusively, or irrationally, or simply too much. As enlightened a figure as Francesco Barbaro insisted on silence in a woman, which he linked to her perfect unanimity with her husband's will and her unblemished virtue (her chastity). Another Italian humanist, Leonardo Bruni, in advising a noblewoman on her studies, barred her not from speech, but from public speaking. That was reserved for men.

Related to the problem of speech was that of costume, another, if silent, form of self-expression. Assigned the task of pleasing men as their primary occupation, elite women often tended to elaborate costume, hairdressing, and the use of cosmetics. Clergy and secular moralists alike condemned these practices. The appropriate function of costume and adornment was to announce the status of a woman's husband or father. Any further indulgence in adornment was akin to unchastity.

THE PROBLEM OF KNOWLEDGE. When the Italian noblewoman Isotta Nogarola had begun to attain a reputation as a humanist, she was accused of incest—a telling instance of the association of learning in women with unchastity. That chilling association inclined any woman who was educated to deny that she was, or to make exaggerated claims of heroic chastity.

If educated women were pursued with suspicions of sexual misconduct, women seeking an education faced an even more daunting obstacle: the assumption that women were by nature incapable of learning, that reason was a particularly masculine ability. Just as they proclaimed their chastity, women and their defenders insisted upon their capacity for learning. The major work by a male writer on female education—*On the Education of a Christian Woman*, by Juan Luis Vives (1523)—granted female capacity for intellection, but argued still that a woman's whole education was to be shaped around the requirement of chastity and a future within the household. Female writers of the following generations—Marie de Gournay in France, Anna Maria van Schurman in Holland, Mary Astell in England—began to envision other possibilities.

The pioneers of female education were the Italian women humanists who managed to attain a Latin literacy and knowledge of classical and Christian literature equivalent to that of prominent men. Their works implicitly and explicitly raise questions about women's social roles, defining problems that beset women attempting to break out of the cultural limits that had bound them. Like Christine de Pizan, who achieved an advanced education through her father's tutoring and her own devices, their bold questioning makes clear the importance of training. Only when women were educated to the same standard as male leaders would they be able to raise that other voice and insist on their dignity as human beings morally, intellectually, and legally equal to men.

THE OTHER VOICE. The other voice, a voice of protest, was mostly female, but also male. It spoke in the vernaculars and in Latin, in treatises and dialogues, plays and poetry, letters and diaries and pamphlets. It battered at the wall of misogynist beliefs that encircled women and raised a banner announcing its claims. The female was equal (or even superior) to the male in essential nature—moral, spiritual, intellectual. Women were capable of higher education, of holding positions of power and influence in the public realm, and of speaking and writing persuasively. The last bastion of masculine supremacy, centered on the notions of a woman's primary domestic responsibility and the requirement of female chastity, was not as yet assaulted—although visions of productive female communities as alternatives to the family indicated an awareness of the problem.

During the period 1300 to 1700, the other voice remained only a voice, and one only dimly heard. It did not result—yet—in an alteration of social patterns. Indeed, to this day, they have not entirely been altered. Yet the call for justice issued as long as six centuries ago by those writing in the tradition of the other voice must be recognized as the source and origin of the mature feminist tradition and of the realignment of social institutions accomplished in the modern age.

We would like to thank the volume editors in this series, who responded with many suggestions to an earlier draft of this introduction, making it a collaborative enterprise. Many of their suggestions and criticisms have resulted in revisions of this introduction, though we remain responsible for the final product.

PROJECTED TITLES IN THE SERIES

Cassandra Fedele, *Letters and Orations*, edited and translated by Diana Robin

Veronica Franco, *Selected Poems and Letters*, edited and translated by Margaret Rosenthal and Ann Rosalind Jones

Lucrezia Marinella, *The Nobility and Excellence of Women*, edited and translated by Anne Dunhill

Arcangela Tarabotti, *Paternal Tyranny*, edited and translated by Letizia Panizza

INTRODUCTION:
ANNA VAN SCHURMAN AND HER
INTELLECTUAL CIRCLE

THE OTHER VOICE

Women who wanted to gain the respect and affection of men in seventeenth-century Europe had to apologize for speaking up. Those who spoke too loudly or too impertinently would never earn favor and might work against the cause of women rather than for it. Anna Maria van Schurman was not a protester, for she had been thoroughly enculturated as a properly modest young woman of conservative seventeenth-century Dutch society. Behind her respectful, demure exterior, however, lay an intensity of purpose and firmness of conviction that belied her apparent submissiveness. While always very deferential to the men who served as her teachers, mentors, publicists, and pastors, she was also conscious of the unrealized capabilities of women in her time, and she lent encouragement to other women attempting to develop their intellectual potential. Insisting that she was not an anomaly but that women in general were capable of learning, she exerted significant influence for the cause of women's education both by advocating it and by serving as an incontestable example. Puzzling and disappointing as it may have been to her admirers that she later rejected the life of the intellect, it was a choice that brought her both social and spiritual emancipation. Her independent act of joining a breakaway religious movement was a bold rejection of the polite society that had shaped and in some ways confined her. In the religious community that she joined, she found spiritual friendship with both men and women which in her view surpassed the value of fame or social status. While renouncing her earlier views, she continued to use her intellectual ability and her supportive personality to influence others to find fulfillment, now no longer in the life of the mind but in a life of love and service to others.

CHURCH AND SOCIETY IN THE NETHERLANDS

Renaissance and Reformation, the two major movements of the Early Modern era, ran parallel in many respects and opposite in other respects. Common to both was a rejection of clerical hierarchicalism and clerical domination of education. The moral shortcomings of popes and priests undermined their authority and encouraged the new belief that every Christian was at least theoretically equal to every other Christian, ordained or lay, male or female. The search for a purer version of Christianity led proponents of this new view to read the Bible and early Christian writers afresh, without the intellectual framework that medieval scholasticism had constructed. Criticism of institutional abuses of money and power led to calls for returning to the core of the gospel as found in the New Testament.

Nevertheless, a basic question of moral theology, whether salvation was initiated by God or the individual, remained unresolved. Renaissance humanists inclined to emphasize the freedom of the human will to turn to God, to cooperate with God's grace, thus to actively accept or reject the salvation God offers. Protestant reformers inclined to emphasize God's omnipotence and human sinfulness, thus the inability of the human will to turn to God on its own strength. Throughout the sixteenth century Protestants tried to refine the meaning of "salvation by grace alone," but the doctrine reached its logical consequence at the synod of Dort in 1619, which placed the Dutch Reformed Church on the side of so-called double predestinarianism, reasoning that if God is both omniscient and omnipotent, he not only knows but also determines in advance who will be saved and who will be damned. The affirmation of total depravity, unconditional election, limited atonement, irresistible grace, and perseverance of the saints was a blow to the Dutch religious party known as the Remonstrants, who held that in principle all could be saved, depending on one's free acceptance or rejection of grace.

Doctrinal victories are often mixed blessings, and such was the case for the Dutch Reformed Church of the seventeenth century. Heresy was clearly defined and to that extent the church was cleansed, but the defense of the official theology resulted in a new scholasticism reminiscent of the medieval system that earlier Protestants had rejected. The original Protestant search for a morally pure form of Christianity was partially diverted into the effort to strengthen the institutional structure and its doctrinal stance against threats from outside. Whether the Protestant spirit could actually survive institutionalization, particularly in a state-sponsored church, is a legitimate question, but in the seventeenth century it was not

yet socially acceptable to leave the state church, even though the Netherlands was more open to dissident groups than were other European countries.

The thriving Dutch economy with its international trade and emerging empire contributed toward the country's openness to new influences.
Having shaken off Hapsburg control, the new Dutch Republic, a confed-
eration of provinces, was more open than was France, where the monarchy
was seeking to reestablish itself after a long period of civil strife, or Germany, which was mired in a thirty-year internal struggle pitting Protestants against Catholics and princes against the emperor. Students came
from throughout Europe to study at Dutch universities, notably Leiden.
The Elseviers and other Dutch printers published books by writers from
many countries where censorship laws were much stricter. Jews and sectarians were allowed greater freedom than in most other countries, and
while the Republic was officially Protestant, Catholics were not prevented
from practicing their religion. The lack of a strong central government and
the commercial interests of merchants led to more religious and intellectual freedom than was legally sanctioned. While Reformed theologians
participated in the intellectual ferment stimulated by the influx of ideas,
they also decried the materialism and secularism of the new bourgeoisie
and sought to maintain or restore authentic Calvinist belief and practice.

Attitudes toward women reflected the ambivalence between endorsing new ideas and maintaining orthodox beliefs. The Dutch church had
fully embraced the spiritual equality of the sexes and inherited Calvin's
emphasis on the value of companionship between husband and wife in
marriage. Protestant insistence that everyone should be able to read the
Bible led to an increasingly literate society, and the Dutch Republic excelled over the rest of Europe in this respect.[1] Public schooling in reading
and catechism was provided for both boys and girls for the first three
years. Well-to-do parents often preferred home tutoring even when
schools were available, and girls in such homes, benefiting from Renaissance humanist advocacy of education for females, were frequently well
trained in arts and languages. Yet the belief in a divinely ordained social
order limited women's vocational options, and the adherence to the injunction against women speaking in church excluded them from positions
of ecclesiastical leadership.

Anna Maria van Schurman was molded by the values of this society
and affirmed many of them while also experiencing the tensions and

1. Jonathan Israel, *The Dutch Republic: Its Rise, Greatness, and Fall, 1477–1806* (Oxford: Clarendon
Press, 1995), 686.

pushing at the boundaries. Her mentor, the Utrecht professor Gisbertus Voetius, was the leading defender of Dutch Reformed theology; like Thomas Aquinas before him, he brought together the accumulated wisdom of the age into a systematic summary of theology. Yet he is also considered to be one of the proponents of a second Reformation, known in Dutch as *Nadere Reformatie*, which would bring to fulfillment the goals of the first Reformation of Luther and Calvin. Still, Voetius was not willing to abandon the state church, and when Schurman's search for the pure church led her outside the state church, she ultimately broke outside the mold of her culture's values.

LIFE OF ANNA MARIA VAN SCHURMAN

Anna van Schurman was born in Cologne on November 5, 1607, daughter of Frederik van Schurman and Eva von Harff, who had married in 1602 and already had three sons, Hendrik Frederik (ca. 1603–ca. 1632), Johan Godschalk (1605–1664), and Willem, who died at the age of five. Frederik's parents had fled to Germany from Antwerp, which had become a Calvinist stronghold, after the Duke of Alva began forcibly to reimpose Catholicism and imperial authority. Eva was of the lesser German nobility and also of the Reformed faith, and as tensions between Catholics and Protestants increased prior to the Thirty Years' War, the family left Catholic Cologne around 1610 for the von Harff castle Dreiborn near Schleiden.

After about five years, in the course of which Frederik obtained a letter of nobility from the emperor, the family resettled in the Netherlands, specifically Utrecht, where Anna Maria spent most of the rest of her life. She was sent to the French school, but after two months her parents decided to have her tutored at home, a decision that enabled her to profit from her brothers' lessons and, after demonstrating her promise, to be included in their studies, which were being directed by their father. Little is known about her father's vocation, but he was clearly deeply interested in learning and was probably the strongest influence behind her academic achievements, aside from her own determination. He was clearly also supportive of his sons' learning, for in 1623 the whole family moved to Franeker in the Netherlandic province of Friesland in order for Johan Godschalk to study medicine. Frederik van Schurman also intended to study with English puritan William Ames, who had become professor of theology in Franeker in 1622, but unfortunately Frederik died soon after the move and was buried in Franeker. The rest of the family apparently remained there until Johan Godschalk finished his medical studies and then returned to Utrecht, probably in 1626, where their household soon expanded to include several siblings of Frederik and Eva who were fleeing the war in Germany.

While still in her teens, Anna Maria was gaining the attention of the literary world. In 1620, Dutch poet Anna Roemer Visscher wrote in praise of Schurman's knowledge of Greek and Latin, her calligraphy, embroidery, and drawing, and her skill in singing, harpsichord, and lute playing. A letter written in 1623 to Daniel Heinsius, poet and classical scholar, demonstrates that she took the initiative in making contact with those whose accomplishments she admired.[2] Popular poet Jacob Cats, to whom she had written a Latin poem in 1622, responded by praising her in his *Houwelijck (Marriage)* (1625), a rhymed description of the stages of a woman's life.

During the 1630s Anna Maria attained such renown for her learning that she won the appellation "The Tenth Muse." Her correspondence with intellectual leaders of the day is our primary evidence for her prominence. Her most frequent correspondent, at least in her extant letters, was André Rivet, professor of theology in Leiden. From about 1632 he encouraged her in her intellectual pursuits, and her logic exercise on whether women should be educated emerged out of this correspondence. Rivet was always her supporter but saw her as an exception to the female norm. Constantijn Huygens, versatile scholar, poet, scientist, and diplomat, befriended her and maintained correspondence with her until the latter period of her life. Gisbertus Voetius brought her into the public eye in 1636 by inviting her to write poems for the inauguration of the Academy of Utrecht. As first rector of this institution, which became the University of Utrecht, Voetius enabled Schurman to attend lectures in a special loge that concealed her from the male students, thus becoming, if unofficially, the first female student at a Dutch university. There she learned the ancient languages that gave her perhaps her greatest intellectual distinction: she knew Greek and Hebrew well enough to write letters in the languages; she wrote an Ethiopic grammar; and she also learned Chaldean, Arabic, and Syriac well enough to utilize them in biblical exegesis.[3] In 1639 another admirer, physician Jan van Beverwyck, publicized her accomplishments in his catalogue

2. Schurman, letter to Daniel Heinsius, September 18, 1623, manuscript 8* F 19, Utrecht University Library.

3. For details on her references to words in these languages in her correspondence, see Anna Margaretha Hendrika Douma, *Anna Maria van Schurman en de Studie der Vrouw* (Amsterdam, 1924), 30–31. Her Ethiopic grammar was not published but was listed among the holdings of Greifswald professor Johann Friedrich Mayer (1650–1712).

of notable women and placed her at the pinnacle of learned women both ancient and modern.[4] Her response to his question whether medicine could extend life or whether the end of life was predetermined by God was published in 1639 both in Latin (*De Vitae Termino*) and in Dutch (*Paelsteen van den tijt onses levens*) (*On the Boundary Marker of Life*).

Anna van Schurman's accomplishments were not limited to languages, poetry, and philosophy, however. From a very young age she had developed artistic skills and had become particularly accomplished in miniatures. She used many different media, such as oil, gouache, pencil, chalk, wax, boxwood, ivory, and engraving. Her paper cuttings, still displayed in the Franeker museum, are of astonishing intricacy. She practiced calligraphy: an extant sample, a page of seven verses in various non-Roman scripts, is preserved in the Royal Library in the Hague. In her letters, she frequently mentions enclosing one of her artistic creations. A number of self-portraits exist which allow us to view a variety of her hair and clothing styles, indicating that she utilized her artistic skills on her own appearance.

In the 1640s she was still very much in the limelight, as indicated by the letters she wrote to men and women far and wide; by the people, such as the queens of Poland and of Sweden, who sought her out in their travels; by her 1643 admission to membership in the Utrecht guild of painters;[5] by the 1641 reprint of her 1638 dissertation in Latin on women's learning and its translation into French in 1646; and finally by the publication of the *Opuscula*, containing many of her letters and poems, in 1648. Yet a shift in her values was already becoming evident, occasioned partly by an upheaval in Dutch intellectual circles, specifically the conflict between adherents of the new philosophy of René Descartes and adherents of Aristotelian philosophy, led by Voetius.

Evidence regarding Schurman's relationship to Descartes gives us a mixed picture. In a 1635 letter to Rivet, she mentions meeting Descartes, who had recently arrived in Utrecht and who, she had heard, was a man of incredible learning.[6] Descartes himself, writing in 1640, charged that she had already by 1635 come under the restrictive influence of Voetius: "This

4. Jan van Beverwyck, *Van de Uitnementheyt des vrouwelicken Geslachts* (Dordrecht, 1639).

5. This admission into the artists' guild may have been comparable to an honorary degree rather than an indication of her artistic activity, for evidence suggests that the period of her greatest artistic productivity was prior to the 1640s. See Katlijne Van der Stighelen, "'Et ses artistes mains (. . .)': The Art of Anna Maria van Schurman," in Mirjam de Baar et al., *Choosing the Better Part: Anna Maria van Schurman (1607–1678)* (Dordrecht: Kluwer Academic Press, 1996), 58.

6. Schurman, letter to André Rivet, March 18, 1635, manuscript 8* F 19 in Utrecht University Library.

Voetius has also ruined Mademoiselle Schurman, for she used to have an excellent spirit for poetry, painting, and other fine pursuits; but for the last five or six years he has possessed her completely. She occupies herself solely with theological controversy, which has caused her to lose contact with all polite company."[7] If we accept this chronology, we would have to conclude that Anna Maria's withdrawal from society had taken place by the time she met Descartes, but evidence from Schurman's later allies places the break between Schurman and Descartes much later, in 1649. Meanwhile, Schurman maintained friendly relations with Princess Elizabeth of the Palatinate, to whom Descartes dedicated his *Principia Philosophiae* (*Principles of Philosophy*) (1644), though she politely disagreed about philosophical method, as we read in her 1644 letter to Elizabeth. Politeness gave way to principle, however, when the issue concerned holy scripture, at least if we are to put credence in a story reported by Pierre Yvon, a friend and pastor from Schurman's later period. He related that in 1649, when Descartes was on his way to teach Queen Christine of Sweden, where he died four months later, he stopped for a visit in Utrecht with Anna van Schurman. Seeing the Hebrew Bible from which she was reading, Descartes remarked that he found reading the Bible in Hebrew a waste of time and not at all illuminating. According to Pierre Yvon, this comment deeply offended her and "gave her such a repulsion toward this philosopher that she took care never again to have anything to do with him."[8] Yvon further generalized that "When she noticed this impious spirit in any one of those with whom she could have had some conversation or correspondence, she immediately broke off all ties with him and refused him all access to her."[9]

Whether from deepening piety or because family obligations began to consume more of her time, Schurman faded from prominence in the 1650s and 1660s. In her later autobiography, she herself wrote of moving "out of the too contemplative and literary life into a more active existence" already with the death of her mother, which occurred in 1637.[10] She had to take care of the household almost entirely by herself, which also drew her into charitable obligations. More consuming, however, was the care she pro-

7. Descartes, Letter to Marin Mersenne, November 11, 1640, in *Oeuvres* (Paris: Victor Cousin, 1842), 8: 388.

8. Pierre Yvon, "Abrégé sincere de la vie et de la Conduite et des vrais sentimens de feu Mr. De Labadie," in Gottfried Arnold, *Unparteyische Kirchen- und Ketzer-historie* (Frankfurt am Main, 1715), 2: 1264.

9. Ibid.

10. Anna Maria van Schurman, *Eukleria, seu melioris partis electio* (Altona, 1673), 133.

vided for two elderly aunts who had been among those who came from Germany to live with the family. For the last twenty years before their deaths in 1661 they were nearly blind, and for the final five to ten years Anna's constant presence and help were required. Although it kept her completely away from her studies, she found such caregiving at this point to be much more meaningful, and saw therein "the remarkable grace of God toward us that he bound us together with such a close and sweet bond of love that so many years passed like a few days."[11]

Anna's surviving brother, Johan Godschalk, had also been part of this loving family unit and shared her wish to find such a sense of Christian community within the church. Shortly after the deaths of the aunts, he embarked on a study tour to Switzerland, the birthplace of Calvinism. He studied Hebrew in Basel under Johannes Buxtorf, who told him of a former Jesuit who was preaching about the need for reform in the church. Johan Godschalk went to Geneva, was inspired by this Jean de Labadie, and stayed with him two months. Upon the enthusiastic recommendation of her brother, who died in 1664 before he could accomplish his goals, Anna became an advocate in the Netherlands for Labadie, and in 1666 he was offered a pastorate in Middelburg, a city in the southwestern coastal province of Zeeland. Labadie's fiery preaching and intemperate plans for church purification alienated even those who had been pushing for church reform. Whatever the drawbacks of a state church, the idea that believers could be clearly distinguished from unbelievers was unsettling to theologians like Voetius, who saw this as the mark of sectarianism. Indeed, Labadie was forced to leave his pastorate and to become a sectarian leader.

Because over the years Anna van Schurman had become more and more disenchanted with the Dutch church, she seems not to have hesitated to continue following Labadie when he was no longer accepted in the state church. Along with another "dear sister in Christ," she followed him to Amsterdam, where they could find no lodging available in his section of town, much of which was still under construction. When he offered them space in his large house on the ground floor, where an old widow and two housekeepers were living, Schurman rejoiced at the opportunity to be so close to this man of God. Unconcerned about the opinions of those who would judge this move by worldly standards, she chose the spiritual edification she would receive from Labadie over the respectability she would retain if she returned home. Turning her back on

11. Ibid., 134.

previous friends and former values, she chose that which for her was "the better part."

> I do not deny that I had all my life placed much weight on bourgeois proprieties, customary manners, and a good name, as if true virtues; but in this case I paid no attention to them; I considered them transient in comparison with heavenly matters or as a heavenly gift and entrusted good which I could give back to God, just as everything that is mine belongs to God and has been given to me by God.[12]

Schurman never regretted her decision and never expressed the slightest discontent or criticism regarding her chosen family. While criticism from the outside forced them from Amsterdam to Germany, she continued to praise the religious leadership of Labadie and coworkers Pierre Yvon and Pierre Dulignon. Schurman was able to persuade her old friend Elizabeth of the Palatinate that Labadie and his community were worthy of protection, and for a time they settled, about fifty in number, in Herford, Germany, where Elizabeth had become abbess. Again they encountered opposition from the surrounding community, however, and after a time they had to move on to Altona, near Hamburg. Here Schurman published her *Eukleria*, which served both as her autobiography and an apologia for the Labadist community. Labadie's death in 1674 was a serious blow to the movement, but it survived into the next century.[13] Under Yvon's leadership they moved back to the Netherlands when war threatened in Altona in 1675 and settled at a country castle in the Frisian village of Wieuwerd, where for a decade or so the community flourished, attracting a few hundred members. There Anna Maria died in 1678.

SCHURMAN'S WRITINGS

That Schurman was not one to inflame passions and incite controversy is evident from the stylized deference with which she addresses her correspondents. Her politeness is both a mark of the age and a personal characteristic, evidence of proper upbringing and feminine submissiveness. Beyond this, the intellectual restraints of her conservative Calvinism prevented her from making radical feminist claims. Thus the format of her defense of women's education is purely academic, a formal exercise in

12. Ibid., 149–150. (The title of this work in English would be *To Choose the Better Part*.)
13. For a thorough history of Labadie and his followers, see Trevor J. Saxby, *The Quest for the New Jerusalem: Jean de Labadie and the Labadists, 1610–1744* (Dordrecht: Martinus Nijhoff, 1987).

logic. The syllogistic reasoning keeps her inner thoughts and feelings at a distance. Only in her letters, when we look underneath the veneer of humble verbiage, do we see her independent spirit and quiet conviction.

Not only the style but also the content of Schurman's argument is shaped by societal conventions. Nowhere does she suggest changes in the power structure of political or religious institutions. A major reason for women of the leisured classes to study the arts and sciences is precisely that they have so few other obligations, not in order to take up positions of responsibility. Carefully distinguishing herself from those such as Lucrezia Marinella[14] who would seek to reverse traditional gender relations by claiming women's superiority, Schurman placed narrow limits on her claims: her cause was the life of the mind, not that of action, and her arguments applied only to those women who would not be neglecting family responsibilities by attending to their minds. As a young woman, Schurman believed that the life of the mind was of one piece with the life of the spirit, that religious and moral virtue would be enhanced by study. Only as she became more involved in service to family did she realize the potential conflict between the two. At the end of her life she became aware that even the claims that had seemed so modest in her youth could encourage an immodest ambition. If learning was represented as unquestionably good, it could detract from the greater good of the soul.

The texts selected for this volume reflect different stages of Schurman's life as well as some of her influence on others. The *Dissertatio logica* with which we begin is her most famous and most influential work. First proposed in a letter of 1632 to Rivet, it was submitted to him for comment and published in Paris in 1638 and in Leiden in 1641 with their correspondence on this question.[15] It is important to note that Rivet was a theologian and that the question posed is fundamentally theological. The issue is not simply whether women ought to study arts and letters but whether *Christian* women ought to study. Because of the centrality of scripture for Protestantism, sufficient learning to read the Bible was desired for all Christians and was thus not in dispute. The question posed, presuming the goal of studies to be the glory of God and the salvation of the soul, is whether the humanistic disciplines contribute to this goal. Schurman argues that they do, though not all equally. Of first importance are grammar,

---

14. A volume on Marinella is forthcoming in this series with the translation of her *La nobiltà et eccellenza delle donne* by Anne Dunhill.

15. Schurman refers to the publication in France in an August 15, 1640, letter to Rivet (Royal Library, The Hague, ms. 133 B 8, no. 22).

logic, and rhetoric, then physics, metaphysics, history, and languages, especially Greek and Hebrew. Certain other subjects such as mathematics, music, poetry, and painting can be pleasant pastimes but do not contribute directly to theology or moral virtue. Some fields of study, such as legal jurisprudence, military affairs, and public speaking, have no practical application for women, but women should not necessarily be excluded from learning about them.

Granting that none of these fields of study is a prerequisite to happiness or to salvation, Schurman nevertheless advances fourteen theses in favor of women studying. The first three come from natural philosophy and might be summarized rather simplistically as making the point that women are human beings. Women have the intelligence and desire to learn, and they belong to the category of upright beings and not prone animals; therefore they have the capacity to understand the arts and sciences. The next two highlight the distinction between men and women not from a biological but from a social standpoint: women of a certain social status often have too little to do and long to do something of greater worth. In such cases, studying avoids the dangers of idleness. Argument six resembles the first three as a claim about women's capability for advanced learning, but the reasoning derives from theology: since all Christians are meant to study and reflect on the Bible, they also have the capacity to study those auxiliary subjects that supplement the understanding of scripture. Up to this point, the theses have the effect of countering negative assumptions; from thesis seven on, Schurman argues for the moral and intellectual virtues that derive from learning. Relying on Aristotelian concepts, she points out that the arts and sciences are habits that serve to perfect the intellect and that by nature human beings take honest delight in the attainment of knowledge, a delight surpassed only by the supernatural delight of Christians. The study of letters also leads to moral virtue, because it provides examples and reasons that prevent one from making mistakes out of ignorance or lack of experience. In the image of virtue as avoidance of ignorance, Schurman relies on Plato, but she then adds the Aristotelian image of a virtuous act as the difficult task of hitting the right mark, while vice is possible in the many ways of missing the mark. Of the theses arguing the positive benefits of learning, only two actually deal directly with the stated goal of God's glory and the salvation of the soul. Her ninth argument is a form of natural theology: to observe God's works more clearly arouses greater love and reverence toward God. The tenth argument defends reason as a tool for warding off heresies.

Rivet in his response seizes on her failure to establish a strong connection between learning and devotion. The magnificence of creation, he notes, could inspire anyone to praise God regardless of whether one understands the rotation of the planets, and many who understand such things intellectually turn away from God and are satisfied with nature alone. If her own studies led her to greater love of God, she should continue them, but often those people whose minds are not occupied with complex questions are more fervent in their devotion. Rivet recommends the plan for female education outlined by Juan Luis Vives in *De institutione foeminae Christianae (Instruction of a Christian Woman)* in 1524, which emphasized practical domestic skills such as spinning and weaving along with a basic plan of study. If women were occupied with their hands, there would not be enough leisure time for idleness to be a moral danger.

In the letter that concludes the correspondence on this topic, Schurman respectfully accepts Vives's plan as worthy of imple-mentation and apologizes to Rivet for any misunderstandings that led him to think she was making immoderate claims, such as of female superiority. No doubt her deferential, submissive approach was part of her appeal and the reason why she was so widely praised by men. Her charm was not only her intellect but also her modesty. Her writings, therefore, may not have done so much to further the cause of women as her example. Indeed, most of the rest of her writings during this period consisted of letters, which constituted the major portion of the volume of her writings published by Frederick Spanheim in 1648.

The letters selected for this volume are those to other women. Even though they by no means dominate her correspondence, they demonstrate that women supported and encouraged one another in their intellectual pursuits. Rivet had already in 1632 mediated contact between Schurman and another highly gifted young woman who was then living in the Netherlands, Princess Elizabeth of the Palatinate, daughter of Frederick V, the "Winter King" of Bohemia who had been overthrown after a year in 1620.[16] The two letters we have from Schurman to Princess Elizabeth are full of recommendations for intellectual pursuits, even though her expressed predilection for scholastic writers in the second letter is a hint of the differences between the two women. The method of Schurman's mentor Voetius is aptly described in this defense of Christian scholasticism, as we may see for ourselves in his chapters on women.

16. There is a possibility that Elizabeth and Anna knew each other through the painter Gerard Honthorst, who had a number of female pupils. Elizabeth is known to have studied with him, but of Schurman's relationship to Honthorst we know only what she reports in the *Eukleria*, that is, that Honthorst greatly admired the boxwood miniature that her brother showed him. See Katlijne Van der Stighelen, "'Et ses artistes mains . . . ,'" 63.

Rivet provided Schurman with an introduction also to Marie le Jars de Gournay, who had written a work on the equality of men and women, *L'Égalité des hommes et des femmes*, in 1622.[17] Schurman wrote a short poem honoring her for her service to the cause of women.[18] Gournay, who was a generation older than Schurman, responded with humble gratitude but also offered some advice: learning Hebrew or other oriental (that is, Semitic) languages consumes time that could be put to better use; anything she needed to know could be read in Latin, Greek, or one of the modern languages. Schurman respectfully declined Gournay's advice, remaining convinced that Bible translations were inadequate to convey the sense of the Hebrew original.

The other letters written to women are less specific in dealing with curricular matters, but they convey the sense of a network of women joined internationally by their love of learning. To Dorothy Moor and to Bathsua Makin she did not need to justify her language study; she wrote to them in Hebrew and Greek, respectively. Makin, tutor for the daughter of King Charles I, was inspired by Schurman's example[19] and wrote her own

17. See Maya Bïjuoet, "Marie de Gournay," in Katharina M. Wilson and Frank J. Warnke, eds., *Women Writers of the Seventeenth Century* (Athens: University of Georgia Press, 1989), 3–29.

18. *Magni ac Generosi Animi Heroinae Gornacensi*
Causam Sexus Nostri Fortiter Defendenti Gratulatur
Anna Maria a Schurman

Palladis arma geris, bellis animosa virago,
Utque geras lauros, Palladis arma geris.
Sic decet innocui causam te dicere sexus,
Et propria insontes vertere tela viros.
I prae Gornacense decus, tua signa sequemur:
Quippe tibi potior, robore, cause praeit.

Anna Maria van Schurman congratulates
the great and noble-minded heroine of Gournay
strong defender of the cause of our sex.

You bear the arms of Pallas, bold heroine in battles
and so that you may carry the laurels, you bear the arms of Pallas.
Thus it is fitting for you to make a defense for the innocent sex
and to turn the weapons of harmful men against them.
Lead on, glory of Gournay, we shall follow your standard,
for in you our cause advances, which is mightier than strength.

(*Opuscula*, 264)

19. A letter from Schurman to Sir Simonds d'Ewes, October 31, 1645, reports that Makin's praise of Schurman had led d'Ewes to write to her and that Schurman was responding, in spite of her intention to limit her correspondence, because she saw him as a supporter of women. See translation of the letter in Wilson and Warnke, eds., *Women Writers of the Seventeenth Century*, 174.

plea for women's education, *An Essay to Revive the Ancient Education of Gentle-women* (1673), in some respects resembling Schurman's dissertation (which had in the meantime been translated into English as *The Learned Maid; or Whether a Maid May Be a Scholar?* and published in London in 1659), yet having the more practical aim of advertising Makin's school. Undoubtedly Makin had Schurman in mind when she put forth the Dutch as worthy of admiration for their care in educating women, "from whence they are to be accounted most virtuous, and to be more useful than any women in the world."[20]

In the same year that Makin published her essay on women's education, however, Schurman published her autobiographical defense of Labadism in which she recanted her earlier approach to learning and asked those who had praised her so highly to retract their praise. That others had placed her within the ranks of the pagan gods by calling her "The Tenth Muse" was now a source of shame, for she had not, in her view, protested strenuously enough against such adulation. We may find such a comment puzzling, for all her earlier writings are so striking for their self-effacing humble protestations. Yet we observed previously that much of what passed for deference was stylistic convention, a required formality in polite culture. This veneer of courtesy prevents us from judging the degree of sincerity of her humble protestations. Granted that there are also stylistic conventions for the writing of pietistic autobiographies, and that the *Eukleria* is at the same time a theological apologia, still we must take seriously her admission that she had to some extent been motivated by fame and bolstered by praise. Not that we would judge these to be egregious faults, but this admission reveals an awareness of the complexity of human motivations and is a more candid instance of self-analysis than was presented in her earlier works.

Religious self-examination was in itself a component of pietism, the larger religious movement of which Labadism was one variety. Puritanism, a related movement in England and New England, had required an accounting of one's conversion experience, and the emergence of autobiographical works and memoirs was an obvious result of such spiritual introspection. On the continent, August Hermann Francke's conversion experience in 1687 became the paradigm according to which his followers should analyze and record their experiences. Schurman's work does not follow a prescribed model unless perhaps that of Augustine's *Confessions* and is thus not a predictable account of prescribed stages on a spiritual jour-

---

20. Makin, as quoted in Kate Aughterson, ed., *Renaissance Woman: A Sourcebook* (London: Routledge, 1995), 190.

ney, but her alternation between personal events and theological issues important during her lifetime reminds us that her purpose was to provide a testimonial for Labadism, not the story of her life for its own sake. The chapters translated for the present volume are those that relate to the time up to which she wrote the other materials included here. The theology of Labadism is not our direct concern in this context, but it is useful to know some of the beliefs, at least as reported by Schurman.

Common to all pietist groups, including Labadism, is the emphasis on practice of religion, *praxis pietatis*. This was directed against those who seemed to require right teaching or orthodoxy but not right living. Recognizing that the intellect could master all the details of theology without affecting the heart, pietists demanded evidence that lives were truly changed by the gospel, that individuals were regenerate. As it was the Holy Spirit working within which brought about this new birth, the Holy Spirit often appeared to be placed in a position superior to the Bible. In contrast to the Quakers, however, Labadists insisted on testing the spirit against the Bible; the spirit did not supersede the Word, as the Quakers tended to think, but must accompany it if the Word is to have any effect. Although Labadists were considered radical pietists because of their separation from the state church and their formation of egalitarian communities, they were in other respects quite conservative. Schurman upheld the doctrines of the synod of Dort and the authority of the Bible against those pietists who drew the conclusion that doctrine was inconsequential and that either all or no teachings could be believed.

Whatever the differences among pietist groups, however, Schurman was now more closely affiliated with them than with those who had supported her for her erudition. Her *Eukleria* was read and approved by pietists in both the Frankfurt and Halle circles, and a correspondence ensued between Schurman and Johann Jakob Schütz, a leader in the Frankfurt circle connected with Philipp Jakob Spener.[21] Of the same circle, Eleonore von Merlau, who was to marry Johann Petersen and with him publish pietistic works, admired and corresponded with Schurman. Connections with others searching for a truly Christ-like community, such as Antoinette Bourignon and William Penn, while at first encouraging, were eventually broken because of doctrinal differences.[22] Gottfried Arnold, on the other

21. See Johannes Wallmann, *Philipp Jakob Spener und die Anfänge des Pietismus*, 2d ed. (Tübingen: J. C. B. Mohr [Paul Siebeck], 1986), 307–324. The manuscript of the letters is in the Basel University Library, ms. G2 II 33.

22. See my article, "Anna Maria van Schurman and Antoinette Bourignon: Contrasting Examples of Seventeenth-Century Pietism," *Church History* 60 (September 1991), 301–315; and Hugh Barbour ed., *William Penn on Religion and Ethics* (Lewiston: Edwin Mellen Press, 1991),

hand, was more inclined to see the similarities and favorable characteristics of pietists and other sectarians and included Pierre Yvon's biography of Schurman in his *Impartial History of Churches and Heretics*.[23]

In the century that followed, catalogues of learned women continued to feature Schurman as an outstanding example of erudition, generally minimizing her later religious shift. During the course of the eighteenth century, on the other hand, representatives of the literary movement of *Empfindsamkeit* ("Sensibility") found Schurman interesting for her expression of feelings and intense emotional life. The poet and writer Christoph Martin Wieland was moved by her writings and called her one of "the most perfect and extraordinary persons of the female sex." His enthusiasm led to the publication in German of the *Eukleria* in 1783.[24]

GISBERTUS VOETIUS

Without the support of Gisbertus Voetius (Gijsbert Voet), Schurman would not have attained such a high level of learning and the prominence that ensued. Voetius is not otherwise known as a promoter of women's causes, but his Calvinistic theology and his personal acquaintance with Schurman combined to lead him to defend women against misogyny.

Born in 1589 near Utrecht, Voetius studied in Leiden during the beginnings of the Remonstrant controversy. Serving as pastor in places where Arminians and Catholics were strong, he had opportunity to hone his skills in argumentation. He also occupied himself with learning Arabic and Syriac, which he later put to use in teaching Middle Eastern languages in Utrecht. His writings demonstrate his vast knowledge and ability to incorporate an impressive number of sources into his arguments.

His career as professor of theology and oriental languages was marked by controversy not only with Arminians but also with Descartes, whom we know as the founder of modern philosophy but who for Voetius was a dangerous skeptic. Descartes's method of doubting everything until he could at last affirm his own existence placed in question the truths of revelation and the principles of natural philosophy. Voetius was an adherent of Aristotelianism, which was the accepted philosophical approach in Dutch universities at this time. He held that Aristotle's use of reason and sense experience complemented the knowledge of nature which could be

---

1:364–367.

23. Arnold, *Unparteyische Kirchen- und Ketzer-historie*.

24. See Mirjam de Baar and Brita Rang, "Anna Maria van Schurman: A Historical Survey of Her Reception since the Seventeenth Century," in *Choosing the Better Part*, 9–10.

gained from scripture. Descartes's rejection of sense experience as a means to knowledge entailed the rejection of the cosmological proof of God's existence, which for Voetius was tantamount to atheism, even though Descartes affirmed God's existence on the basis of the innate idea of God.[25]

Another major ideological opponent was Johannes Cocceius, who developed covenant theology in such a way as to deemphasize the Old Testament. In Cocceius's view, the covenant of works which promised salvation for obedience ceased to be in effect after the Fall and was replaced by the covenant of grace, which reached its culmination in the work of Christ. Thus the law, which played such an important role in Calvinist theology, was downplayed, and all scripture was interpreted in relation to Christ. Cocceius's method of biblical interpretation was thus quite different from that of Voetius and other Calvinist scholastics who used scripture passages to demonstrate theological points within a logical system. In deemphasizing the law, Cocceius also abandoned the strict observance of the Sabbath, which was stressed by Voetius on the basis of the continuing validity of the moral law.

In spite of Voetius's legalism and scholasticism, however, he also emphasized devotional life and insisted that piety and knowledge develop together. His insistence on purity of life encompassed even the smallest details of behavior, as characterized by the term "Precisianism," the Dutch equivalent of English "Puritanism," with which Voetius was sympathetic. His concern for genuine reform of life led to advocacy of small gatherings for scripture study and prayer, such as would later characterize pietist conventicles. When Jean de Labadie, therefore, came to the Netherlands, Voetius at first supported him but soon recognized his potential for sectarianism, always the danger of movements that formed *ecclesiolae in ecclesia*, small churches within the territorial church. By denouncing Labadie and bemoaning Schurman's affiliation with him, Voetius allied himself with the state church. With all the tendencies that identify him as a forerunner of pietism, therefore, Voetius is most representative of Calvinist scholastic orthodoxy.

VOETIUS ON WOMEN

Calvinist scholasticism may have used the formal structure of medieval

---

25. For a study of Descartes's reception in the Netherlands, see Theo Verbeek, *Descartes and the Dutch: Early Reactions to Cartesian Philosophy, 1637–1650* (Carbondale: Southern Illinois University Press, 1992).

scholasticism, but the content of Voetius's thinking, particularly in regard to women, was quite different. Although Voetius defended Aristotle's philosophy in general, he abandoned Aristotle on the question of woman's nature and her role in procreation. Endorsing the emerging consensus of Renaissance physicians, who relied more on Galen than on Aristotle, Voetius and other Calvinists regarded woman as contributing seed in procreation, rather than being mere matter that the male seed fertilized.[26] He also followed Calvinist tradition in emphasizing the companionate nature of the relationship between Adam and Eve. His focus in the first chapter is entirely on the essential nature of woman at creation, affirming that she shares with men the image of God, even though in relation to men she may be subordinate. Striking to us is the amount of space devoted to the question whether woman was created on the sixth or the seventh day, a question that arose only because of Jerome's Vulgate translation of the Bible. In order to make sense of the statement that God finished his work on the seventh day, Jerome and those who followed him concluded that woman, the final work of creation, must have been made on the seventh day. Voetius and other Protestants, however, interpreted the Hebrew to say that the work of creation had been completed by the seventh day and that nothing was created on that day. The significance of this debate has less to do with the nature of woman than with the observance of the Sabbath. Noteworthy by its absence in any of the three chapters is any blame on women as the source of sin.

Having observed that Schurman accepted the subordinate status of women in society and in the church, we should scarcely be surprised that Voetius regards women as by nature inferior to men. What is remarkable is the extent to which he restricts men's authority over women and also opens the door to women in public office under certain unusual circumstances, such as a hereditary monarchy lacking a male successor or a crisis situation in which a woman happens to provide wise counsel. In the area of education, Voetius does not even bother to weigh differing opinions but merely appeals to Schurman's arguments in her *Dissertatio* and to the examples of learned women given in the catalogues of Beverwyck and Johann Heinrich Hottinger, adding some who had not been included in these catalogues. In his treatment of women and religion he is as favorable to women as was conceivable in his church at the time. Respect for the authority of the Bible did not allow him to ignore Paul's injunctions against

---

26. See my "Embryology and the Incarnation: A Sixteenth-Century Debate," *Sixteenth Century Journal* 9.3 (Fall 1978): 93–104.

women speaking in church, but he pointed out the situations when women were permitted to lead in discussions or devotional exercises. The conclusion that women are more religious than men puts women in a positive light, but it is counterbalanced by the related conclusion that women are more inclined to superstition. Nevertheless, Voetius refuses to blame women for the majority of heresies in spite of several examples of their complicity in heresy.

On balance, Voetius's position on women is quite positive, though not particularly unusual and by no means revolutionary. His major contribution is that of assembling so many sources from so many areas of scholarship. His theological sources range from patristic to medieval to post-Tridentine, from Catholicism to Protestantism to Judaism. His political, medical, and historical sources show him to be widely read in areas outside theology. The result is itself a rich source of information concerning different perspectives on women during the sixteenth and seventeenth centuries. To have presented the positions of so many authors in such a concise manner is a major contribution.

Outside Dutch Reformed circles, however, Voetius's treatise on women probably had very little impact. The treatise, after all, was buried in his multivolume systematic theology, *Politica Ecclesiastica*, in which all doctrinal issues were discussed with the same thoroughness. Participants in the *querelle des femmes* were unlikely to discover it or to be drawn to the scholastic mode of presentation. Reflecting his conservative position in debates against progressive or innovative thinkers, Voetius's image was that of a narrow-minded legalist, not a person likely to endorse new ideas. Indeed, what we learn from Voetius is that few of the ideas were new, that differences of interpretation had existed for centuries, and that some schools of thought were more favorable to women than others. Calvinism was moderately favorable within biblical and societal limits, neither as open-minded as some humanist writers nor so negative as popular culture.[27] Voetius serves as an example of Dutch Calvinism in its sober but solid support of women's spiritual and intellectual equality in spite of social inferiority.

27. The suggestion by Jane Dempsey Douglass in *Women, Freedom & Calvin* (Philadelphia: Westminster Press, 1985) that Calvin opened the door slightly to women's leadership in church has been effectively countered by John Lee Thompson in *John Calvin and the Daughters of Sarah: Women in Regular and Exceptional Roles in the Exegesis of Calvin, His Predecessors, and His Contemporaries* (Geneva: Librairie Droz, 1992). More research remains to be done before we have a complete picture of the theology of women within Calvinist thought.

SUGGESTIONS FOR FURTHER READING

The two major published works by Schurman, *Opuscula* (Leiden, 1648; reprint, 1650) and *Eukleria seu melioris partis electio* (Altona, 1673; part 2, Amsterdam, 1684), provide the primary sources of information about her life. A number of unpublished letters are held in various libraries, primarily the Royal Library in the Hague; to read the original manuscript copies of her printed letters is a pleasure because of the beauty of her handwriting. The most meaningful sources written by her contemporaries about her life are various poems and letters written by Constantijn Huygens, an entry by Jacob Cats about her in his *Werelts begin, midden, eynde, besloten in den Trouringh* (Dordrecht, 1637), and a description of her life in Jan van Beverwyck's catalogue of learned women, *Van de Uitnementheyt des vrouwelicken geslachts* (Dordrecht, 1639). From a different perspective, the biography by Pierre Yvon cited in footnote 8 gives considerable insight into her life.

Most secondary studies of either Schurman or Voetius are in Dutch or German, but one full-length biography of Schurman appeared early in this century entitled *Anna van Schurman: Artist, Scholar, Saint,* by Una Birch (the pseudonym of Constance Pope-Hennessy), published in London in 1909. In 1924 A. M. H. Douma wrote a thesis in Dutch, *Anna Maria van Schurman en de studie der vrouw,* the bibliography of which is valuable even for the non-Dutch reader, as it lists Schurman's published and unpublished works and letters as well as writings about her from her century to ours. Similarly, Katlijne Van der Stighelen's study of Schurman as an artist, *Anna Maria van Schurman (1607–1678) of 'Hoe hooge dat een maeght kan in de konsten stijgen'* (Louvain, 1987), provides extensive bibliographical references and information on Schurman's extant artworks. Fortunately, a most valuable collection of essays which originally appeared in Dutch has now been translated into English: *Choosing the Better Part* (Dordrecht: Kluwer Academic Publishers, 1996), edited by Mirjam de Baar and others, offers essays by highly competent scholars of Schurman from several perspectives as well as a very thorough bibliography. Clearly, interest in Schurman has become much more widespread since I published my first article on her in 1977 in *Church History* ("Anna Maria van Schurman: From Feminism to Pietism"), and we can look forward to more studies of her in the near future.

Voetius also has attracted renewed attention recently both from historians of theology studying the *Nadere Reformatie* and from historians of philosophy interested in his opposition to Descartes. Still, only one selection of his writings is available in English, in *Reformed Dogmatics,* edited and translated by John W. Beardslee III (Oxford University Press, 1965). A chapter in a book in German on major figures in church history, *Gestalten des Kirchengeschichte,* edited by Martin Greschat (Stuttgart, 1982), provides a general study of his life and thought. A recent specialized study by Theo Verbeek, *Descartes and the Dutch: Early Reactions to Cartesian Philosophy, 1637–1650* (Carbondale: Southern Illinois University Press, 1992), places Voetius in the context of debates about Cartesianism. One of Verbeek's students, J. A. van Ruler, has pursued the philosophical differences between Voetius and Descartes to greater depth in *The Crisis of Causality: Voetius and Descartes on God, Nature, and Change* (Leiden: E. J. Brill, 1995). The five studies of various aspects of Voetius's theology which have appeared in the last decade are all in Dutch, but this indication of renewed interest in his thought gives grounds for hope that the English-speaking world will soon recognize his significance not only as an opponent of modern philosophy but also as a major religious leader of the seventeenth century.

SELECTIONS FROM THE WRITINGS OF
ANNA MARIA VAN SCHURMAN

A PRACTICAL PROBLEM

by Anna Maria van Schurman

For the venerable and distinguished theologian, Mr. André Rivet

WHETHER THE STUDY OF LETTERS IS FITTING
FOR A CHRISTIAN WOMAN

We will attempt to defend the *affirmative*.

We advance these presuppositions, first concerning the subject, then also the predicate:

The terms of the subject are free of all ambiguity; for when I say *Christian* woman I understand such a one by profession and in fact.

The terms of the predicate are, first, "the study of letters." *Study*, I say (to omit its other meanings), is here assumed to be the diligent and eager application of the mind. By the word *letters* we understand the knowledge of languages, history, and all disciplines, not only the higher, which they call faculties, but also the lower, which they call philosophic sciences. Only scriptural theology, as it is properly called, do we exclude, since we believe that its fitness for all Christians is beyond controversy.

Second, there occurs the word *fitting*, that is, whether it is right, expedient, appropriate, and proper.

The terms thus having been defined, the issues themselves have to be clarified. For among *women*, some are naturally capable, others more dull-minded; some poorer, some richer; some more involved in business or domestic cares, some less. *The study of letters* is divided either into universal principles, when indeed we work at the same time on all disciplines, or into particular subjects, when we learn some single language or science with a certain facility.

This translation of the *Dissertatio logica* and the letters that follow is based on Schurman's *Opuscula Hebraea, Graeca, Latina, Gallica, Prosaïca et Metrica* (Leiden, 1650), 28–95.

Let us apply the following limitations:

First, in respect to the subject, it is presumed that our woman have at least a mediocre ability and not be utterly inept at learning.[1]

Second, we presume that she will be instructed by the necessary means and that the limited wealth of the household does not altogether stand in her way. I introduce this exception because few are fortunate to have parents who either want or are able to educate them themselves, and it is not possible to contract for the work of tutors in this region without expenses.

Third, we presume that the circumstances of her time and fortune are such that it is possible sometimes to be free from any general or special calling, and certainly from the exercises of devotion or from the duties of the household. As follows easily from this, what helps is, in part, in child-hood, immunity and freedom from cares and responsibilities and, in part, in a more advanced age, either celibacy or the attendance of servants who usually free wealthy women in large part from domestic duties.

Fourth, the goal of studies is presumed not to be vainglory and show or idle curiosity but rather the general goal of the glory of God and the salvation of one's soul in order that she may also emerge the better and happier and may educate and guide her family (if that duty falls to her) and even be useful to her whole sex, to the extent that that is possible.

Limitations of the predicate

I limit *the study of letters* in such manner that I think all honorable disci-plines, or the whole circle of liberal arts,[2] as it is called, is entirely fitting to a Christian woman (just as it is a proper and universal good or adornment of humanity); but it must be in accordance with the dignity and nature of the science or art and also in accordance with the girl's or woman's capa-bility and fortune so that what is to be learned may follow in its own or-der, place, and time and be properly connected. First of all, account should be taken of those sciences or arts that have the closest connection with theology and moral virtue, and which primarily serve them. We consider grammar, logic, and rhetoric to be of this sort. Among these first disci-plines, however, some expressly identify logic as the key to all sciences.

1. Schurman's marginal note: "On the instruction of girls, who among the wealthy are taught partly at home, partly outside the home, read Liv. lib. 3, Plin. Epist. 17. lib.1, Athen. lib.1, Plut. lib. de Educ. liber, Gordia.1.15 de negot. gest, Forner. ad Cassiod."
2. Schurman uses here the Greek term *encyclopaedeia*, a term found in classical writers Quintil-ian, Pliny, and Galen to refer to the circle of arts and sciences considered by the Greeks as essential to a liberal education. *Oxford English Dictionary* 5:219.

Then come physics, metaphysics, history, etc., and also knowledge of languages, especially Hebrew and Greek. All of these things are able to move us to easier and fuller knowledge of Sacred Scripture, to say nothing of other authors. Other subjects, namely mathematics (to which music is also assigned), poetry, painting, and similar things, may be pursued as liberal arts, as an excellent adornment or pastime. Finally, we do not especially urge those studies that pertain to the practice of trial law and the military or to the arts of speaking in church, court, and school, as they are less fitting or necessary. Nevertheless, we do not by any means concede that women should be excluded from scholastic or, so to say, theoretical knowledge of those things, least of all from knowledge of the most noble discipline of politics.

Let us define the phrase *fitting or expedient* not as whether the study of letters is appropriate, requisite, or precisely necessary to eternal salvation, nor indeed as a good that makes for the essence itself of happiness in this life, but as an occupation or means that can contribute to our integrity in this same life and, to a degree, through the contemplation of very beautiful things, move us that much more easily to love of God and to eternal salvation.

Let this then be our thesis: the study of letters is fitting to a Christian woman.

To confirm this we present these arguments, first from the side of the subject, then also of the predicate.

I. *Argument with reference to the subject*

Whoever is instilled by nature with the first principles or the power of the principles of all arts and sciences is suited to study all arts and sciences: but women are instilled by nature with these powers or principles.

Therefore all arts and sciences are fitting to women.

The *proposition* is proved, because if the principles or powers of principles are fitting, the knowledge of the conclusions that are drawn by their nature from those principles is also fitting.

The *assumption* may be proved both from what is specific to the form of this subject, that is to say, human reason, and also from the acts or effects themselves, since it is evident that women learn all kinds of arts and sciences in actuality; and indeed no acts can be without principles.

II. *Argument with reference to the subject*

Whoever by nature has a desire for sciences and arts is suited to study sciences and arts. But women by nature have a desire for arts and sciences. Therefore . . .

The reason of the major premise is obvious since nature makes nothing in vain.

The minor premise is proved because what belongs to the whole species also belongs to single individuals. But every human being (as the Philosopher clearly established in *Metaphysics* book I, chapter 2) desires by nature to know.

III. *Argument with reference to, or externally associated with, the subject*

Whoever is created by God with a countenance raised and erect toward the heavens is suited for the knowledge and contemplation of lofty and heavenly things.

But God created woman with a countenance raised and erect toward the heavens. Therefore . . .

And while other animals look with downturned head to the earth, he gave a raised countenance to humans, etc.

IV. *Argument*

Whoever longs greatly for a solid and enduring occupation is suited for the study of letters. But woman longs greatly for a solid and enduring occupation. Therefore . . .

The consequent of the major premise is proved, since nothing in like manner directs all movements of the soul to itself and, as the great Erasmus says,[3] nothing so occupies the whole mind of a girl as does study: to which, as to a place of refuge, she may be allowed to flee on any occasion.

The minor is proved by this twofold reason:

1. Whoever is in greatest danger of vanity on account of weakness or inconstancy of intellect or temperament and also because of the innumerable attractions of the world is in greatest need of a solid and constant occupation.

And because of the weakness of a woman, etc. Therefore . . .

The major can again be proved, since opposites best cure opposites, nor does anything withstand emptiness more effectively than a serious and perpetual occupation.

The minor we consider beyond dispute; since scarcely any virtue, however heroic, is able to conquer the Sirens of the world and youth unless it is occupied with serious and solid things.

---

3. Schurman's marginal note: "In the letter to Guillaume Budé in which he discusses the education of the daughters of Thomas More." *The Correspondence of Erasmus* (Letters 1122 to 1251, from 1520–1521), trans. R. A. B. Mynors (Toronto: University of Toronto Press, 1988), 8: 297.

2. The reason by which the assumption or the minor premise of argument IV is proved:

Whoever has abundance of leisure is greatly in need of a solid and enduring occupation.

But those women who enjoy wealth as their lot in life most of all abound in leisure. Therefore . . .

Again the consequent of the major is proved: first, since leisure in itself is tedious, and even burdensome. As Saint Nazianzus rightly said, "Better action than inaction." And second, since leisure gives way to vices; for "By doing nothing human beings learn to do ill."[4]

V. Argument

Literary study is fitting for someone who has a more tranquil and free life; but women generally enjoy a more tranquil and free life. Therefore for women generally the study of letters is fitting.

The reason of the major is clear since nothing is as favorable to studies as tranquillity and liberty.

We prove the minor with this argument: To whomever it befalls to be as free as possible from work and exempt from business and public cares, to that person befalls a more tranquil and free life.

And it often befalls a woman (especially in an unmarried state) to be as free as possible from work, etc. Therefore . . .

VI. Argument

Whoever is fit for the study of the principal sciences is also fit for the study of instrumental or auxiliary sciences. But study of the principal sciences is fitting for a Christian woman etc. Therefore . . .

The consequent of the major is valid, since to whomever the end is fitting, the legitimate means by which one may most easily move toward following that end are also fitting.

But instrumental or auxiliary sciences are legitimate means, etc. Therefore . . .

The minor is proved by the study that is fitting to a Christian woman, namely diligent and serious meditation on the divine word, the knowledge of God, and the consideration of his most beautiful works, as these things apply equally to all Christians.

The study of letters is appropriate for anyone who needs to fol-

---

4. St. Gregory of Nazianzus (329–389), one of the Cappadocian Fathers who led in the defeat of Arianism at the Council of Constantinople in 381, had entered the monastic life but was pressured to become priest and ordained against his will.

low a pastime at home by oneself rather than outside among others.

But for a woman at home by herself rather than outside among others etc. Therefore . . .

The major is very true since studies possess the advantage of always providing a source of pleasure for a companion, even if no other comrades beyond that are available; whence according to the wise Greek Proverb it is said, "Self-choice is also self-experience."

The reason of the minor is no less obvious, since the Apostle wants women to be homemakers, Titus 2:5. Next, experience itself shows that those women whose tongues, ears, eyes are more accustomed to wander and to watch for outside delights, have their faith, diligence, even their chastity called into question by many.

VII. Argument from the genus of the predicate, that is to say, of science

Arts and sciences are fitting for those to whom all virtue in general is fitting.

And all virtue in general is fitting to a woman. Therefore arts and sciences are fitting to a woman.

The major is apparent from the division of virtue into intellectual and moral, under which, namely the first, the Philosopher included the arts and sciences.

The minor needs no proof since virtue (as Seneca says) chooses neither rank nor sex.

VIII. Argument from the goal of sciences

Whatever perfects and adorns the human mind is fitting for a Christian woman.

But the sciences and arts perfect and adorn the human mind.

The argument of the major is that their own highest perfection is proper to all creatures and that toward that end it is necessary to struggle with all their strength.[5]

The minor is proved since the sciences and arts are habits by which the natural powers of the human intellect are perfected.

IX. Argument

Whatever things by their nature contribute to arousing in us greater love and reverence for God are fitting for a Christian woman.

But the sciences and arts contribute by their nature to arousing greater love and reverence for God. Therefore . . .

5. Schurman's marginal note: "A good added to a good thing," as the Philosopher [Aristotle] says in his *Topics* [bk. 3, chap. 3], "makes a greater good."

The truth of the major is clearer than light since the most perfect love of God is fitting for all people as is the highest reverence, so much so that in this matter no one can sin in excess.

The minor is proved by the following argument: whatever causes us to observe and recognize God and divine works with a greater degree of clarity contributes toward arousing in us a greater love and reverence for God. And certainly sciences and arts cause us to observe and recognize God with a greater degree of clarity. Therefore . . .

The major again is proved by an argument such as this: whatever is in truth most beautiful, best, and most perfect is loved more and held more worthy of reverence or celebration to the extent that it is better known. But God and all his works are most beautiful, best, etc. Therefore . . .

The minor can also be proved from the goal or effects of the sciences, of which there is none that may not contribute greatly toward an easier and more distinct knowledge of God and divine works.

X. Argument

Whatever fortifies us against heresies and discloses their traps is fitting for a Christian woman.

But the sciences etc. Therefore . . .

The reason of the major is evident since no Christian ought to neglect his duty in this common danger.

The minor is proved since that sounder philosophy is like a breast-plate and (if I might use the words of Clement of Alexandria) a fence for the lord's vineyard, that is to say, the teachings of the Savior;[6] or—a simile that pleased Basil the Great—in conjunction with the gospel, it is like leaves that are an ornament and support to their own fruit.[7]

Certainly with right reason it is easily possible to refute spurious or corrupt reason, by which heresies are chiefly nourished.

XI. Argument

Those things that teach prudence without any detriment to reputation and modesty are fitting for a Christian woman.

But the study of letters teaches prudence without any detriment, etc.

6. Clement of Alexandria, *The Stromata or Miscellanies* (bk. 1, chap. 20) in *The Ante-Nicene Fathers* (reprint; Grand Rapids, MI: Wm. B. Eerdmans, 1983), 2:323: "and the Hellenic philosophy does not, by its approach, make the truth more powerful; but rendering powerless the assault of sophistry against it, and frustrating the treacherous plots laid against the truth, is said to be the proper "fence and wall of the vineyard."

7. Basil the Great (c. 330–379), having been educated in the best classical and Christian culture of his day, became instrumental as a theologian and bishop in bringing the fourth-century disputes about the nature of Christ to a conclusion.

Therefore . . .

The major is generally acknowledged, since everyone knows that the honor of the female sex is very delicate and that there is almost nothing that it needs more than prudence. And furthermore, everyone knows what a difficult matter it is and how full of risks, as they say, to derive prudence from use or experience itself.

The minor is proved, since the writings of learned men produce for us not only excellent precepts but also very beautiful examples and lead us as if by the hand to virtue.

XII. Argument

Whatever leads to true greatness of soul is fitting for a Christian woman.

But the study of letters leads to true greatness of soul. Therefore . . .

I prove the major since to whatever extent one is by nature inclined toward the vice of pusillanimity, the more one needs the aid of the opposing virtue. But woman by nature, etc. Therefore . . .

The minor is proved, since science raises a person's mind and takes away the hobgoblin from those things that are usually feared or striven after ineffectively.

XIII. Argument

Whatever fills the human mind with exceptional and honest delight is fitting for a Christian woman.

But the study of letters fills the mind with exceptional and honest delight. Therefore . . .

The reason of the major is proved, since nothing is more suitable to human nature than an exceptional and honest delight, which represents a certain likeness to the divine rejoicing in humans, which Aristotle described splendidly with these words: Delight is a divine thing implanted in mortals by nature.[8]

The minor is proved, since, with the single exception of that supernatural delight of Christians, there is no greater delight and none more worthy of the noble mind than that which comes from the study of letters. It is easy to show this with various examples as well as reasons.

XIV. Argument from the opposite

The study of letters is fitting for those to whom ignorance or lack of awareness is not fitting.

---

8. See Aristotle, *Nicomachean Ethics*, 1.9 (1099b) and 10.8 (1178–1179).

But ignorance is not fitting for a Christian woman. Therefore . . .

The major is confirmed with this argument: Whatever in itself is not so much a cause of error in the intellect but of defect in the will or action is not fitting to a Christian woman.

And ignorance in itself is a cause of error, etc. Therefore . . .

The reason of the major is again shown, first with respect to error in the intellect, because ignorance or lack of skill in the intellect, which is the eye of the soul, is nothing other than blindness and darkness, which stand forth as the cause of all error.[9] Second, it is shown with respect to defects in will or action, since whatever in itself renders men proud, arrogant, etc., is the cause of defects in will or action. But ignorance or lack of awareness in itself renders men proud, etc. Therefore . . .

The reason of the greater is evident.

The minor is proved, since to the extent that each one knows himself less, he will be more pleased with himself and will scorn others: and the person who does not know how much he does not know will think himself perfectly fine. Finally (to reply concerning barbarism), nothing is more intractable than ignorance, which Erasmus testifies he has experienced more than once; and as the holy Plato said, "The man who receives a proper education is wont to become the most divine and civilized of animals; insufficiently or badly raised, however, he is the most savage of any creature on earth."[10] Add to this that when one has faithfully learned the liberal arts, one's character is refined and one cannot remain uncivilized.

Finally it is possible to show the danger of ignorance with respect to vice from the very nature of virtue and vice. For while a great deal of precision is required for every virtuous act in order for it to conform to right reason, even the smallest lack of discipline, which follows spontaneously after ignorance, is sufficient for a complete accounting of vice.[11]

Evidence and examples I omit here for the sake of brevity.

Refutation of the Adversaries

We think these presuppositions should be set forward first:

9. Schurman's marginal note: "If the light that is in thee be darkness, how great is that darkness! Matthew 6 [:23]."

10. Plato, *Laws* 6.766a. Schurman's citation of the Greek original leaves out some words.

11. Schurman seems here to be referring to Aristotle's *Ethics* 1106b:29–35: "There are many ways to be in error . . . ; but there is only one way to be correct. That is why error is easy and correctness hard, since it is easy to miss the target and hard to hit it. And so for this reason also excess and deficiency are proper to vice, the mean to virtue: "for we are noble in only one way, but bad in all sorts of ways.'" Aristotle, *Nicomachean Ethics*, trans. Terence Irwin (Indianapolis: Hackett Publishing Co., 1985), 44.

1. There are certain adversaries who, for whatever prejudices, as if deprived of eyes, do not limit our subject; but they think it follows from our thesis that there is to be no distinction [among women] from the perspective of either natural abilities or social status which would render the aforesaid less suitable.

2. There are also those who seem not to know any other goal of studies than either profit or empty fame, unless they serve a public function. This is the first and rather shameful falsehood, as if it were utterly superfluous to philosophize *"in order to flee ignorance."*[12]

3. There are, finally, those who do not necessarily deny that studies are fitting to a woman, but only that a higher level of knowledge is not fitting. These people are vexed perhaps by jealousy, otherwise certainly by the fear that it might sometime happen that "many students are better than their teachers." And again that saying of the ancient poet: "You youths carry minds of women, the heroic woman that of a man."

Thesis of the Adversaries

For a Christian woman the study of letters is not fitting unless she be divinely inspired to this by a certain special motion or instinct.

First argument from the part of the subject.

Whoever has a weaker mind is not fitted for the study of letters, but the mind of a woman is weaker.

The major they will prove since for the study of letters a strong and healthy mental ability is required, unless we should wish to labor in vain or fall into danger because the intellect is incapable.

The minor they consider to be generally acknowledged.

We respond to the major: by our limitations we declare those to be excluded who on account of weakness of mind may be wholly unfit for studies in view of the fact that at least average minds are required here. Next we say a heroic mental ability is not always precisely necessary for studies, since we see a number of learned men gathered indiscriminately from among the average.

To the minor I respond that it is not absolutely true, but only compared to the masculine sex. For even if women are not able to compare in mental ability to the more excellent men (who are as eagles in the clouds), nevertheless the argument itself states that not a few such women are found who may be admitted to studies with some benefit.

12. Aristotle, *Metaphysics*, 982 b 20.

But indeed we infer from the contrary: whoever is less capable in mental skills is most suited to the study of letters. But a woman is less capable in mental skills.

The major we prove, since those who are less furnished with the gifts of nature are most suited to those means and aids by which these defects may be alleviated. And the study of letters is that means and aid. Therefore . . .

Second Objection

If one's mind does not incline to studies, one is not fitted for them. And the mind of a woman does not incline to studies. Therefore . . .

They prove the major since nothing is to be done against the will of Minerva, as they say.

The minor they will prove out of custom itself, since very rarely do women apply their minds to studies.

Let us respond to the major: it should have been stated, "If a person's mind does not incline to study by all legitimately attempted means, the study of letters is not fitting for that person." Otherwise the consequent is denied.

To the minor we say, no one can properly judge of our inclination to studies before he has prodded us to undertake studies by the best reasons and means and has also given a certain taste of their sweetness; meanwhile, however, we are not lacking examples that show that the contrary is true.

Third Objection

Whoever lacks the necessary means of study is not suited to the study of letters. But women lack the means, etc. Therefore . . .

The major is not disputed.

The minor they try to prove on the grounds that today there are no colleges or academies in which women can be trained.

But we deny this consequent for it suffices that they be trained at home under leadership of parents or some private tutor.

Fourth Objection

Those whose studies fail their proper end are little fitted for them.

But women's studies fail their proper end. Therefore . . .

The major can be proved, since all things are done on account of their goal.

They demonstrate the minor in that women's study very rarely or never advances toward public duties, whether political, ecclesiastical, or academic.

We respond to the major that in the speculative sciences women are by no means frustrated of their goal; even in the practical sciences, which we have just mentioned, if they do not follow that primary or public goal, nevertheless they pursue the secondary and, as I would say, more private goal of these sciences.

Fifth Objection

If for the serving of one's vocation it is sufficient to know little, the curriculum of the liberal arts or a higher level of knowledge is not fitting for that person.

But to serve their vocation women need to know little. Therefore . . .

They prove the consequent of the major on the grounds that it is not fitting for anyone to do unnecessary things or those foreign to one's vocation.

They prove the minor on the grounds, namely, that a woman's vocation is confined within narrow boundaries, certainly within the limits of private or domestic life.

Omitting the major, we respond to the minor that there is ambiguity in the terms, first in the term "vocation"; for if they understand here the vocation of private life, as opposed to public duties, we say that for the same reason men in private life would be denied the curriculum of the liberal arts or a higher degree of knowledge; whereas nevertheless the most weighty opinion of Plutarch on all individual men of whatever status rightly declares that the perfect man necessarily is capable of studying all things and of doing all that ought to be done. If they mean a special vocation that serves either family or household matters, we say that the universal knowledge that pertains to all, and by which we are Christians or at least humans, is by no means thereby to be excluded. Let me dare to assert that an unmarried woman can and ought above all to have time for the latter inasmuch as she is usually much freer from the hindrances of the former. "The unmarried woman cares for the things of the Lord" (1 Corinthians 7:34).

Second, there is ambiguity in the words "it is enough"; to remove the ambiguity, what we said above on the limitations of the phrase "whether it is fitting" in respect to the necessity of literary study will suffice.

Our thesis therefore stands: the study of letters is fitting for the Christian woman.

From this we draw the conclusion: women can and ought to be stimulated to embrace this kind of life by the best and strongest arguments, the testimonies of the wise, and finally the examples of illustrious women. This is especially true, however, for those who are better provided than others with leisure and other means and supports for the study of letters. And since it is preferable to imbue the mind with better studies from infancy itself, we think parents themselves should be the first to be urged and seriously admonished concerning their duty.

SOME LETTERS CONCERNING
THE SAME PROBLEM

*Between the Most Excellent Maiden Anna Maria van Schurman
and Dr. André Rivet, Doctor of Most Sacred Theology*

To the most distinguished gentleman, Dr. André Rivet, salutations,

Whenever I think to myself, venerable Sir, how much your kindness has obliged me to you and with what honor you have expressed your opinion of me to others, I confess nothing is more pleasing and no greater fortune has ever befallen me than from so slight cultivation to obtain such abundant fruits. But by now whoever knows and reveres these virtues of yours ceases to wonder what reason impelled so many good things to be granted to me. And since in this age the stars are especially inconstant and fleeting, I shall resort to this unique support of friendship.

Nor am I so ignorant of this world as not to believe that there exists some ill-willed person who would declare that I had been led to this point in the vainglorious hope of displaying my mental ability. But God is my witness how far removed from this kind of ambition is my purpose in the kind of life I have undertaken. Although I bear these things rather lightly when I know myself to be otherwise, I rejoice nevertheless that you have given no room for scruples. For out of your kind disposition toward me you have interpreted everything so favorably that the great hope that I had harbored up to this point in one person you have never disappointed. Therefore from now on, as our trust is increasing, I do not think it right for me anymore to conceal from you any of my studies, or rather, trifles. It is a year, or about that, since someone tried to put into French (because the charm and elegance of that language usually strike a responsive chord in young women) the book in which I try to persuade them, albeit more by the effects [that would result] than by the power [of my eloquence], of the best way to make use of our leisure. Since, however, nothing in the book was in final form except its general form, nor, moreover, were its images and conceits to be taken as anything but shadows and darkness, I did not think it was worthy yet of [being submitted to] your criticism or in any way capable of [receiving] such a light. Nonetheless, by I know not what secret direction of its guardian spirit, it has hastened to you as if to its guide and protector; indeed, [under your protection] someday, if God wills, it will overcome all obstacles. Meanwhile I shall make supplication to him with inward prayers, that he may keep you and yours safe and sound as an example to individuals and an ornament to all, that is, of his Church. Farewell, most fair man, esteemed not the least by me among your lovers and admirers.

> *Desirous of pleasing you and similarly*
> *every good man,*
> Anna Maria van Schurman
>
> *Utrecht, January 12, 1632*

To the most excellent and erudite maiden Anna Maria van Schurman,

Most noble maiden, if I have published your praises among others, I have done what I ought. For an honest and sincere heart does not close inside and admire within itself alone what, if it becomes known to others, is a cause of honor to the one whose gifts are being praised; and it can also be useful to others both as an example that they may be incited toward honorable emulation; and that they may pay tribute gratefully to God that he has adorned also your sex with such splendor of letters and good arts. It can also serve as proof for the living and for posterity that it is not by a defect of mind or judgment that most women do not deal with such things but because they do not want to apply the mind to them, or because they are not free on account of other and more humble occupations. Nor may it be expedient for many to choose this kind of life; it may suffice if some, called to it by a special instinct, sometimes stand out, especially in our time, in which many young men profess studies more than they seriously cultivate them and, content with the name alone, scorn the thing itself; certainly someone such as you helps to expose them and fill them with shame. These reasons moved me to bring into the open those things that your modesty almost hides, insofar as I was able, just as I will do again when occasion arises. I should add that I am looking to my own interests in this matter, for I indeed pride myself not unjustly that a girl of such mental ability and such piety should moreover entreat my friendship and so kindly provoke me to this communication. I feel myself so moved by this kindness that I bestow my paternal affection upon you whom I do not yet know by sight. Would that I might someday be able to make this affection have its effect! An occasion will be given, if God wills, that in each other's presence I may be able to open my heart and gaze on the face that such an elegant mind adorns. A mind, I add, that is so sincere and so modest in its own self-estimation. I have thus far not heard of anyone who would despoil you of this virtue. As far as I am concerned, I thought you had sinned more by lack [of self-estimation] than by excess except that I think even that defect leads to perfection.

I handed over your French verses to Princess Elizabeth, and she read and praised them in my presence and promised that she would render thanks in her own hand. But the work that you are considering in that same language, I ask you not to subject me to desiring it any longer: I would read it most eagerly. And if there is anything in my maternal language, learned by you as a foreign language, of which you should be advised, know that I will speak clearly and freely. However, having seen specimens of your style, which satisfied me completely, I should not think there would be any need of my comments.

Undoubtedly you know I am going to move within two months to the Hague, where a new occupation calls me, in which I must become a boy again, but in conjunction with a grand boy.[1] If I can give him to the country and to the church as a man, I shall consider my work not badly spent. Whether I live there or elsewhere, you will always have, as long as I live,

> *my admiration for your virtues and*
> *above all for your exceptional piety and modesty,*
> *André Rivet*
>
> *Leiden, March 1, 1632*

To the most distinguished man and a father to be venerated in Christ, Sir André Rivet,

Nothing could please me more, revered sir and a father to be venerated in Christ, than to know that you welcome with such good will however small that thing was which we could through our mediocrity bestow on your granddaughter. Because if you want to consider only the item itself, it truly was not enough; if, however, you consider the weight of our affection, there is indeed nothing that I think is not due you by right of our long-time friendship.

I received most happily, as was appropriate, the volumes with which

---

1. Having been professor in Leyden since 1620, Rivet moved to the Hague in 1632 to become tutor to the future prince of Orange.

you wished to adorn my library. The gift was indeed very pleasing to me when I turned my eyes toward the person of the giver and when I turned to the argument itself, that is, to the subject matter of your triumph. What should I answer? Nothing precisely is at hand by which I might offer recompense, even if I wanted very much to do so; unless perhaps the one who feels gratitude be thought to have requited his debt. Further, I think it not less of a kindness that you deign to offer your services, both by aiding with all my studies and also by resolving more serious doubts. Most assuredly, as is fitting, I highly value your judgment because where I do not grasp matters sufficiently, I hesitate uncertainly and am forced to proceed, as it were, with a suspended step. But for a long time now I have avidly desired your opinion in a weighty matter (as something that especially touches upon the office and condition of unmarried women), and I do not think anything would be more illustrious or more glorious than for my opinion to be confirmed by your judgment as almost by a rescript from you.[2] But if indeed you feel otherwise, it will not fill me with shame, after I am instructed otherwise, to sound the signal for retreat.

I question, however, what you put forward in this matter as a general principle. You provided an opening in the letter you previously sent me, in which, after you have praised many things regarding me and my studies lovingly and honorably, as you are accustomed, you write thus: "Nor may it perhaps be expedient for many to choose this kind of life; it may suffice if some, called to it by a special instinct, sometimes stand out." If married women involved in household affairs or any others who by necessity look after the interests of family matters are understood here, I assent immediately; but if we mean girls endowed with mental ability who are to be educated more liberally—such as our age produces in large numbers—, I will accede less easily. An enormous admiration of sciences or the justice of the common law moves me not to set down as rare in our sex that which is most worthy of the desires of all. For since wisdom is so much an ornament of the human races that it ought by right to be extended to one and all (as far as, in fact, one's fortune allows) I do not see why the most beautiful adornment of all by far is not fitting for a maiden, in whom we allow diligence in tending and adorning herself. Nor is there any reason why the Republic should fear such a change for itself, since the glory of the literary order in no way obstructs the light of the rulers. On the contrary, all agree that that state in the end will flourish most which is inhabited by many

2. In the Roman Empire and in Roman Catholicism, a rescript was an official written response to a private question or petition.

subjects obedient not so much to laws as to wisdom. Add to this that neither virtue nor the chorus of the learned can gain their honor or dignity unless the more influential portion of them knows how to esteem the glory and splendor of letters not with blind admiration but with true estimation.

But in order not to linger further in the entrance hall, I approach the crux of the debate itself. If this is well worked out, the whole truth of the matter will be apparent. The principal question therefore is whether it is fitting for a maiden, especially in this day and age, to study letters and fine arts. Weighty arguments have led me to find the affirmative more attractive. For indeed, to begin with civil law, I remember reading somewhere that according to Ulpian women were barred from all civil or public office. By what justice this was decreed I will not now laboriously inquire, save that I think it is clearly proven from this that the leisure in which we pass time was praised and legitimate. From this arises a large supply of time and quiet leisure friendly to the muses. But most of all, by a certain special privilege, freedom from necessary work and also immunity from cares and domestic matters may be granted to us. To be sure, this wide and empty space of life, where it flows into luxury and negligence, where it is not laid to any good cause, may become the opportunity for all vices. Basil said admirably, "Idleness is the beginning of vice."[3] And in whatever manner we may avoid this Charybdis, is not the mind effeminized little by little and dissolved into the likeness of the leisure and ignorance in which it lies? What then? Observe how Seneca, cultivator of the more sublime mind, opens the way between the rocks. For, he says, of all men only those who are at leisure (that is, those putting their leisure to excellent use) have time for wisdom;[4] they alone live. For they not only look after their own age well, they also bring all ages to bear on theirs. For one must not seek leisure away from the best things but seek the best things when at leisure. Thus a deeper tranquillity in seclusion will occasion for us neither distress nor weariness. Indeed, leisure and solitude, the two things, as Cicero says, which bring lassitude to others, heighten the alertness of the wise.[5]

But they are apt to argue that pulling the needle and distaff is an ample enough school for women. I confess many have been thus persuaded, and those of today who are maliciously inclined agree with them in many cases. But we who seek the voice of reason, not of received custom, do not accept this rule of Lesbos. By what law, I ask, have these things become

3. Basil of Caesarea, *Homiliae in Hexameron*, 7.5.11.
4. Seneca, *Dialogues*, 10.13.9.6; 14.1.1.
5. Cicero, *De officiis*, 3.1.9, 10.

our lot? Divine or human? They will never demonstrate that these limits by which we are forced into an order are ordained by fate or prescribed from heaven. For if we seek testimony from antiquity, examples from all ages and even the authority of the greatest men demonstrate the contrary, as she who is the noblest glory of the Gournay family shows with both wit and learning in the book that she entitled *The Equality of Men and Women*. But in order not to say what has already been said, I will refrain from enumerating these examples and authorities. It suffices for me to add to these clear words that higher things are not merely fitting but to be expected in this kind of life. For the more noble-spirited natures do not allow their talents to be confined within such narrow limits, nor do they let the sharpness of their higher intellect always be drawn down beneath their ability.

Indeed, if these Draconian laws ought to prevail, it would seem to me no wonder that many are sometimes seized by the attractions of the coaxing world because of contempt for this less valued work. No respect, no dignity, finally no reward for virtue, by which worthy souls are customarily urged on to pursue praiseworthy things above all else, leaves us any hope here. In vain do we boast of the nobility that we have received from our forebears, since a useless obscurity soon envelops the same. Hence it is that to one reading the history often of very long expanses of time the monuments of our name seem no greater than the traces of a ship passing in the sea. "But," they ask, "whence does glory come to you? Whence immortality? Surely not from leisure?" Why not? But it would be from a leisure illuminated by the light of knowledge. It is fitting for us to become illustrious with the aid not so much of Athena in armor as by Athena in citizen garb. Moreover, where true philosophy occupies the throne of our mind, no opening is ever given to useless or aimless activities of a wandering mind. This also Erasmus, distinguished patron of all finer literature, eloquently observed with these words when he discussed the education of the daughters of Thomas More: "Nothing so occupies the whole heart and soul of a girl as study." For how do we not safely spurn the trappings of this world, the specious authority of examples, and the foolishness of an unrestrained age when we look down on these earthly things from the heights of wisdom?

Further, since it pertains no less to the duty than to the happiness of all to struggle toward the original perfection of our beginnings (from which there is none who has not fallen short) we must strive at all costs so that the image of him who is light and truth may begin to shine more and more in the supreme governing seat of our mind. I do not deny that theology fills both sides of the account here (as that which greatly perfects the mind); nevertheless those who want theology to walk alone and unescorted seem to me to have insufficiently perceived the majesty of such a queen. For indeed when we look into the book of nature, who does not see by what a beautiful harmony the parts of each of these sciences [theology and physics] fit together? How much support the one brings to the other, how much light? Nor should it hinder us that some confine this study in such narrow limits, thinking it makes little difference to us whether the machine of this world flowed together from atoms; whether it emerged from unformed chaos; whether certain bodies take as their lot celestial nature, certain terrestrial; whether the uppermost mass of the world revolves in an orbit or whether rather those things spin which strive to turn not around the highest but around the lowest mass; whether the setting sun is immersed in the ocean; whether it owes its light also to the antipodes; whether the earth has taken a square or round shape; finally, whether the entire earth or just the perception of our eyes is bounded by the horizon of the world. If we should listen to such statements, which are commonly tossed about for the purpose of disgracing us, then we ourselves would be sanctioning that God, creator of all, who introduced us into this theater to show forth, know, and celebrate his most beautiful works, would be frustrated in his ends. For nature was not a stepmother to us to the extent that she wanted to prevent us from inspection of her. To what purpose otherwise would we have been endowed with that which the Philosopher affirms to be in all humans, namely the desire to know?[6] To what purpose would he have given erect stature unless to direct our eyes and minds toward contemplation of him? Certainly we would be tree trunks, not humans; guests, not inhabitants, of this world, if we did not bring an excited mind, as if fired by divine love, to such beautiful, august things in which the Majesty of the eternal divinity shines forth. Nor may we think we perform our duty commendably if we do no more than look at these a few times as if through latticework. For in this case we do not look in order to know but rather show by this that we do not see because we do not desire to know further. Nothing more marvelous is subjected to our eyes than a human being, nothing more beautiful than the home of the soul. But how small is that which is judged solely by its skin, or only by external appearance. How miserably we should blush at such superb hymns of the pagans in which, while they probe the depths of nature and, in probing,

6. Aristotle, *Metaphysics*, 1.980a22.

approach the first cause of all more closely, they are accustomed to sing the praises of the highest maker. Furthermore, whenever our minds are turned to the constellation of sacred letters, who would deny that we are obliged to pay the same gratitude by so many examples of holy men who appropriated material from this work to celebrate their God.

Moreover, to say nothing in general concerning the study of history that today obtains for the most part in women's chambers and the courts of the nobility, we shall examine only in passing whether the knowledge of public affairs is fitting for any private person. Indeed for the practice and use of the Republic I would easily concede it to be directly relevant: but on account of theoretical and special benefits that redound from history to individuals we think no one should neglect this knowledge. The sacred writings lead the way here; but they not only lead the way—they lead us by the hand. There the succession of the ages are connected through the reigns of monarchs; there the rise and fall of the greatest peoples is either described or announced. Nor is it surprising, since the marvelous judgments of God, which we ought to heed constantly, appear there in a more splendid subject matter; and since these universal judgments cannot occur in the space of a single person's lifetime. If God wishes this study to be dear to everyone, can it not be that contemplation of this marvelous government will stir our lyres? About this the royal Psalmist, spellbound with his whole mind, always exclaimed, "How very great are your deeds, O Lord, how deep your thoughts."[7]

Perhaps some will object here, This is all nothing else than to commend monastic life or to restrict our duty to contemplation alone. Indeed reason seems to argue thus, so that first we look out for ourselves, as much as is necessary for our happiness; then for our neighbor. In vain does one who never had time for oneself assume the responsibility of being free for others. In vain does one who has not been helpful to oneself concern oneself with being helpful to others with advice or deeds. In vain, finally, will one who is a stranger in one's own home aspire to civil community or the bond of the higher polity of Christians. For, I beseech you, would it not be ill-considered to want to build the whole economy of moral virtue on the ignorance and opinions of the crowd? Indeed, if you make an exception for chance, the examples of every age teach us that no one gets what one wants when sacrificing to the mighty gods unless one comes instructed in great and solid knowledge. That knowledge very much prepares, disposes, and renders us fit for doing well and lifts the mind to undertake more ex-

7. Psalm 92:5.

cellent deeds. Besides, nothing is more useful for a young woman, nothing more necessary than to distinguish wicked from honest, harmful from harmless, appropriate from inappropriate. But how much skill in discernment this activity demands of us! But since it is not practical or safe for us women to learn prudence of this sort by experience, we must necessarily flee to history," as in a mirror to beautify and make our lives like the virtues of others." It is never permitted, I say, for us women to return to grace and good reputation when dishonor begins to cling to us out of some base suspicion, so much so that indeed the great concern incumbent on girls is not so much to avoid bad things after they have broken out as to take precautions lest they at some time become a problem.

Finally, I am not able to pass in silence over the arts and instrumental sciences (as they call them), which follow the principal sciences just as footservants necessarily follow their queen, without saying a word about the delight we should have in the capacity to speak in many languages, especially if they are held for use, not for show. For languages are faithful caretakers, nay rather interpreters, of those things that a wise antiquity leaves to us. When antiquity speaks to us in its own idiom, it reveals to our minds a genuine likeness of itself and touches our senses with a certain marvelous grace and charm that with good reason we find missing in all translations, however good they may be. If to provide you with a peroration I were to explicate and prove how profitable it is to draw from the original sources their heavenly teachings, that would be nothing else than what the proverb calls "lending light to the sun."

But in order to bring this discussion to an end, let me cite one example that is constantly in my mind. One example, I say, of the incomparable princess Jane Grey, to whom no people, no age (which I say by the leave of everyone) will provide an equal. The Florentine Michelangelo, who describes the history of her life and death fully and compassionately in a discussion that took place between him and Feckenham,[8] who brought the news of her recent death, noted among other things, namely this, that she considered of less account, in addition to those other notable gifts she had received from God, her noble blood, her beautiful form, her vibrant youth by which she would otherwise have been able to achieve for herself glory

---

8. John de Feckenham (1515–1584/5), an English priest who remained steadfastly Roman Catholic yet worked against persecution of Protestants during Queen Mary's reign, was sent to interview Lady Jane Grey in prison to attempt to get her to recant her Protestant beliefs, which she refused. The transcript of the dialogue is found in *The Acts and Monuments of John Foxe* (New York: AMS Press, 1965), 6:415–417.

and favor in this world; instead, she affirmed magnanimously that nothing in all her life had been so gratifying as the fact that she had knowledge of the three languages that are called learned; furthermore, that if the desire or delight that can accrue to us in this life from that matter should come in the name of true happiness, she confessed that for herself she has concealed that pleasure in the study of good letters and especially Holy Scripture. And although many might greatly censure studies of this kind in a woman, nevertheless, on account of the great consolation of mind that in the last analysis she had derived from that source and still felt inwardly, she judged their opinion out of harmony with reason. Behold the words of a swan issuing forth not under the shadow of the schools, but in the final act of a glorious martyrdom. Who, I beseech you, will not venerate them as an oracle?

And so I have not hesitated to babble these things before you concerning by no means trifling matters, relying, to be sure, on the indulgence of your paternal love toward me. But I break off here lest I seem to have wished to leave nothing unsaid or indeed to have been unmindful of your responsibilities. Farewell, dear father to me in many respects, and please do not disdain to extend my greetings to your most beloved wife.

Anna Maria van Schurman
who depends completely on your support

Utrecht, November 6, 1637[9]

To the most noble virgin who excels in every form of virtue, Anna Maria van Schurman,

Your most elegant dissertation on behalf of your sex and the aptitude of women's minds for undertaking all the liberal arts and sciences, equaling and perhaps even surpassing the minds of men, has kept me in a state of uncertainty for some time. On one side was the shame of jumping bail and leaving our cause undefended. On the other side was ingratitude toward that adversary whom I would rather help, conquest by whom would be a thing most pleasant and sweet, especially since you argue your case with such modesty and without omitting any of those things that contribute to your cause in a most eloquent and tightly argued discourse.

---

9. I choose the date according to the handwritten letter in manuscript 133 B 8 of the Royal Library at the Hague ("VII Ides of November"), rather than the printed date in the *Opuscula* and the manuscript copy in the University Library in Utrecht ("VIII Ides of March"), because Rivet's following letter indicates a lapse of time prior to his response.

The occasion arose for you from my words in a certain letter in which, while I praised your undertaking and admired your success, I did not admit that what I considered appropriate for you and a few others should be done by all. You therefore did not want to have me mention among other admirable things what we see in you. You wanted this [education] to be of the many so that you might hide in the crowd and have nothing singular attributed to you. You are able to be very persuasive, but here you act in vain; you will not draw to your opinion anyone who knows you. But this is also part of your modesty, that you want the eyes of all turned away from your virtues that they may turn toward many others. Forgive me if I say reality will not follow the lead of your words, and, even if you obtain from us what you intend, you will not be able to draw the female world into your opinion. And so you fight either alone or with a few, deserted by all others whose talents and sentiments do not incline to such. You say the will is lacking, not the capacity, which even happens in men. In some I don't deny this, but yet if conduct and studies follow the makeup of the body, it is certain that the author of nature so formed the sexes differently in order to signify that He had destined men to one set of things and women to another. You are not ignorant by what reason the wise Ithacan separated out Achilles from the daughters of the foreign king even though he was clothed with a woman's toga.[10] I will not say with the old poets, nature gave "intelligence to men, but it does not have it for women." I am not so unfair to your sex nor so unjust to God, but it seems certain to me that practical civic knowledge ought to be as different as possible from that of women; and the description of a strong and active woman whom the Holy Spirit praises through Solomon was laid out in this way in order that the things that he attributed to her most in praise be greatly distant from the study of these liberal subjects.[11]

The hypothesis of mine that you cite was, "nor is it perhaps expedient for many to choose this kind of life; it may suffice if some, called to it by a special instinct, sometimes stand out." In what? Clearly in philological,

10. According to Greek legend, Achilles, son of the goddess Thetis and the mortal Peleus, was sent to live in disguise among the daughters of Lycomedes, king of Scyros, because an oracle had foretold that he would die in the Trojan War. Ulysses, king of Ithaca, learned of this and, wanting to recruit Achilles for the war, visited Lycomedes disguised as a merchant of fine cloths and ornaments. As the king's daughters, with Achilles among them, were admiring the wares, Ulysses suddenly brought out arms to the sound of war calls. While the girls fled, Achilles rushed enthusiastically toward the weapons, thus revealing his male identity.

11. Proverbs 31:10–31.

philosophical, and similar studies, which involve knowledge of various languages and of the whole collection of those disciplines that are called "encyclopedia" or "liberal learning." And so I persist in my opinion that it is neither useful nor appropriate. There is already much that, as you say, you immediately assent to, if I am thinking of women involved in household affairs or any others having to take care of essential family matters. Certainly those upon whom this is incumbent make up the greatest part of your sex; the portion remaining for these studies is small. Nor do I even think you wish to argue that all who are exempted from the necessary care of domestic matters are qualified for the study of letters.

And so, if you only look at what I have written, there will be no controversy between us, or it will be very small, even if the question is posed which you subsequently said is the principal one, namely, whether in these times the study of arts and letters is most fitting for a maiden. That is unless you understand the term "maiden" as a universal, to be applied without precise specifications, or unless you take it as referring to all alike. If the latter is not the case, I have easily conceded this education to some women "called to it by a special instinct." What if I add that I concede or rather desire this for as many as possible? But I should wish that that study first be limited with respect to how far it ought to proceed, in which arts and sciences it should consist, and by what method it is to be instituted and advanced, so that it should hold to the adage "nothing in excess." I should wish besides that a goal be established for women's studies, on the basis of which those elements might be chosen which would be suitable or necessary to that end. For since it is placed beyond dispute that the feminine sex is not suited for political and ecclesiastical duties, especially for public teaching, why should young women work to acquire that erudition which looks to ends from which they are barred (unless perhaps you exempt the few who are admitted in several countries to the succession of monarchies where masculine offspring are lacking). "I do not permit a woman to teach," said the Apostle, "or to have authority over man, but to be in silence."[12] If this is enjoined upon women, you will not deny that it is especially appropriate for maidens. Consequently, if you consider utility, precise instruction aimed at the principles of speaking well is not necessary for them; unless perhaps you object, which you also do, that the art of speaking well is useful to the end that they may judge concerning the diligence of others who exercise this practice. But among whom? For that judgment ought to hold fast to honorable modesty. I shall

12. 1 Timothy 2:11–15.

say the same concerning the art of discussion; indeed you will easily grant that it is not sufficiently in keeping with all maidenly conduct to aspire after verbal cleverness and to take the lead in argument in a crowd of disputants. Let it suffice that a woman have some practice in argumentation from natural skill and let there be added the experience arising from both ordinary conversation and the public teaching that takes place in the church, where women are not prevented from hearing the Word.[13]

What you conclude from this, however—that they are most suited for the learned studies or at least plentifully supplied with opportunities not available to men, since they are engaged in honorable leisure, exempt from civil cares—, this does not seem to me to prove what you intend. First, since if we look at that age which is most fitted for learning, the male sex is on the same footing up to the completion of youth, before which time it is not thrust into public responsibilities. Second, maidens ought not to be brought up in such leisure that they might always have time for the cultivation of the mind; for they also have those things that they do at home as long as they are under the power of the parents, so that they may not be able to take for themselves that leisure of which Seneca said, "Leisure without letters is death and the burial place of a living man."[14] But I would not wish to condemn all to the distaff and the spindle, so that they might never admit more serious concerns, even though previously princesses—whether among Greeks, Romans, pagans, or Christians—did not scorn this. I assume you have read the elegant book of Ludovico Vives on the Christian woman. Consider, if you please, the whole third chapter of book 1 concerning the first exercises of girls: there you will see that it has always been regarded as praiseworthy, even in the estimation of the Holy Spirit, that not only matrons but most of all maidens, even of the royal court, occupied themselves in those workshops that require working with the hands. But yet we do not for that reason go to the other extreme, nor did he do so where he adds the fourth chapter on the teaching of girls, in which he eloquently and sensibly treats this question: "What type of learning is fitting for the lesser sex?" You will not be angry with me, however much Gournay resists, if I express the opinion with the Apostle, "The woman is the weaker vessel."[15] If you agree with Vives's position, agree-

---

13. See. for example, Matthew 13:23.

14. Seneca, *Epistles*, 82.3.4; 82.3.5; 82.4.1.

15. 1 Peter 3:7: "Likewise, ye husbands, dwell with them according to knowledge, giving honour unto the wife, as unto the weaker vessel" (KJV).

ment between us will be easy, and we will not begrudge you the Sempronias, Cornelias, Laelias, Mutias, Cleobulinas, Cassandras, Hortensias.[16] Nor the Christian Enonias, Paulas, Albinas, Pellas, Zenobias, Valerias, Probas, Eudocias.[17] Nor the Greys, nor the Olympia Moratas[18] or whomever you might wish to add to the ancients from those who have adorned your sex within our memory or that of our fathers. Provided that we all agree that they are rare birds on the earth—not because there could not possibly be more, but because it may not be useful or in the public interest. And whereas what ought to be common in men, if we look to the benefit of the Republic and the Church, may in women be less frequent and have the effect of a prodigy, such as it was in former times when women were

16. Cornelia (2d c. B.C.E.) was the daughter of Scipio Africanus and wife of Tiberius Sempronius Gracchus. Sempronia, her daughter, married the national hero Scipio Aemilianus. After she was widowed, Cornelia devoted herself to the education of her sons Tiberius and Gaius Gracchus, bringing in Greek philosophers to teach them. They became noted for initiating social reforms in the Roman Republic. Laelia and her daughter(s) Mutia were known for their eloquence in speaking. Cleobulina was the daughter of the philosopher Cleobulus (6th c. B.C.E.), who advocated that girls be educated. She was noted for composing riddles in verse. In Greek legend, Cassandra, the daughter of Priam and Hecuba, received the gift of prophecy from Apollo but refused to comply with his wishes. As a punishment he decreed that no one should believe her prophecies. When captured from Troy by Agamemnon, she warned him of his fate, but when he failed to heed the prophecy, both were slain by Clytemnestra. Hortensia (1st c. B.C.E.) was the daughter of a great orator and became noted in 42 B.C.E. for pleading successfully before the triumvirs for removal of special taxes being imposed on women whose male relatives had been proscribed.

17. Enonia is presumably the daughter of Nazarius, rhetorician in the time of Constantine, whose daughter was identified as Eunomia in Prosper of Aquitaine's *Chronicle* (see *Paulys Real-Encyclopädie der Classischen Altertumswissenschaft*, art. Nazarius) and as Eumonia in Beverwyck's *Van de Uitnementheyt des vrouwelicken Geslachts*, 111. Paula (347–404), mother of Eustochium (both sainted), followed Jerome to Palestine where she founded a convent. Albina was the mother of the philosopher Seneca. Zenobia, queen of Palmyra c. 268– 272, was regent for her son and virtually ruled Syria. She was learned in Greek, Egyptian, and Latin, wrote history, and was responsible for the education of her sons. Proba Valeria Falconia, wife of a Roman proconsul in the time of emperors Honorius and Theodosius II, wrote a life of Christ based on Virgil's poetry and sent it to Eudocia, wife of Theodosius, who did the same with Homer's poetry.

18. Lady Jane Grey (1537–1554), one of the best educated girls of her age, spoke and wrote Greek and Latin and also studied Hebrew, Chaldee, and Arabic. Manipulated by English nobility in the struggle for the crown following the death of Edward VI, she was queen for nine days but was overthrown and executed for treason. Olympia Fulvia Morata (1526–1555) was the daughter of a humanist teacher in Ferrara and was educated at the court he served, receiving very strong classical training. A Calvinist, she found it necessary to leave the court; she married Andreas Grundler, doctor of medicine, and went with him to his German homeland but survived only five years in the war-ravaged country. Her letters depict not only her thoughts but also the political and social conditions of the time.

seen to stand in arms and go to oppose and fight men on the battle line. Among the people of God, Deborah and Jael were rare; nor did that palaestra that the Angles designated for burning people alive submit very happily to Joanna of Lotharingia. Similarly, however much the other Pallas is honored by our Aurelians, nevertheless her modesty is in doubt even among her admirers.

But this kind of life you have not undertaken to advocate—I am well aware of that. What you are striving for is something else and more fitting, I confess. But before you persuade me, I should like you to establish for me colleges of learned women, in whose academies the maidens whom you would dedicate to these studies would be refined. For you yourself would not readily admit that all these women might be self-taught or have parents at home who would themselves undertake this responsibility, as happily befell you. But it would not be appropriate for them to attend the schools of men, mixed with boys. You will concede to me that however much the study of good literature and languages, especially of those in which God recorded his Word for us, may greatly aid those who ought to dig out the true sense of the Spirit, still it is not given to just anyone to drink directly from the fountainheads themselves and that not just anyone has the judgment needed to be able to distinguish ambiguous words or phrases and select the most appropriate meanings. For many it is more wholesome if they are content with the streams. To them it often happens that as they read in their own vernacular tongue furnished by others, provided that they read humbly, quietly, and attentively, calling on the name of God, they investigate and draw forth meanings that have escaped those skilled in the [sacred] languages. But nevertheless I do not say this in order to diminish the praise of those women who with you have advanced to the point that they are able to understand the sacred books in their original language, but lest the arguments that you use create scruples in the souls of those women who despair of equaling your accomplishments. The magnificent works of God, concerning which the Psalmist speaks, may be celebrated by all, although there are few who have expert knowledge of the rotation of the heavens, the appearance of the planets, and the influence of the stars or similar things. Indeed, it often happens that those who are considered greatly versed in such things you may see turning from God, with the result that they attribute all things to nature. And on the other hand those who employ a simple outlook may be inspired to sing the praises of God's wondrous works and may wholeheartedly find comfort in their author when all the most learned weary their minds in vain in such things and after long disquisitions feast upon the wind; concerning their wisdom, that interpreter for the most wise king said, "In a multitude of wisdom is a multitude of pain; and he will add pain."[19] But you seek and approach that true wisdom that consists of the fear of God and observance of his commandments, from which be it far from me to divert or discourage you or any others thus disposed. I have no greater desire than that what was foretold by the prophet and was partly fulfilled at the start of the preaching of the gospel might be frequent among us: "your sons and daughters shall prophesy."[20] I rejoice that you are among them and that such a daughter has befallen me in accordance with my wish and her consent, whom

> *I both cherish with true paternal affection*
> *and court with that attention*
> *which her virtues deserve,*
> *André Rivet*
>
> *The Hague, March 18, 1638*

To the most distinguished man and my reverend father in Christ, André Rivet,

That you, reverend and venerable Father in Christ, while occupied with so many and such great affairs, should have deigned to respond so fully to my trifles, I owe especially to your kindness. Indeed at first your opinion unnerved me somewhat, as it seemed to oppose our cause not a little; but after examining everything thoroughly I understood that in respect to its main thrust your opinion accorded wonderfully well with my desires.

Yet in the meantime, I suffered no small pain in seeing that either because of the obscurity of my defective writing style or because of my lack of skill in distinguishing, I have managed to impress on your mind a meaning far different from my intention, as if, that is to say, I so thoughtlessly favor that invidious and groundless assertion of the preeminence of our sex compared with yours that I would blithely dare to raise it with you, whose precious time is almost too sacred to take even a little away. For I perceive that you have thus interpreted the whole position of the controversy that I introduced against today's customs: "Whether in these times the study of letters and fine arts is above all fitting for maidens?" Here this term "above all" you would interpret as if I employed it not in

19. Ecclesiastes 1:18.
20. Joel 2:28; Acts 2:17.

comparison to occupations or concerns accepted by today's customs, but as compared to your sex, to the extent that I would contend that women are more suited to study than men. If this hypothesis were to be put forward, the arguments that I would introduce for my thesis would not only seem feeble and foolish but could also deservedly be accused of a new and haughty vanity. It is so far from me to consider this in keeping with maidenly modesty or at least with my innate shyness that it troubles me, for instance, to read through that otherwise outstanding treatise by Lucrezia Marinella, to which she gave the title *The Nobility and Excellence of Women, along with the Defects and Deficiencies of Men*. Just as, on the basis of its elegance and wit, I can by no means disapprove of the little dissertation of the most noble Gournay *On the Equality of Men and Women*, at the same time I would certainly not dare nor would I want to approve of it in all things. Yet for the sake of brevity I may appeal to the testimony of the wise authorities which she presents to us. Admittedly, if the virtues of our order (i.e., maidens) ought to be preached rightly, I very much desire that that role be handed over to you who are a sublime herald of the virtues. For us it is appropriate that the more solitary theater of conscience suffice. The goal at which I was aiming here, however, was none other than to know your judgment clearly and precisely concerning the best possible use of our leisure time. And in order to more easily attain that goal, I seized the occasion from the words that you put forth problematically, "nor is it perhaps expedient for there to be many such." Not in order to attack them, but to inquire more carefully into the genuine intention of your mind. Beyond that I put forth my opinion—which I thought to be consistent with what is fair—or, rather, illustrations of my feelings. Finally, I brought forward the various arguments meant to illustrate our position with no other aim than that you may discern through the acuity of your judgment whether they seem to you to be valid against the usual voices of ignorance and tyrannical laws of custom. These few things I thought should be pursued further so that you might be fully informed about my thinking, which I know for you takes the place of every argument. The two chapters of Ludovico Vives that you indicated I should read, I read again with great pleasure along with the preceding chapters. There an excellent and neatly ordered scheme for the instruction of a Christian woman is outlined, which I would deem most worthy of being applied as closely as possible to the studies of women today. On which account I am very pleased that he came along for us as an interpreter of your opinion, the authority of which I most willingly embrace in this case as I do in most other circumstances. Farewell, dearest Father. I ask and pray the supreme power, now that you have lately been restored to health, that you might continue to enjoy it to the full,

> *I who cherish and hold you dear*
> *in the inmost disposition of my soul,*
> *Anna Maria van Schurman*
>
> *Utrecht, March 14, 1638*[21]

21. The date is given in Latin as *pridie Idus Martii*, which seems to place it on March 14, prior to Rivet's letter to which it is a response. Perhaps she was using the Julian calendar and Rivet the Gregorian calendar, or perhaps one of the printed dates is erroneous.

CORRESPONDENCE WITH
OTHER WOMEN

To Madam the Princess of Bohemia[1]

Madam,

I cannot express the abundance of joy and happiness I felt in reading the letter Your Highness was so gracious to write to me. For beyond its inventiveness, wit, and structure, which could fill a more learned ear [than mine], it was a marvelous pleasure to consider the musings of your noble spirit. For my part, I am very eager to become capable of all that pleases Your Highness; and although I could not hope, in [all] modesty, fully to do your bidding, I shall at least try to demonstrate the devotion and love that I bring to your service. Among those authors who have interpreted the unique genius and character of great personages, it is commonly agreed that Xenophon admirably described the life of Cyrus, the first Persian monarch, although it seems that sometimes he devoted more [attention] to the elegance and beauty of his work than to the truth about his subject. Alexander [the Great], who subsequently initiated the Greek empire, is depicted perfectly by Q. Curtius,[2] but he commonly interweaves fire, sword, and bloody victories into his discourse. For a quick introduction, I find nothing as suitable as Plutarch,[3] who presents to us illustrious men as in a perfect tableau while drawing a serious and very beautiful com-

Letters in this section are translated from the Latin, Greek, Hebrew, and French originals found in the 1650 edition of Schurman's *Opuscula* on pages 158–160, 164–166, 195–199, 281–287, 293–303, 309–312, 318–320.

1. Original is in French.

2. Quintus Curtius Rufus, a rhetorician and historian of the first century, published a ten-volume history of Alexander the Great.

3. The Greek biographer Plutarch (c. 46–c. 120) is best known for his *Parallel Lives* (c. 100), paired biographies of Greek and Roman political and military leaders.

parison between the Greeks and the Romans. Suetonius[4] presented to us in lively manner the twelve Roman emperors whose lives (I speak of the majority) were so extraordinary that our minds can reach no other conclusion than that the emperors exhibit conflicting virtues. One must not forget that Tacitus[5] amused himself similarly by describing some of the early emperors; and we may get to know Tacitus better if we read the Italian essay on his histories written by Scipione Ammirato.[6]

If we wanted to consider the value we derive from this and to examine it in detail, we would find that it is almost limitless, especially in the livelier way the examples strike the senses and the imagination than do the precepts of philosophy. Moreover, the knowledge of past matters which is acquired by this means is without partiality and without bias toward a faction, which is almost inevitable to those who let themselves be led by experience alone. We can see in such works all the past centuries as in a clear mirror and make fairly accurate conjectures concerning those that are to come. As a result we will succeed to that perfect state of regarding nothing on the earth as new, and we shall say with the wisest of kings: "What has been done is what will be; and what has been done is what will be done; and there is nothing new under the sun."[7] It is indeed true that there is some difficulty in arriving at a specific application, primarily because the ancient world is generally harsher and more severe; but the essence of things always remains the same, even though certain formalities and circumstances may be accustomed to change often. We can easily apply the necessary moderation if we know more closely the genius and temperament of their century and of ours. J. Lipsius outlined this method more fully in his book entitled *Admonitions and Political Examples*,[8] showing both public personalities and private individuals the uses they can make of ancient and modern examples. And in fact, it seems to me that the latter are in no way inferior to the former if we consider not so much the force and eloquence of the historians as the material. I would dare to set a single Elizabeth in her life as Queen of England and a Jane Grey over against all

---

4. Roman biographer Gaius Suetonius Tranquillus (c. 69–c. 140) wrote *Lives of the Caesars*, biographies of the Roman emperors from Julius Caesar to Domitian.

5. The major works of Roman historian Cornelius Tacitus (c. 56–c. 115), *Annals* and *Histories*, delineate the history of Rome in the first century.

6. Scipione Ammirato (1531–1601), *Discorsi su Cornelio Tacito* (Florence, 1594).

7. Ecclesiastes 1:9.

8. Justus Lipsius, *Monita et exempla politica* (Antwerp, 1605).

the illustrious women of ancient Greece and Rome. One finds some admirable things in certain centuries beyond that, namely before and after the decisive change of the reformation of Christianity; and the breadth of the subject is put forth quite straightforwardly and accurately by the Italian Guicciardini[9] and, in its third phase, by Sleidanus[10] and Auguste de Thou.[11]

Physics is a little dry if we limit ourselves to its bare speculation: but there is one part (concerning which St. Augustine has written in his 21st book, chapter 4, of the *City of God*, also Cardan,[12] Wecker,[13] and several others) called natural magic, which is more pleasant since it unites with experience some works wonderful to the eye and nevertheless remains within the bounds of laudable curiosity. But astrology (I do not take this to mean astronomy, as was customary in ancient times; that is a noble science and very worthy of our contemplation) goes further and usually degenerates into superstition because it attributes more to secondary causes than the order and properties of nature permit. For if we say that the human will and contingencies depend on the constitution of the heavens and on the aspect or conjunction of the planets, we introduce into the world a necessity greater than that of the Stoics. The causes that act freely and fortuitously cannot be determined by natural causes, that is to say, by the influence of celestial bodies. But because of their excellence they are directly subordinate to the first and sovereign cause. Besides, it is both dangerous and pointless to seek to predict future contingent events, something that belongs properly to divinity alone, as we see in Isaiah 46:9–10, and cannot be communicated to mortal creatures except through special revelation.

I would not have dared to entertain Your Highness so long if Made-

9. Francesco Guicciardini (1483–1540) wrote a history of Italy covering the period 1494 to 1534.

10. Johannes Sleidanus (1506–1556), a lawyer and diplomat, was appointed historian of the Reformation by Philip of Hesse. His major work, *De Statu Religionis et Republicae Carolo V Caesare Commentarii* (1555) is the most valuable contemporary history of the Reformation, containing a large number of documents.

11. Jacques-Auguste de Thou (1553–1617), French statesman and historian, published several volumes of the history of his time, ultimately collected into the one work, *Histoire universelle de Jacques-Auguste de Thou depuis 1543 jusqu'en 1607.*

12. Jerome Cardan (1501–1576), Italian physician, mathematician, and astrologer, wrote popular works dealing with scientific and philosophical questions.

13. Johann Jacob Wecker (1528–1586) taught dialectic in Basel and also published works on medical practice.

moiselle N. N. had not assured me that You would consider this importunity agreeable. However that may be, I desire utterly to testify that I am and will always be, Madame,

> *Your very humble and devoted servant,*
> *Anna Maria van Schurman*
>
> *Utrecht, September 7, 1639*

To the great city Dublin, to the honorable Lady Dorothy Moor, to the widow of the honorable nobleman Moor, from the city of Utrecht.[14]
To my honorable Lady, peace.

I have heard about you, my beloved friend, honorable Lady, and I am happy and joyous for the one goodness that Heaven has borne us in our days, to renew the glory of your people. For I said: For want of knowledge wisdom has gone into captivity[15] from the midst of the women of England after the death of Lady Jane Grey and Queen Elizabeth, may their memory be blessed! But wisdom has entered your heart, and knowledge has been pleasing for your soul. God has chosen you to be a crown of glory for all women! You have a goodly heritage,[16] and you have found hidden riches in secret places.[17] Therefore I rejoice as for the light of the sun upon its rising. I long for your love, and I said to myself: I will come toward your excellent majesty with these ten statements, in all humility, to make a covenant of salt[18] between myself and yourself. Let us join together to trade and to acquire wisdom and understanding, for the merchandise of it is better than the merchandise of silver, and the gain thereof than fine gold.[19] Now, if I have found favor in your eyes, let me know of all your desires. You are blessed to God; majesty and glory to your people.

> *Your beloved friend and your servant,*
> *Anna Maria van Schurman*
>
> *From the city of Utrecht, in the year*[20]

14. Original is in Hebrew.
15. Isaiah 5:13.
16. Psalm 16:6.
17. Isaiah 45:3.
18. Numbers 18:19.
19. Proverbs 3:14.
20. The meaning of the Hebrew is unclear as to the date.

To Dorothy Moor:[21]

Most noble lady,

Your letter seemed sweeter than nectar to me, and because I take great delight in your correspondence, I would have responded sooner had not my brother, who will bring this to you, long since intended to come to England. He will make known to you the manner of my life and will disclose the inner chambers of my heart to you. Nevertheless I can scarcely restrain myself from writing about the weightiest points of your letter.

You ask how I order and dispose my affairs so that I pass with least offense through the cares of this life, especially in this miserable age. Even if I owe the credit to your singular kindness and modesty that you consider my example not unworthy of imitation; still, if we were at some time permitted by the grace of God to enjoy one and the same companionship, I do not doubt that in such a union of minds and studies we could better encourage one another to virtue. However, I will tell you in a word not what I have always achieved but what target I set for myself to be attained as nearly as possible. The polestar of heavenly truth shows us the short path and by far the safest; as was best stated by the great Count Mirandola, "Philosophy seeks truth, theology finds it, religion possesses it."

But in order not to digress further from the subject I say not without cause along with the distinguished philosopher Epictetus that mortal affairs have two handles; not, however, as he, that one is suitable, the other unsuitable, but that both are suitable, only that they are to be grasped properly and in order. Of course, whatever pertains to living well and happily must be assigned either to divine providence or to our duty. Touching the first I do that one thing in order that, in those matters that are beyond our power, I may have one concern only, namely to throw all concerns onto God, according to that admonition of the Apostle, "Cast all your anxieties on him, for he cares about you."[22] Certainly the source of all our inquietude is that we are accustomed too anxiously to turn over in the mind the occurrence of things that depend solely on the will of the highest deity.

Our duty is what remains; only those parts that fall under our deliberation are to be regulated with our industry and prudence. Nothing so dislodges us from the bulwark of tranquillity as the perverse example and

21. Original is in Latin.
22. 1 Peter 5:7 (RSV).

the false attractions of this century, not to speak of the nuisances and an-
noyances that perpetually accompany the condition of those who take
part in the theater of this world. But for this evil I find no other remedy
more expedient than the retreat of studies. For indeed, since the most corrupt morals are practiced everywhere today, it is hardly possible for anyone to kindle in others as much enthusiasm for pursuing virtue as one
yields of one's own enthusiasm when engaging in frequent interactions
with people. Here, in this retreat, with those deceptions of this age removed, we judge more correctly of all things and we safely despise those
things that fill the profane minds of men with admiration. Here one can
direct the mind to higher things in the convenient leisure of the Muses
and undertake the study of wisdom without impediment—about which
more is written in the printed letter I am sending to you. I have added also
my image depicted true to life with my own hand, by which I may become
known to you in all ways, insofar as is possible.

Farewell, immortal ornament of our sex, and continue to love in return
her who is so fond of you.

Anna Maria van Schurman

Utrecht, April 1, 1641

To Madam Anne de Merveil, dowager of Prosting[23]
Madam,

I do not know whether I should have more compassion for your ad-
versity or more joy for your victory. For the letter that you have done me
the honor of writing assures just as much of one as of the other. It is true
that you have had to surmount very great difficulties and I would wish you
a purer and more perfect happiness if our condition in this world made
that possible. But given that the evils of this life are the material for the
triumphs that await us in heaven and that God wants, by means of proofs
and exercises proportioned to their strength, to make the excellence of the
gifts burst forth which he has placed in the spirit of the faithful, placing
your Christian struggle in the ranks of miseries or misfortunes would be to
take these measures in the wrong way. But you will say that I have
thoughts too abstract for your tangible worries and that the wisest of kings
knew the strains thereof better when he says, as if by exclamation, in his
proverbs: "Who will lift the dejected spirit?"[24] I concede to you, Madam,

23. Original is in French.
24. Proverbs 18:14.

that I judge your afflictions more freely when I regard them as past matters that were indeed adverse but hardly superior to your virtues, which were able to combat them, yet without altogether conquering them. In another way I am well aware that contemplation and rejoicing at the heavenly privileges that we obtain through Christian faith are not always so vivid and constant that they can divert all the blows of our adversities or remove the sensation from them. Experience itself easily teaches us the contrary, because the Spouse of our souls remains behind the wall and chooses for a time to hold back the influence of his grace and divine consolation. In truth, as the royal Psalmist says, his "steadfast love is better than life."[25] From this it happens that the faith and virtue of the dearest friends of God—David, Job, Jeremiah, and others—have sometimes had grand eclipses and that the force of their temptations caused them to utter laments closely resembling those of people in desperation; these have been recorded in Holy Scripture for our consolation. Thus it often comes about that our victories are just as bloody as they are certain, and the crowns of Paradise are given only to those who have fought valiantly. As far as your opinion is concerned that I might be able to contribute to your peace of mind through my presence, that gives me cause to rejoice greatly, as an infallible proof of your affection. But for my part I cannot conceal from you that the ardor and the strength of the desire that I have of one day being able to offer you my very humble service makes me hope and sometimes even believe that you will choose to establish your residence here in our city, especially since you have developed uneasiness about your overly large household. And having the pleasure of enjoying sometimes the sweet company of Madame ———— your daughter, we have quite often conversed about these very pleasant talks, from which we will await confirmation of your good resolution and of divine providence. To whose protection I commend you, remaining always

> *Your most humble and very affectionate servant,*
> *Anna Maria van Schurman*
>
> *August 13, 1642*

---

25. Psalm 63:3.

To Princess Anne de Rohan[26]
Mademoiselle,

I was previously of the opinion that in order worthily to esteem and revere your very distinguished virtues, I should cover them with a veil of sacred silence rather than reduce their price by the baseness of my style. But after Monsieur Rivet communicated to me the letter with which you recently honored him, I had to confess that your goodness, which shines so clearly there, was more forceful in making me set pen to paper than these respectful considerations were in making me hold onto it longer. For to tell the truth, I would be ignoring my happiness and the value of your good graces not to accept them promptly when you are so generous as to offer them to me, when I am so incapable of deserving them. To be assured of being admitted into communication with so great a good is to participate in the most precious treasures of the virtue itself, which has no need of giving us other laws than those that form from your example. I do not presume to wish to draw up a catalogue of your praises, but I shall simply say that you have joined two things that are ordinarily incompatible, namely the knowledge of the grandeur of this world and Christian wisdom. Yet although the high rank of your very illustrious house does not permit me to join my soul with yours through an alliance of friendship, which requires equality of parties,—if it is equality that binds souls in a firmer knot than that of political societies—to this extent all my wishes conspire with yours in love of this heavenly quality, which, as the wisest of kings says "is better than jewels, and all that you may desire cannot compare with her."[27]

I do not deny that the progress I have made in this debate is but a little; but that will not hinder me from putting forth your example as a brilliant star amidst the darkness of this corrupt century and to remain all my life

> *Your very humble and very devoted servant*
> *Anna Maria van Schurman*
>
> *Utrecht, August 19, 1643*

---

26. Daughter of René de Rohan and Catherine de Parthenai and sister of Duke Henri de Rohan, Anne de Rohan endured the siege of the Protestant stronghold of La Rochelle in the 1620s and was for a time a prisoner of war along with her mother. Like her mother, she was a woman of remarkable spirit and learning. Original is in French.

27. Proverbs 8:11. Schurman renders this verse in the Hebrew original.

Letter from Mademoiselle Anne de Rohan to Mademoiselle van Schurman[28]
Mademoiselle,

Even though the sincere friendship that the eminent Monsieur Rivet bears toward me accounts for the favor of your letters, I do not cease to be extremely obligated to you for making me a participant therein, and I take pride in being in the memory of a Lady whose compassion, knowledge, and merit have the approval of the most virtuous. But what troubles my contentment or this happiness is that I feel more suited for admiring you than I am useful for serving you. Furthermore I believe that being satisfied with your own virtues you have no need of assistance from anyone. Thus I offer you nothing, nor can I give you anything, but I ask that it please you to remember in your dear country that in France there is a person of your sex and of your name who honors you as she should and wishes you that happiness which you deserve, who is

> *Mademoiselle,*
> *at your service, your very humble and devoted*
> *Anne de Rohan*
>
> *Paris, September 20, 1643*

To Princess Anne de Rohan[29]
Mademoiselle,

It would be a great presumption to want to attribute to my merit and not to your pure goodness your graciousness in receiving the offers of my very humble service, and what is more, in rewarding them with a letter from your hand, which bears as many marks of your illustrious favors as it has lines and phrases. If Monsieur Rivet has painted me with a brush of Apelles[30] and there has given some beautiful strokes of his eloquence, you must excuse the affection of such a friend, who perhaps made use of this artifice for acquiring your affection toward me, given that there was no evidence of being able to attract it by means of vulgar things. However that may be, since neither the law of prudence nor that of sincerity commands me to uncover an error, the knowledge of which would not increase anyone's happiness but rather diminish ours, I carefully refrain from

---

28. Original is in French.
29. Original is in French.
30. Apelles, who lived in the time of Philip of Macedon and Alexander the Great, is considered one of the greatest painters of the ancient world, noted particularly for his portraits.

defaming myself lest, for the sake of an unnecessary truth, I run the risk of losing your good favor. That is a treasure of which I think more highly than the riches of the Orient and the Occident. And if I am able to preserve it for myself, I shall be rich and happy, even amidst the disgraces of the world. In fact to respect and admire your excellent qualities out of love for the qualities themselves is a duty that justice generally requires of all people; but to be respected by a Princess such as you is a prerogative or rather an act of grace so rare that it is desired by all those who are accustomed to aspire to exalted matters. But although for a long time I have regarded France as one of the most beautiful parts of the universe and as the mother and nurturer of wisdom and of virtue, it is at the present that I love and honor it most particularly, because it possesses the glory of our sex, which spreads so agreeably to our Provinces. And if there is any conformity between things that have the same name (I interpret thus your sweet observation advantageously) and if I may be permitted to search for some secret in words and syllables, in imitation of the Cabalists, how shall I remember myself without reflecting back on my Original, that is to say, Your very illustrious person whose name and image I bear, as the one who is truly, Mademoiselle,

Your very humble, very obedient and faithful servant
Anna Maria van Schurman

Utrecht, Nov. 13, 1643

To the Princess of Bohemia:[31]
Madame,

It would be to ignore the greatness of Your Highness and the lowliness of my condition to attribute to my merit rather than to your pure grace the fact that it has pleased you to honor me with a letter from your hand, and to inquire so graciously concerning my health and occupations. As for my disposition, it belongs (by the grace of God) to a temperament proper and suitable enough to receive the honor of your commands: but the progress of my studies is not so notable that I could render an account of them to my advantage. At least I am not of the opinion that they live up to public expectations, as your good will tries to persuade me.

It is true that I have high regard for the Scholastic Doctors and that without doubt they could provide me with worthy occasions for exercising my mind if I were not frequently diverted from them by more necessary

31. Original is in French.

exercises. I do not wish to deny that they sometimes go astray through vain and dangerous speculations, which have brought upon them the censure of a number of learned people of our time. Nevertheless that ought not to prejudice either the solidity or the excellence of their ideas, which we are accustomed to admire in their works, when it is a question either of clarifying the secrets of philosophy or of sustaining the highest points of the Christian religion against secular skeptics and atheists. It would be hard to tell whether they have been more ingenious in conjuring up doubts and objections or more adept in resolving them; whether they have been more rash in undertaking lofty and difficult matters or more fortunate and capable in clearing them up. Thus, in my opinion, they have combined well these two qualities rarely associated, the subtlety of reality. And in fact it is not strange that they have arrived at such a high degree of perfection, inasmuch as they have not scorned the legacy of their predecessors or the heritage of all the past centuries; and because it is easy, according to the rule of the Philosophers, "to add something to the discoveries of others." It was enough glory for them to let themselves be led by those two great stars of the divine and human sciences, St. Augustine and Aristotle, whom none have been able to obscure, no matter what chaotic muddles of errors people have tried to set over against their brilliant light.

In order not to engage Your Highness too long, I will finish after you have given me permission to say that I am still the one who has been and all her life will be, Madame,

> *Your very humble,*
> *and very obedient,*
> *and very faithful servant,*
> *Anna Maria van Schurman*
>
> *Utrecht, January 26, 1644*

To the most honorable and wise lady Bathsua Makin,[32]
Greetings.

Even if I write a letter that does not come up to your expectations, nonetheless I prefer to ruin my reputation for learning than to be cavalier

---

32. Original is in Greek. Schurman's Greek rendering of the name suggests that she was more familiar with the alternate spelling "Machin." Frances Teague speculates that Cambridge University records naming John Machon as "clerk" and Thomas Machon as matriculating in 1655 may refer to her son and husband. Frances Teague, "Bathsua Makin: Woman of Learning," in Katharina M. Wilson and Frank J. Warnke, eds., *Women Writers of the Seventeenth Century* (Athens: University of Georgia Press, 1989), 286.

in my duty. I enjoyed your letter immensely, for it shows that you have attained no superficial level of Greek eloquence. This is all the more admirable, since, while you are prevented by many domestic cares from devoting almost any time to philosophy, your muse has in no way become silent amid the din of armed camps. Hence I value your essay concerning the beautiful, so much so that I especially praise you for having placed the humanities in the service of theology, the greatest of the sciences. Besides, you must strive above all to invest your talent in educating the young princess so that you may succeed in producing a second Elizabeth, under whose holy and glorious reign your island once so extraordinarily flourished.

> *Farewell and return to me the love I have for you.*
> *Anna Maria van Schurman*
>
> *Utrecht, in the year 1645 of the Incarnation, on the sixth day of the rising month of Pyanepsion.*[33]

To the most estimable lady Bathsua Makin,[34]
Greetings.

I wrote you, most honorable of women, not long ago, but I have not yet had a chance to learn whether you received my letter or not. For on the one hand it is not right that we have to let this fine season pass by in silence; and on the other, you have often given me great pleasure writing me about your activities. Inasmuch as I am completely in sympathy with your marvelous work, of necessity I am especially keen to learn the state of the church and how go your labors concerning virtue and the education of your royal pupil.

> *Farewell.*
> *Anna Maria van Schurman*
>
> *Utrecht, on the third day of the dying month of Mounuchion in the year 1646[?] of our Lord's Incarnation.*[35]

---

33. The date was probably in late October or early November, following the Athenian calendar, which began with the first moon after the summer solstice. See Frances Teague, "New Light on Bathsua Makin," *Seventeenth-Century News* 49 (1986): 16. I suggest that it might have been on or about the same day (October 31, 1645) that she wrote to Simonds d'Ewes and referred to Makin.

34. Original is in Greek.

35. Probably in April, though there is reason to question the year. While the letters in the *Opuscula* are not arranged strictly chronologically, those addressed to a single recipient generally appear in chronological order, and these two letters are preceded and followed by

To Mademoiselle du Moulin[36]

My very dear sister,

Since we have the same concerns in joy and sadness, we have been quite delighted to see in your letter the true marks of a serene face, and not only in the act of laughing but also in such a way as to make even sorrow laugh. And in fact the gaiety of your heart awakening and breaking out after a great eclipse can only produce in us pleasant and refreshing thoughts, such that if you find me at present in a more cheerful humor and more extravagant than usual, know that it is you who have put me there. You will pardon me therefore if I happen to divert you a little from the serious instruction of your father and of the company of philosophy, to which (as I understand) you have given my place. And although in order to take away my jealousy of this rival you would try to persuade me that you adhere to none of its charms except its mien and appearance, I know not whether I can persuade myself that she has not given you her caresses. Because if you have resolved not to reveal to me any of her secrets and mysteries, I am of the opinion that she did not want to communicate them to you except under a bushel of silence and by a secret confession. Yet I do not wish to deny that in common with the wisest people you mingle a little folly with your wisdom, by taking pleasure in abusing the world, and by appearing less than you really are. Furthermore, when I consider the advantages that you give me, I have reason to believe that the portrait that I recently sent you flatters me too much and that the Idea of the original is nearly effaced from your mind, in such a way that it is not surprising that your Flemish (as you say) has almost escaped you. As for me, I see well that my French is already about to embark and seek elsewhere better provisions than I know how to give it. And if you do not wish for me hereafter to write long letters in Flemish or for us to need an intermediary in order to understand each other, you must soon plan for your return. Now to

---

other Greek letters from the years 1645–1647. Furthermore, the reference here to a previous letter Schurman had written makes most sense as a follow-up to the letter of 1645. Hence, it is plausible to argue that the word "sixth" was inadvertently omitted, giving the correct year as 1646. Internal evidence would support this, as Schurman in 1640 would have had less reason to ask about the state of the church in England than in 1646 when the civil war was well underway. Also, Makin's royal pupil, Princess Elizabeth, would have been only five years old in 1640, and Makin herself indicates that Latin and French instruction should begin around the age of eight or nine. (Kate Aughterson, ed., *Renaissance Woman: A Sourcebook* (London: Routledge, 1995), 191.) Finally, if Schurman's first letter to Makin coincided with her letter to d'Ewes, the second letter may have coincided with a letter to d'Ewes written on April 5, in the likelihood that whoever was traveling to England would carry more than one letter at a time.

36. Original is in French.

finish on a serious note, I desire greatly to hear from you the continuation of the good news concerning the convalescence of your father and about the current status of our religion in France, troubled (as they say) by changes, which, as a result, can only be very dangerous in a kingdom where there are so many adversaries. I am and shall remain, as long as I live,

My dear sister,

> *your very affectionate sister and very humble servant,*
> *Anna Maria van Schurman*
>
> *December 8, 1646*

To Mademoiselle de Gournay,[37]
Mademoiselle,

If I have testified to the sense I have of the advantages that your heroic qualities have procured for our sex, it has only been to discharge a duty that justice has rendered necessary for me. Indeed the letter that you have done me the honor of writing demonstrates well that your courtesy is not measured out according to its objects and that it accepts no limits other than its own.

Hence it seemed to you a small matter to thank me for that which is legitimately due you, if you had not given me hope that my name would one day be ordained to immortality by the favor of your Muse. Certainly I would wish to be just as worthy of this happiness that you are quick and generous in promising me; and that you might find some harmony and balance between the lofty character of your style and the lowliness of the material. But, however that may be, I imagine by a sweet dream that the marks of your affection which will here be read without misgivings will not be less glorious than the honor of a praise that I might have merited.

With regard to your opinion that I occupy myself too much with the study of languages, I can assure you that I contribute only my leisure hours to them and sometimes after rather long gaps of time, if you permit me to make an exception of the sacred language. Beyond the fact that it has as its subject the word of God, which ought to be the first object of our thoughts, and that there is no translation that can express so well the simplicity and dignity of these Holy Mysteries, it has the properties and ornaments that cannot be equaled by all the elegance even of Greek or

---

37. Original is in French.

Latin. The words of Jerome, "Let us learn those things on earth of which the knowledge will persist with us to the heavens," can well be applied to Hebrew, the use of which (according to the feeling of the most learned) will endure into the next life. Now it is an infallible proof of your good graces that you believe my spirit was born for better things. As for me, if I cannot satisfy the grand designs that you have made of my abilities, at least I shall try to conform to your good advice, which it is, Mademoiselle,

> *Your very humble and very obedient*
> *and very faithful servant,*
> *Anna Maria van Schurman*
>
> *Utrecht, January 26, 1640*[38]

38. The date given in the *Opuscula* is 1647, but this is evidently a typographical error, as Gournay died in 1645. Schurman's letter is a response to Gournay's letter of October 20, 1639 (Royal Library, The Hague ms. 133 B 8, no. 76). In a letter of December 1639 to Rivet (same collection, no. 19), Schurman writes that she has not yet replied to Gournay's letter but intends to do so as soon as she has opportunity.

EUKLERIA

CHAPTER ONE

Universal and Genuine Explication of
My Past and Present State

Everyone is aware from their publications that some renowned men who in the recent past were quite favorably disposed to me now find my new manner of living very displeasing.[1] And no one at this time can be unaware what bitter prejudice and unfair judgment some churchmen hold against the good cause of God for which I have openly declared myself. Therefore, I am glad that this occasion has arisen, on which these outstanding witnesses to the truth and faithful shepherds of our church—Mr. de la Badie, Mr. Yvon, and Mr. DuLignon—have publicly expounded the declaration or defense of their orthodoxy and have opposed the dark missiles of calumny.[2] On this occasion, I say, I am glad to happily achieve my aim, which does not differ from theirs. That is to say, I will pay some of my debt and give public testimony to the same celestial truth and piety for the sake of which these men do battle in the company of a few friends and cultivators of truth and piety. By this work I also hope once and for all to explain briefly and candidly to all who love truth and justice the reasons for the remarkable change of my station in life. Through this work, even if I should not change the opinions of these great men, I may at least fortify the hearts of the little children in Christ against all future prejudice. And if perhaps some false conception of this matter (which the malice of these

---

1. See T. J. Saxby, *The Quest for the New Jerusalem: Jean de Labadie and the Labadists, 1610–1744* (Dordrecht: Martinus Nijhoff, 1987), 176–191, on Labadie in Amsterdam, Schurman's affiliation with him, and the reaction of Schurman's friends such as Voetius and Constantijn Huygens to her move.

2. *Eclaircissement, ou Declaration de la Foy et de la pureté des sentiments en la doctrine des Srs. Jean de Labadie, Pierre Yvon, Pierre Dulignon* (Herford, 1671). This declaration of faith appeared the same year in German and the following year in Dutch.

times, so fruitful in imaginings and monstrosities, could instill in anyone) should still remain in the heads of honest men, let me place in front of it a genuine image of truth, or at least faithfully set the true over against the false.

I. In the first place, I think that I must explain here that I not only consider the doctrines that these teachers of our church present to the world through this work[3] as well as others to be correct, but I also find that their whole teaching, which they impart to us daily, in public as well as in private, agrees in all ways with Holy Scripture. Further, I see—both in the whole elaboration of divine truths and in the particular articles thereof as well as in the manner of presenting them—so many marks of divine teaching—a great and very pure light, a marvelous ease and simplicity and, as I would say, an ointment-like pleasantness and sweetness, and finally, such an insuperable force—that I could not doubt them, even if I wanted to, any more than I doubt the daylight itself when it envelops and brightens our eyes. Not only am I obliged to assert these things according to the inmost feelings of my heart; but also all hearers of this holy teaching who cherish even a spark of the divine light will testify as if with one mouth that they have been touched no less forcibly than sweetly by the pure and simple explanation of that teaching and that they have felt vividly the fiery power of its truth and holiness, like a coal brought by a flying angel from the altar into their hearts, as if they had been touched by some kind of thing recognizable to the external senses. And no wonder, for the more spiritual something is, the more real it is and the more effectively it works.

Nevertheless, if indeed we seek scientific and invincible proof of the divinity and effectiveness of this ministry, we should not depend on these sudden or even fiery movements, which often occur in cases of temporary faith. These movements seem to arise at the hearing of the Word and fade completely away when they encounter hostile times and events (as our Savior in Matthew 13 and his Apostle in Hebrews 6 teach). But we may glory purely and truthfully in the Lord on account of the surest and eminently proper effect of this divine teaching, which the royal Psalmist attributes to Jehovah, namely, that "he restores souls."[4] Of this we have as many examples and witnesses among us as our church has members.

---

3. According to the Dutch translation, Schurman is referring here to *Veritas sui vindex, seu solemnis fidei declaratio* (Herford, 1672), written in reply to a variety of opponents. This volume contained *Eclaircissement* as well as some other writings by Labadie. For a complete list of works by Labadie and his circle, see Saxby, *Quest for the New Jerusalem*, 441–453.

4. Psalm 23:3.

Not in vain will our pastors have spoken honestly of each and every one of them in the words of the Apostle: "You are our letter of recommendation; indeed you are a letter of Christ prepared by us, written not with ink but with the spirit of the living God."[5] For it is also beyond dispute that this holy and true reputation applies to them, inasmuch as they feed their sheep by the apostolic method, namely, as much by example as by word: "having themselves been converted, they convert their brothers." Thus they may justly make use of the exhortation of St. Paul, "Be imitators of me, as I am of Christ,"[6] since they present themselves in all things as models of good works to their flocks, showing integrity in teaching and gravity in behavior. For no one will disagree with me that this is greatly demanded of a minister of the New Covenant and shepherd of Christ's sheep. For this reason I have always liked that old saying of the holy man, "Whoever's life is a flash of lightning, his words are blasts of thunder," and that clever couplet of the English theologian,

> *Hos ego Doctores soleo laudare docenda,*
> *Qui faciunt, plusquam qui facienda docent.*

> I am wont to praise those teachers who do what ought to be
>   taught
> More than those who teach what ought to be done.

II. These few pages to which I intend to confine my writing do not permit me to make it my purpose here to describe the gifts and Christian virtues of our predecessors. But there is one thing I shall willingly and truly say about them nonetheless, namely, that in my whole life I have found no one among mortals who so genuinely and so ardently expressed the spirit and manner of life of the early church or the condition of the first Christians as they have. Anyone who examines with a pure and simple eye the whole course of their lives will admit that he observes with his heart and eyes a kind of living gospel of Christ and a likeness of the first church of Christ. And anyone who follows Christ truly and inwardly and strives to be like him in all things will also confess with full assent that the life and lot of this primitive church, just after it had received the glorious and plentiful first fruits of the Spirit of Christ, was the best and happiest of all, that is, the most Christian. When I had seen the rays of that simple, free life fully devoted to God shining forth from the lives of our Pastors, and when I had perceived in them those living waters which our Savior said

5. 2 Corinthians 3:2–3.
6. 1 Corinthians 11:1.

would gush forth into eternal life, I certainly could not but unhesitatingly follow Christ, my Rock, to the place where he poured out and manifested the rivers of his divine teaching and grace—especially when I saw that these kinds of clear waters no longer followed us everywhere in this desert of Christianity, as they once did in the figure.[7] I do not regret what I have done in the slightest since I hold the true lot of Christians, though despised by others, to be the happiest of all and through the grace of God will hold it to be so into eternity.

III. Since now for some years I have looked with sorrowful eyes at the almost total deflection and defection of Christianity from its origin (I attest to this fact among other things in the letter I wrote five years ago to a preacher in Julich, which was published in part by the author of that outstanding book *On the propagation of the Faith*),[8] and since I am left without any hope of its restitution through that common path on which the churchmen of our age walk (most of whom are themselves in need of Reformation), who could fairly blame me for having chosen for myself and joyfully welcomed pastors who are reformed and divinely instructed toward the goal of reforming deformed Christians? And when the wonderful providence and goodness of God, so worthy of devotion, showed me the correct and direct path to the true practice of the original life of the gospel through the singular Mr. Jean de la Badie, who is well practiced in the ways of the Lord and a faithful servant of the Lord, and his partners in grace, who likewise follow in the footprints of Christ, both in teaching and in working and suffering, how could anyone justly reproach me for following them as the best teachers and leaders? Or that I am also supported by the company of many faithful who all with the same mind and zeal look to Jesus the guide and perfecter of our faith, as we strive toward our heavenly homeland, aiming for the same and only goal of all, namely the glorification of our God and of Jesus Christ the king of glory?

IV. Nevertheless, since there are learned and eminent men who consider my old state of life to have been so excellent and admirable that I was not justified to have exchanged it for another except perhaps with the consent of all my friends or even to the applause of the whole literary world (inasmuch as to it I owe the little fame I enjoy), I think I should give here, as I have said, my reasons, along with supporting arguments. These reasons

---

7. Using the term "figure" to refer to Old Testament imagery, Schurman has in mind such prophecies as Isaiah 35:6 and 43:19.

8. I have been unable to identify this work or the name of the preacher.

will very easily prove the contrary against them. The first reason concerns religion, where the justice and honor of the Divine Majesty as well as the service and imitation of Christ are at issue. It is not to be debated with flesh and blood, as the apostle Paul taught us by example. Indeed, reason and human, that is to say, carnal, wisdom neither savors of the things of the kingdom of God nor understands them. Furthermore, self-love is the worst advisor for making progress therein. It erects as many idols for itself as there are creatures, which it can exploit to its imagined good, honor, advantage, or pleasure. Rather we must listen only to the voice of God and Christ. It will instruct us that "all nations are as nothing before him and that they are accounted by him as less than nothing and emptiness";[9] and that God is pleased with those who with Levi "say concerning their father and mother, 'I do not acknowledge them' and who do not recognize their brothers and pay no regard to their sons, for they abide by God's word and keep his covenant."[10] This our Savior demanded of his disciples with other words: "Whoever comes to me and does not hate his father and mother, his wife, children, brothers, and sisters, and even his own soul, cannot be my disciple" (Luke 14:26). Or more concisely: "If anyone wants to follow me, let him deny himself and take up his cross and follow me" (Luke 9:23).

V. As far as that little bit of fame that the learned world has bestowed on me is concerned, I confess that I am greatly indebted to these scholars because through that reputation I have from their good opinion, they have provided me with a great treasure, and they have presented me with ample material for exercising virtue, including renouncing this beautiful ampule of fame and, among other things, dispersing or selling off things that used to be dear to me in order to possess the most precious pearl of the gospel more securely and purely. I exchange this ampule happily for the reproach of Christ which Moses, that great servant of God, preferred to all the riches of Egypt. But let the learned consider their favor amply repaid if I here make known that truth which I have learned from actual experience, namely, that if anyone should through self-love take unto himself even the least part of the glory that belongs to God alone, he who does not vainly call himself a jealous God will avenge this plunder with the supreme and perhaps eternal disgrace unless averted through true penitence.

VI. Before I proceed to more specific matters, I think I should reveal some-

---

9. Isaiah 40:17.
10. See Deuteronomy 33:9.

thing that has been almost a universal principle entering into all the acts of my life and rightly serves to demonstrate the vanity of that life. Although quite often a certain hidden ground of conscience protested, nevertheless, under the appearance of some virtue or duty and the supposed common good of learning, I have allowed myself to be led step by step into that theater of a more conspicuous fame, from which the departure has been difficult. I do not know through what carelessness or blindness of mind I have furnished an argument, that is to say, an occasion for literary idolatry, of which all who cultivate vainglory are guilty. Lying eulogists, as some-one has not unfairly called them, as they sing each other's praises, trans-form themselves into mere animals, living for glory. I recognize that I was caught in this grossest of faults by certain extravagant singers of my praises. They exalted me to the heavens, though I am a mortal human be-ing, a worm of the earth, worthy of eternal chains and of the prison of utter darkness because of the manifold sins I have inherited and committed against heaven. They not only set me profanely within the ranks of pagan gods but also blasphemously loaded me with divine attributes of the true God such as omniscience and I know not what other offensive titles, Never in all this time did I emphatically enough contradict their foolish-ness, or should I say godlessness, with any public protest or apology. It is this that I now, late but all the more earnestly and with a kind of abhor-rence of my neglect of duty, have brought myself to do here. In the full light of day, therefore, I retract (after the example of Augustine, the most candid of the church fathers) all those writings of mine which exude such a shame-ful slackness in my soul, or, if you will, a vain and worldly spirit. I no longer recognize them as mine. Also, I hereby reject and remove far from myself as alien to my condition and profession all the writings of others, especially the panegyric poems, which are marked with that sign of vainglory and godlessness. I should also like to ask their authors, if any of them are still alive, to weigh such things in the scales of the sanctuary it-self and to determine whether they will have to give an answer to the Su-preme Judge concerning these words, which are not only pointless, but in some instances also perverse and harmful by their example, unless they condemn them with me or even retract or correct them.

VII. Someone might object that this was not a use but an abuse of learning and of fame and that, as in other things, even the best, the abuse must be removed but the substance of the matter should be retained. I cannot bring myself to mount a full and accurate response since all that needs to be said is that this axiom applies only to those things that are truly good and necessary and to those that pertain to God purely and truly, not to us outside him. I have no wish to spend time criticizing the vanity of studies or to reenter the labyrinth that learned and intelligent men have already described skillfully and widely enough in their published writings, the best of them being the priestly Preacher, who gave us this wisest of sayings: "Of the making of many books there is no end, and much reading is wearying to the flesh. The highest cause is to worship God himself and observe his commands, for this is the whole of man."[11]

I will not waste my time and that of others (here parsimony is utterly justified) by being too distracted by the vain depiction of past things at the expense of the present. Let that simplicity which I think must be preserved for receiving better things be the rule. It is enough for me here to point out briefly what necessarily happens to all others who are seized with a desire for learning because of the general darkness of the human mind and deviation from the true and good. I have not been either so prudent or so fortunate as always and everywhere to have separated abuse from use in the course of my studies or to have observed equal proportion in all things. Nor have I consistently devoted the best hours to the best and most necessary matters. On the contrary, if I were to observe diligently all the stages of my life along with the studies that occupied them and to expose to everyone the complete shape of the whole, it would be like a monster. But there are enough monsters in the world.

CHAPTER TWO

A Quick and Specific Description of My Past Life,
Beginning with the Tender Years of My Childhood,
When I Inclined to Piety and Began to Devote Myself
to Languages, Arts, and Sciences.

[1.] I now return to the comparison of my present condition with the past and thus to a short sketch of my life insofar as it should serve this purpose. I shall not deny that I felt some small sparks of genuine piety in my heart from a tender age; during the whole later course of my life these could easily be seen at times to glow and even to break out in flames. One instance among others that comes to mind was when I was a little girl of scarcely four years. While collecting herbs with the maid whose chore this was, I sat down on the bank of a certain stream. When she suggested it, I recited from memory the response to the first question of the Heidelberg

11. Ecclesiastes 12:12.

Catechism. At the words "that I am not my own but belong to my most faithful servant Jesus Christ," my heart was filled with such a great and sweet joy and an intimate feeling of the love of Christ that all the subsequent years have not been able to remove the living memory of that moment.

To add another example, I remember that when I was about eleven, I first happened to read the history of the martyrs.[12] At the contemplation of the example of so many faithful servants of Christ and witnesses to his truth, such an ardent desire for martyrdom seized my mind that I fervently longed to exchange even the sweetest life for such a glorious death. After that during my whole life nothing seemed to me more intolerable or more unworthy of the Christian name than that mentality of Erasmus expressed in his writings to Eck. There he stated openly that he did not aspire to the glory of martyrdom (as it exceeded too much the sphere of his ambition), and that he was unwilling to approve it for anyone.

Beyond this I thirsted constantly from childhood on with an honest and sincere desire for the true practice of devotion, according to the understanding I had attained. But how poor and feeble that was I shall later indicate more accurately. Here at least I must note in passing that, even though I always conferred first place to piety (as to the highest virtue) beyond what was popular opinion and the common practice and manner of the youth of my status and condition, nevertheless this was not taken by anyone to be the primary reason for praising me. Either it was not sufficiently recognized and admired by others as the supreme virtue, or I did not show it forth purely and firmly enough in my life; or perhaps they judged nothing worthy of observing and celebrating except what was rare in our sex and valued for that reason. So let me return to those studies which rendered me famous and happy in the opinion of nearly all; and let me not detract from their esteem, beyond telling the truth of the matter. Nor shall I misrepresent my present cause.

II. I must therefore go back to the first scene in my life and at this point give faithful testimony with filial gratitude to my parents that they sought to educate their children not only in humane letters but also in the faith as

---

12. Schurman probably is referring here to John Foxe's *Commentarii Rerum in Ecclesia Gestarum* (Strasbourg, 1554), a widely read history of Protestant martyrs during the reign of Queen Mary in England. Published in English in 1563 as *Acts and Monuments*, it received official church approval during Elizabeth's reign and appeared in four editions during Foxe's lifetime (1516–1587).

they understood it. This was a matter of such earnest concern to them that they had us instructed from childhood by an excellent domestic tutor, since we lived in the country. This met with such success that as a child of only three years (as was told to me later by others) I could read German accurately and recite part of the catechism from memory. That I, or rather God Himself as the author of Nature, contributed a special readiness to learn, I gladly recognize. But lest anyone think that I strove of my own accord or choice for things too exalted and out of the ordinary, I must touch briefly on the circumstances, trifling though they be, which led to the beginning of my studies.

When I was in my eleventh year (A.D. 1618), it happened that my brothers (one of whom was two years older than I, the other four years older) were given exercises in Latin and I in French by our father. By I know not what chance or, to be more accurate, by divine providence, it happened that I sometimes assisted them when they overlooked something. This prompted my father to think that I might successfully be instructed with them in the same letters. And when he encouraged me to believe this and saw that I cheerfully followed his desire (surely only out of a wish to please him), he began from then on to initiate me in the study of letters.

III. In order that I not be put off at the outset by the prickly points of grammar, he prudently set before me instead the philosopher Seneca (whom I enjoyed very much) to read and explicate, saying, "The eagle catches no flies." The most essential elements he taught me thereafter, but only while playing or walking in the garden, so that I easily endured the bitterness and tedium in studying the rudiments. Meanwhile, in order that the charms of this heathen writer not hinder Christian devotion (which is in conflict with all wisdom of the flesh), he had me moderate the reading of the former by combining it with the reading of Holy Scripture.

IV. First off, however, I must acknowledge with thanks as a sign of God's beneficence to me that my parents, who were most con-cerned for honor and decency, instilled in me from an early age a great horror of those authors and all those things that could divert the mind from chastity and virginal purity. So throughout my life I consistently abstained from the reading of all those books, especially of poets, both Latin and Greek, as if from a kind of poisonous potion; and I scarcely read any with care and attention except Homer and Virgil, whom my father recommended to me as easily the princes of all the poets. The contemporary poets, on the other hand, I acquired only with great selectivity. If some texts containing worldly or contaminated arguments were presented, even if their authors were very famous (out of respect I spare them here the mention of their names), I either did not read them at all or read them only in bits and pieces, sampling them with just the tips of my lips. Today, in-deed, you will find few who merit that tribute which someone deservedly paid to the French poet Bartas, that he did not befoul his laurel crown with, as it were, the rotten leaf of a single licentious verse.

V. An additional merit of my unusual education was that my parents did not send me to the French school until I was seven and then only for two months, so that I might suffer little corruption from childish games and from the contagion of impure words, which are easily imprinted on a deli-cate memory as on a blank slate. They preferred that I be taught the arts of writing and arithmetic, as well as both instrumental and vocal music, by tutors together with my brothers. In addition, they let me pass my leisure time in various kinds of arts (to which my natural inclinations led me) and thus to temper the more serious studies with that more pleasant seasoning. This training did not seem so worthy of censure, since it later kept me also from foolish company and from involvement in the amusements and adornments of worldly girls, except that at a later age and naturally gifted for better things I overly indulged this inborn impulse and carried out great frivolities with great intensity. For in truth there is scarcely anyone who, when eager to please himself and others in the world, will use something correctly or in moderation; and the rarer and nobler the gift is, the more easily and harmfully it is abused.

VI. I shall not deny that artistic skill is to be included among the gifts of God and that the spirit of God itself is credited as the author of the arts. For example, in Exodus 31 Bezalel and Oholiab are said to be capable and skilled in accomplishing any work whatever. But the use of the arts at that time served the outward and childlike worship of the Jews, from which it derived its worth. Meanwhile I have indeed often wondered what place my study of the arts should hold for me; even from early childhood my talent inclined to and expressed itself in a remarkable variety of things. When I was scarcely a girl of six years, I cut out, without any example, outlines and figures from discarded scraps of paper so skillfully with scis-sors that almost no one could be found, even among adult friends, who tried it with similar success. Then four years later I learned the art of em-broidery in three hours, at which everyone marveled. This was after I had spent a few weeks tracing the outline of flowers with Spanish lead. And this is to say nothing about the nobler arts, which I carried on in seclusion after the death of my father, without any teacher, in various materials.[13] I should not dare to mention all this, lest I seem to overstep all bounds of modesty, if I did not now think that there had been more vanity than true cause for praise in them. For if we believe the philosopher, no one is worthy on account of natural gifts; and no one is accustomed to praise them as virtues.[14]

VII. I confess that sometimes, when I painted flowers and insects with water color (which seemed a simpler and more innocent kind of picture than others), my mind was no less occupied with heavenly thoughts than my hand with earthly exercise. But sometimes the same activity so filled my whole brain and even my heart itself with new discoveries that I was not able easily and unwaveringly to contemplate or enjoy God either in himself or in his creatures. This clearly demonstrated to me the vanity of this art. But since I now want to show that the world held this child's play to be of some value and that I may be said to have abandoned something for the sake of God, and also because I do not wish to conceal any of my early happiness, I shall offer here an example or two of my skill which was so renowned. The first example concerns three figures that I carved out of boxwood with an ordinary knife (for there was no other instrument or teacher available for aid or advice). One figure was of my dearest mother, the second of myself, and the third of my one and only brother.[15] When my brother himself later showed this last one to the highly celebrated painter Honthorst, he declared seriously that it could not be worth less than a thousand florins. The second example I wish to mention is (or rather was) a wax image of myself, which I had produced by depicting myself in a mirror; I did not expend thirty years, or as many as Albertus Magnus devoted to his talking statue, but at least thirty days on it.[16] There

13. Not everyone is convinced that she was uninstructed in art. Katlijne Van der Stighelen, in *Anna Maria van Schurman (1607–1678) of 'Hoe hooge dat een maeght kan in de konsten stijgen'* Leuven: Universitaire Pers, 1987), 15, cites evidence that Schurman did receive artistic instruction.

14. Aristotle, *Nicomachean Ethics*, 2.1 (1103a, 18–25).

15. According to Van der Stighelen, this indicates that the portraits were made after the death of the oldest brother, which took place around 1632. See 14 and also 97 and 153–158 regarding these three miniatures and the genre of *Dosenköpfe*. On 155, photographs of the surviving two (of her mother and herself) are to be seen.

16. Van der Stighelen discusses this on 146; see also G. D. J. Schotel, *Anna Maria van Schurman* ('s-Hertogenbosch, 1853), 14–15.

were many things to be discovered in that art which I could not learn from anyone. Its eyes, moreover, not only resembled my own in miniature, but because of the vivid brightness and roundness of the pupils they seemed to turn on their own when the case was rapidly turned. The wax locks of hair were attached to the head only with their most delicate ends, so that they adorned it, it seemed, with freely flying garlands. Most difficult of all were the eyelashes of very fine hairs, which I fortified with prolonged effort like an upright palisade. And, to mention one more thing concerning the vanity of this ornament, the jewels that encircled the neck so ingeniously simulated nature (because of a new discovery of mine) that scarcely anyone believed me when I asserted the contrary. For no other reason than to distinguish art from nature, I pierced one of them with a hairpin at the request of the astute Countess of Nassau.

VIII. But what fruit do I really seek from this unless I might buy penance for the loss of that most precious time, which followed a little later in its falling and breaking? For a little afterward one of my mother's sisters, while surveying it with curious eye, allowed it to fall carelessly from her hand. I had inscribed these verses on the margin:

> I do not propose to mock human fate
> or to sculpt my features in bronze.
> Behold my likeness which I have expressed in wax.
> Verily I have given it over to a fragile material
> that is about to perish.

That is, I had imagined the likeness of my life (as we are accustomed to do with life itself) not that it was soon to disappear or be broken but as fragile (that is, remaining fragile, but remaining nonetheless permanent). Thus by this breakage as by a serious and unexpected accident, I was not a little dismayed. This shows that I held foolishly in some way to a thing of no value, which was nothing but a shadow of me, as I am nothing but the dream of a shadow, as the Poet [Euripides] elegantly described human beings: *skias onar anthropos*. In this he does not differ from the meaning of the words of the Psalmist which compare the life of mortals to a dream and to a thought, or, as others translate, to a tale that is told.[17] And who would believe that men, who think they are placed above the sphere of the moon and can look from above on changeable things left under their feet, could fall back so deeply into the mud that they are occupied or disturbed by

17. Psalm 90:5, 9.

these insignificant kinds of things? This folly of the human mind is as laughable in the philosophic life, because with their meditations and exalted dicta concerning the contempt of external things (of which the paradoxes of Seneca used to please me above others) they seize upon it as the very condition and constitution of the soul. So should we laugh or cry about the spiritual and religious life of those who pretend to be Christians? In thinking and speaking the noble thoughts and spoken pronouncements that circulate in thought and conversation (especially concerning the renunciation of outward things and concerning the practice of faith, hope, and charity) they dream that they possess them. They embrace them as real truths and virtues and settle into this imaginary happiness. Whence many have been made fools, as were once the philosophers concerning whom the Apostle spoke in Romans 2:21, because they came to nothing in their ratiocinations; while all the while saying that they were wise, they made themselves fools.

IX. Other things of this sort I shall pass over. I began to lay aside both the love and the memory of such things as the divine image of the life of Christ came into my mind, which I judged to be alone worthy of imitation. But still I could not preserve a sufficiently clear and constant image of this in my soul. So I thought to capture in writing a certain very defined picture of it for my good and that of others. The excellent little book of Thomas à Kempis, *On the Imitation of Christ*, pleased me; but I wanted in it more agreement between its title and the treatise proper. For some reason I hoped I could attain this. To tell the truth, I was never able to satisfy myself in that work both because my mind and eyes were often blinded by the splendor of this divine theme and also because I seemed only to be depicting the sun with charcoal. I found that the life of Christians is alone the most excellent image of the life of Christ, but it is not within easy reach in these times. When afterward I saw the most vivid outline of this in our pastors, I believed their living examples had to replace for me the mechanisms of all the arts. Because I expressed my serious undertaking briefly and in a manner suitable to my point here in a letter written before I left Utrecht to an illustrious patron of the arts and sciences (who asked my opinion concerning some splendid paintings), I transcribe here the following words taken from that letter:

> Another kind of picture I guard in my soul. Through it I can depict or even imitate the celestial image of the divine virtues of our highest and most beautiful King and Savior Jesus, if not with pen and paper (something I have tried in vain to do for some time) certainly in

my soul in some manner. I see more and more that this art is long while life is short and circumstances difficult; also that the entrance to the heavenly court is open only to those who shine with some of the radiance of that divine mark. If, however, anyone learns to trace successfully in this tablet [of the soul] even the faintest lines [of the image of Christ], he will leave behind him easily all Protagorases and even Apollos by an infinite distance. I, for my part, inasmuch as I wish to dedicate the rest of my life to this pursuit, end this letter with the wish that God, who is the Highest Good and only teacher of this art, may teach it to you, me, and all his own to the glory and the reformation of the true church. Utrecht, 13 September 1669.[18]

Assuredly we will treat all works of art as small if we see with a spiritual eye and feel and taste with divine senses that the Creator has impressed on all creatures some likeness of himself, in accord with the well-known verse, "Every blade of grass teaches the presence of God." Certainly, if we become accustomed to lifting up all created things as if they were veils opaque to all, under which divine goodness, wisdom, power, beauty, and majesty are concealed, or if we penetrate them with the keen eye of the spirit, we will through right use elevate all things with us to God (which is the duty of rational creatures). and will be engulfed in his immense beauty. But even if we lack this practice and look only at the surface of things, why not rather gaze at the works of God than of man, and most of all at those endowed with life? For these leave the excellence of all paintings behind by a vast distance. What painting can imitate either their life, their motion, or even the surface of the things—even granting that once, as antiquity testifies, this art was brought to such perfection that both people and animals were deceived and, if we can believe it, those looking at the art took it to be nature itself? Nevertheless today, if you compare even an excellently painted fruit or animal with a live one and hold one next to the other, soon the deception is uncovered and one is ashamed of the very ridiculous and foolish comparison. But such is human nature that, as if God had not made enough creatures or had not made all things beautiful in their own time, we strive in winter after green meadows and flowers produced by us in paintings—which in summer we often ne-

---

18. The person in question was Constantijn Huygens, who had been a friend and supporter of Schurman for decades. Huygens's letter of September 8, 1669, and Schurman's response of September 13, 1669, are reprinted in *De Briefwisseling van Constantijn Huygens* (1608–1687), pt. 6, 1663–1687, ed. J. A. Worp ('s-Gravenhage: Martinus Nijhoff, 1917), 253–254 (nos. 6722 and 6723). The artists mentioned by Huygens are Caspar Netscher and John Hoskins.

glect in nature—and almost admire more and praise our fantasies more than the real, very beautiful, useful, numberless works of God, which cannot be imitated by any art or adequately celebrated by speech in any language. But since I am declaring painted images to be close to vanity, it is fitting for me to abandon the image of images and progress to more solid matters.

X. I already said above that through this delight in studies and arts, I was easily drawn away and made a stranger to children's games and other false amusements. Let me add also that I had been to a certain extent armed against idle and worldly associations, which awaited me in subsequent years, partly through my father's precise instruction in the duties of devotion (to which ought to be added the care of my wonderful mother), partly through his frequent warnings, by which he deterred me from contamination by the spirit of the times and from the company of worldly people. And in order that I might not become imprudently entangled in the snares of this world, he especially warned me with great ardor even up to his death against the inextricable, highly depraved bond of worldly marriage (which is commonly found). I did not throw this fatherly advice to the winds when thereafter the world attempted in various ways to bind me to it by this method.

XI. But would that I had protected myself just as faithfully from the vainglory of men as from the special association of the worldly. Many things prevented me, which would take too long and be superfluous to recount here. I will therefore note only briefly how I was brought forward onto the world stage. This happened chiefly at the time when I was urged by some patrons of learning, and especially Mr. Gisbertus Voetius, the first professor of theology, to celebrate the inauguration of the University of Utrecht with my verses. After this I began more than ever to dedicate myself willingly to the vanity of the sciences, which I thought I should hold in reverence as if they were distinguished handmaidens to Queen Theology; indeed I considered it my duty to preserve carefully the little honor of my fame as a common good of the republic of letters and, as much as modesty would permit, to increase it, so that among the other great lights I too, as a star of the sixth magnitude, might contribute some brightness to that sphere of vast knowledge or Encyclopedia. I confess that before this time I had not allowed myself to be snatched away by such thoughts. For although the famous professor and doctor of theology André Rivet, among some other famous friends, sought very eagerly to bring some fame to my name, nevertheless by my innate modesty and a sincere desire to keep out of the public eye, I strove to shun the celebrity of my name as a great burden. And I would have been content in this hiddenness and quietude if thereafter not so much by popular sentiment as by the extraordinary good will of some of the illustrious men in society I had not been drawn away from my intention. Only too late did I recognize how much this ran counter to Christian humility and renunciation of all created things. But afterward it would have been futile to try to place limits on the fame that was extending far and wide and which gained strength as it went, had not the rather assiduous hatred of worldly theologians (as is worth noting) taken care of it. Their hatred arose from the fact that I constantly fled their company and their sermons, for which perhaps they had burned the midnight oil, so to speak. This I did, not only because they contained not a whit of solid learning or genuine eloquence, but primarily because they did not savor or give off the scent of even a drop of that oil that the Spirit of Christ pours into the hearts of his own, whereby all weariness of the devout listener is usually prevented. This, as I say, was the reason why, through a kind of law of retribution, they believed they should scorn and denigrate me and my studies by their slanders; and through envy, or whatever else, they got a ready hearing and attained their goal with many, thereby lifting from me the burden of too great a fame and freeing me from the many tiresome visits, especially of people who lived in my immediate area. I would have wished, however, that I could have spurned with equal ease the worldly well-wishing of other worldly men, especially the famous, as I did the ill-wishing of these clerics, whom I regarded not as ministers of Christ but as traitors to his grace and glory since they worked openly for the world. Nor did I expect any fruit from their sermons; rather it seemed to me that Jehovah was speaking primarily to them in Psalm 50:16–17: "What right have you to recite my statutes, or take my covenant on your lips? For you hate discipline, and you cast my words behind you." For I cared nothing about their outward vocation among men, since their works testified that they had not been inwardly called by God. I was strengthened in this opinion by experience, and no one could easily persuade me, since it was truly most false, namely, that the words of life that are dead in the mouth of a dead preacher (as someone said more elegantly than accurately) bring life to dead listeners. For the preacher can indeed say the words but not grasp and give voice to the meaning and life or Spirit of Scripture; the listeners, moreover, have not the ears to hear spiritual things in a spiritual manner or to grasp them inwardly. But how would the Holy Spirit plausibly attach himself to a dead person as a tool of his grace for bringing souls to life? Certainly not more, indeed less than to the crowing of the cock, which our Savior wanted to be a reminder to the turncoat Peter of his words in order to call him back from his special sin. In such a preacher the rule of sin stands in the way, but not in the cock or Balaam's ass, which accused his master of his sin. For what does the light have in common with darkness, or Christ with Belial? If, however, someone should use against me by way of objection the example of Balaam himself, who in his rapture uttered very holy words, I would respond that these words were not uttered for the conversion of Balaam but for his condemnation and a more serious judgment on him, and to be read in Scripture as if they were prophecy. I shall say further that such prophets are born perhaps not like the phoenix every 500 years but scarcely every 5,000 years. Moreover an unclean vessel cannot produce a pure drink; and the purest words and thoughts, if they flow through the unclean throats of the unregenerate (which Holy Scripture compares to open graves) cannot safely be swallowed as living and pure spring water. The Apostle says, "We have this treasure in clay jars,"[19] but they were cleansed by the blood of Christ and the water of the Holy Spirit. For earthen vessels that were unclean and contaminated by leprosy were not even to be brought into the house of Israelites but had to be broken; much less could they be used in worship of God and in his temple to store blood or water or oil. No one calls into question that these things were types or prefigurations of the state of the New Testament church. Everyone who knows me knows that as soon as I began to form spiritual judgments I always hated and fled as worse than the plague such blemishes of the Christian faith, especially of the sacred ministry. And by contrast I have always regarded and still regard with both great honor and love as worthy teachers of the church those who have proved and continue to prove themselves faithful servants and followers of Christ not only by words and dispositions but through deeds and effects. But let this be said only in passing. I return to my situation at that time.

XII. Here I shall bring to light only two or three more things that give evidence of my earlier wanderings from the right path and my servitude to the world, even though I seemed to many to be wise and happy. First, as fame itself showed the way and guided me (for it seemed I ought to keep that which was said favorably about me from being a lie), I turned my mind and efforts to too many different and idle—indeed worthless—

19. 2 Corinthians 4:7.

matters. Second, that in respect neither to time nor to knowledge itself did I maintain a proper proportion; I did not always give first place to the things that could glorify God, edify my neighbor, and make my soul more pleasing to God. Third, following mostly human instinct, which drew me more to human than to divine matters, I clung with too much affection to various sciences and arts and in them sought, even if I did not find, some pleasure and repose. All these things will easily be recognized by anyone who observes the course of my life.

XIII. In truth I was recently astonished at my earlier lack of moderation in studies on the occasion of looking through my dissertation to Mr. André Rivet on the learning of a Christian woman, where I read the words, "I think all honorable disciplines, or the whole circle of liberal arts, as it is called, is entirely fitting to a Christian woman (just as it is a proper and universal good or adornment of humanity)." At that time I believed that I must learn everything that can be known, indeed, "in order to flee ignorance," in accordance with the words I quoted there from the Philosopher. But I did not want to recommend to others anything of which I myself was not fully persuaded. Yet how far my thoughts were then from the admonition of our Savior that "one thing is necessary,"[20] anyone can see from all that has been said.

XIV. Further, as far as the order and proper proportion in my studies are concerned, even though I did strive for it, nevertheless the following words from the same dissertation show that I did not attain it:

> First of all account should be taken of those sciences or arts that have the closest connection with theology and moral virtue, and which primarily serve them. We consider grammar (I mean general grammar), logic, and rhetoric to be of this sort. Among these first disciplines, however, some expressly identify logic as the key to all sciences. Then come physics, metaphysics, history, . . . and also knowledge of languages, especially Hebrew and Greek. All of these things are able to move us to easier and fuller knowledge of Sacred Scripture, to say nothing of other authors.

It is evident from this that I did indeed subordinate everything to theology as preeminent but that this subordination extended almost ad infinitum before one would reach the goal of pure theology, since I consid-

20. Luke 10:42.

ered so many and such different aids necessary for understanding Scripture that this study would easily exceed the bounds of the very brief life of mortal human beings. In truth, had not the grace of God ordained otherwise, death would have overtaken me while still in these preparations.

XV. For example, let us look solely at the study of languages, which the learned call vehicles of the sciences, and to which indeed, even though I found that they often were hindrances, I devoted very many hours. But to what end, I ask? So that with Cato, who studied Greek at sixty years of age, I might respond to one who inquires, "that I may die more learned"? Or, since I was younger, that I might live more learned? At least I did not imagine my primary ornament to lie in this study, but because I respected the Greek as well as the Hebrew language and esteemed them as the original languages of Holy Scripture; and because I considered the other Oriental languages to be daughters or branches of Hebrew and for that reason lovable and, by the recommendation of learned men, worthy, I was persuaded that I should acquire them with inexhaustible efforts, especially Syriac, Arabic, and Ethiopic, because they have the most root words, of which only the derivatives are in Sacred Scripture, and consequently shed a bit of light in my quest to unearth its deepest meaning. But, if we love the truth, was this not lighting torches in the sunlight? or making an elephant from a fly?[21] or, in order not to say anything worse, playing games with a serious matter? For there are very few words which in our day are obscure in the learned translations and unknown to the experts in the Hebrew language. Furthermore, a certain spiritual gift for interpretation is required most of all, toward which this knowledge contributes little or nothing. For either the Scripture is read in the light of the Holy Spirit, or it is not. If not, it is futile to employ a grammatical explanation of one word or another in order to grasp its innermost spiritual meaning. But if you are taught by that Master, then its true and complete or universal meaning will not depend on the knowledge of some word or unusual root. In his universal light the whole context of the discourse manifests the truth since God alone through his Spirit is the sole infallible and real interpreter of Sacred Letters.

XVI. I am happy, nevertheless, that I attained some knowledge of various languages so that at least I do not think temples should be built for them, as for an unknown God, in the way the Athenians once did.[22] Rather I

---

21. These or similar sayings may be found in Erasmus's *Adages* 1.9.69 and 2.5.5.
22. Acts 17:23.

think that the great textual apparatus, like some rehearsal hall of vainglory adorned with imposing sentences of rare erudition as if with splendid tapestries and like an overly furnished house, with which Christians (at least in a private capacity) would burden themselves, should be left to literary scholars—unless perhaps some child of God who has been divinely awakened and gifted with spiritual proficiency and fluency produces for the Christian world some universal grammar that has for a long time now been desired by wise men or some spiritual lexicon that could be used toward the conversion of Gentiles or Jews. I am indeed now of the persuasion that the slightest experience of the love of God gives us a truer and deeper understanding of the sacred page than does the most complete knowledge of the sacred language itself. And I believe that the same judgment should be made concerning all sciences.

XVII. I know, admittedly, that if human affairs, both civil and ecclesiastical, are to be preserved in the same condition as they now are, all those theologians and preachers who are instructed little or not at all by the Spirit of God will have no less need of this great support of external aids than human and worldly orators themselves in order to gratify and satisfy the human and worldly taste of their hearers, that is, to fill their ears with rare inventions of the human intelligence, beautiful images, and rhetorical flowers and thus feed and delight their empty minds with a methodical elegance of speech and arouse various human emotions, or treat controversies and objections of all sorts with logical arguments and syllogisms and refute them in a human manner. In short, like the whole world, they too put on an act. If, however, the teachers are truly taught by God and are instructed and led by the strength of his Spirit, three books are more than sufficient for them, namely the book of Scripture, the book of Nature, and the book of inward grace, in order to know God and themselves—and thus also humankind—thoroughly; in this knowledge all true wisdom is located. On this point history supplies us with examples of the martyrs, the Albigensians and, in the last century, of simple people—the unlearned, so to speak—who in one talk convert more people to God, or discover those already converted, than most of today's preachers with a thousand of their learned and well-prepared sermons. Those who lack this inward Teacher can only borrow a kind of barren and false knowledge from a human school, which the Apostle elegantly calls "the form of knowledge";[23] this they also transmit and inflict upon their students.

---

23. Romans 2:20.

XVIII. Memorable in this respect were the dying words of Rivet (whose memory I take pleasure in recalling here), when at the end of his life he felt in his soul the light and power of divinely imprinted experiential knowledge. He considered knowledge drawn from books like dung or filth, and he broke out in these savory words greatly worthy of all our attention: "You are the teacher of spirits. I have learned more theology in these ten days in which you have visited me than in the space of fifty years. . . ."[24] Since these words especially deserve to be read there in their context, I direct the reader to it.

XIX. This is not to say, however, that we should utterly reject all true sciences and useful or necessary arts indiscriminately. Nor should we deny that the pure can make use of some of them in a pure and useful manner. But it is to say that most of them are vain and superfluous, fully occupying people's foolish minds and hindering them from aspiring to more enduring things, and that even good things are not good for everyone. For just as all things work together for good for those who love God, so all things work together for evil for those who do not love God. So that all the worldly, since they lack the eyes of faith and do not see God in his light, since they are not instructed by the love of God (which Augustine rightly calls the great Teacher) and they are devoid of the Spirit of God, change all teachings, even Holy Scripture itself, into a fragrance of death (to use the words of the Apostle)[25] for themselves and those who follow them. For that reason they ought rightly and prudently to use as few things as possible lest they abuse many, in order not to bring greater damnation on themselves.

XX. Whether indeed they treat the truths themselves and pursue positive and, as they call it, didactic theology, or whether they practice polemical theology, in all these they sin, since with regard to Scripture and didactic theology they seize not the Spirit of the letter, but, legalistically and perversely, they seize the letter of the Word of God, which kills, for killing the old man and conquering Satan.[26] Thus it is for them not the sword of the Spirit but an empty sheath or rather an iron sword in the hand of a fool, with which they wound themselves and others while mixing their own corrupt reason with divine matters and raise it up as administrant, interpreter, and judge of Holy Scripture. As much as in them lies, they

24. Footnote in original cites p. 65 of the 2d edition of *Dernières Heures [de monsieur Rivet, ministre de Jesus Christ, et professeur en théologie* (Geneva, 1666)].

25. 2 Corinthians 2:16.

26. 2 Corinthians 3:6.

thereby dislodge the Holy Spirit from his throne and turn the weapons of erudition against the simplicity of faith. But as regards their elenchtic or eristic exercises (to use scholastic terms in scholastic matters),[27] they often erect a theater pleasing to the devil, since he not seldom presides at their disputations and forges or supplies arms or arguments for his champions of errors to fight truth; he provides them material to nourish ambition, envy, anger, and other such monsters of the human heart or else to establish the reign of and love for reason and human argumentation, by which he may then triumph, if not in full, certainly in part, over the actors in this kind of pretense. And those who think they have turned out victors will find they have attained nothing except human assent or, in any event, the stopping of the mouth and the restraining of the tongue of their adversary.

XXI. For it is not that anyone should believe that truth is established or anyone correctly taught by human reasonings or artificial arguments or that errors can truly and in a wholesome manner be overcome through subtle disputations. For it is not a divine faith that depends on human reason, and the devil does not find it difficult to weaken the convictions of reason by new stratagems. Whatever the so-called angelic doctor[28] may assert concerning the defense of religion by reason unless it is established by the grace of God, I know for certain the one argument that is most effective against the errors of atheists or contentious men is a blameless life striking by the brightness of Christian virtues. Such was that holy martyr in England who denied that she was able to dispute for Christ but confirmed strongly by words and deed itself that she was able to die for him. I have experienced for myself that those human and satanic artifices and endeavors against the doctrine of Christ are often mocked and destroyed only by contempt and abhorrence.

27. "Elenchus" is a refutation in syllogistic form; "eristic" is the art or practice of disputation and polemics, esp. as based on specious grounds.

28. Thomas Aquinas believed that reason could provide a basis for knowledge of God, though some central Christian teachings could be known only by faith.

CONCERNING WOMEN
Gisbertus Voetius

CONCERNING WOMEN
Gisbertus Voetius

In Treatise II above we distinguished between members of the church according to various qualities, both internal and external. Among these is one that distinguishes members by sex into men and women. At this point, since we have to consider several things concerning women in relation to the body and state of the church, it will be worth our while, or at least we will seem to be doing nothing inappropriate, if, like scholastic theologians and also our own writers of commonplaces who treat the nature, parts, essences, affections of humans, we thus here expound on at least some selected questions relating to the

I. Natural
II. Secular and Political   } Status and Condition of Women
III. Spiritual and Ecclesiastical

CHAPTER ONE
Questions surrounding the natural status and condition of women

Question 1. Whether a woman is human

Response: More than sixty-four years ago a book was published by an anonymous author who attempted to show by resorting to certain scriptural texts that women are not human.[1] But to such absurd and stupid

Note: This selection comes from Voetius's major work, *Politica Ecclesiastica* (Amsterdam, 1663–1676), bk. 1, treatise 4.

1. *Disputatio nova contra mulieres, qua probatur eas homines non esse* (1595), possibly written by Valens Acidalius (d. 1595), though he denied this. The work is a satirical attack on Anabaptist biblical interpretation; what position the author actually took regarding women is not clear. See Ian Maclean, *The Renaissance Notion of Woman: A Study of the Fortunes of Scholasticism and Medical*

questions and disquisitions, we must apply the words of the Apostle, "Avoid the profane chatter and contradictions of what is falsely called knowledge" (1 Timothy 6:20), and "Have nothing to do with stupid and senseless controversies" (2 Timothy 2:23).

Plato indeed did not openly deny that women are human, but in the *Symposium* in a less than philosophical way he wavered in his opinion whether they are to be placed in the genus of rational or irrational animals. Nor was he philosophical and accurate in the *Symposium* when he identified three kinds of humans: male, female, and a third composed of both.[2]

But this doubt or false knowledge is overcome through Scripture and reason:

1. Genesis 1:27: "And God created humankind in his image, . . . male and female he created them." Genesis 5:1–2: "When God created humankind, he made them in the likeness of God. Male and female he created them."

2. From the Incarnation of Christ, who is and is called human and the son of a human, and who was made from woman (Galatians 4:4). Therefore the most holy virgin Mary, his mother, who was a woman, was human.

3. From the salvation of Christ the mediator, which was of humans, not of other creatures. "For there is one mediator between God and humans," etc. (1 Timothy 2:5 with Titus 3:4). Now, women assuredly are saved through Christ the mediator (1 Timothy 2:15, Acts 16:14–15 & 17:34).

4. Since no creatures are members of the church or constitute the mystical body of Christ, and none are subject to baptism and the supper, unless they are human. But women are members of the church and of the mystical body of Christ since they are subject to baptism and the supper (Acts 14:14 [*sic*])[3] and are part and members of the visible church or the outwardly gathered assembly (1 Corinthians 11:5 and 14:34).

5. From the fact that just as male and female are not species of animals, so too neither are man and woman species of humans or belong to different species. We take it as proven from philosophy and by the philosophers.

Science in European Intellectual Life (Cambridge: Cambridge University Press, 1980), 12.

2. The discussion of three original types of humans occurs in the speech of Aristophanes in Plato, *Symposium* (190 A-B). Whether women are rational or irrational is not debated explicitly in the *Symposium*, but in two instances (181 B and 209 A) love of women is associated with the body, a lower form of love than that of the soul.

3. Voetius may have intended to refer again to Acts 16:14–15, although the passage mentions only baptism, not the supper.

6. Since the same essential parts constitute a woman as well as a man, namely a human soul and a human body. It is therefore by essence and species the same composite, that is, a human, or a human being, constituted of those essential parts. There can be no doubt concerning the human soul of a woman, since woman is said to have been created in the image of God (Genesis 1:27) and renewed through Christ according to the image of God to have faith, holiness, etc. (1 Timothy 2; 1 Peter 3). These things could never be said of her unless her soul were human and endowed with intellect and will. From the investigations of anatomy it is clear that she essentially has the same human body as that of a man, while the difference to be observed is only of accidental attributes relating to the functions of generation and to certain kinds of qualities. And let these reasons suffice.

Among his arguments the author of the 1595 pamphlet, reprinted at the Hague in 1638 with the title *Pleasant disputation that women are not human*[4] puts forward the reference to 1 Corinthians 11:7, as if it were Achilles, to prove that woman was not created in the image of God.[5] Therefore. . . . But on this see the separate question below.

From the various acceptations[6] of the word *Adam* nothing can be proven. For sometimes, as a proper noun, it signifies some individual, namely the first human being (Genesis 4:1). Sometimes, as an appellative,[7] it denotes a human being of any sex, status, or condition. And this necessarily is how we must take Genesis 1:26–27 and 5:1–2. Sometimes it is a shorthand way of referring to the ordinary people of the common sorts and condition, those whom the Latins called the *plebes*, in contradistinction to *'ish* and *bene 'ish* in Hebrew. See Psalm 49:1–2.[8] Many other arguments that depict faults and diseases of the mind in women (according to the

---

4. *Disputatio perjucunda qua anonymus probare nititur mulieres homines non esse: cui opposita est Simonis Gedicci . . . defensio sexus muliebris* (The Hague, 1638). On the many printings and translations, see Maclean, *The Renaissance Notion of Woman.*

5. Voetius alludes here to Achilles' reputation as an invincible warrior; the pamphlet's author placed his confidence in the single biblical verse "The man is the image and glory of God, but the woman is the glory of the man."

6. A technical term referring to "the sense in which a word or sentence is accepted or received; the received meaning" (*Oxford English Dictionary*, 1:71).

7. An appellative is a common noun or name that may be applied to any member of a whole class.

8. The Hebrew word *'ish* can be translated as "man," "husband," and "mankind." Modern commentators are not certain whether the terms *bene 'ish* and *bene 'adham* as used in Psalm 49 are meant as parallel or contrasting terms. See G. Johannes Botterweck and Helmer Ringgren, editors, *Theological Dictionary of the Old Testament*, trans. John T. Willis (Grand Rapids, MI: William B. Eerdmans Publishing Co., 1974), 224.

authors to be indicated below) work to deny their human nature only as much as would the almost limitless diseases and defects of the body work to deny the human nature of men, and the poisons of many animals or the savagery of beasts to deny their animal nature.

Question II: Whether woman is a mistake of nature, a misbegotten male, is generated by accident and to that extent is a monster

Response: Such is what Aristotle lets slip out in *On the generation of animals,* book 2, chapter 3; and book 4, chapter 2.[9] Thomas adopts this opinion in part I, question 92, article 1 (of the *Summa Theologica*) and book 3, chapter 94, of the *Summa Contra Gentiles.*[10] Following him Viguerius in his *Institutes,* chapter 21, paragraph 2, verse 4.[11] Also commentators on Thomas's *Summa,* Cajetan, Medices, and Alagona, and Ferrariensis on *Contra Gentiles,* book 4, chapter 94;[12] also commentaries on the *Sentences,* bk. 2, distinction 20, by Bonaventure, Giles, Richard.[13] But they think this crude opinion is softened by the cure-all of a distinction that the woman is misbegotten not in herself in respect to the particular agent (which aims at its likeness) and that she comes into existence out of the weakness of the acting force, the disposition of matter, or some external change; but that in herself woman comes about from the intention of the universal agent and of nature. But this distinction presupposes and assumes what is to be proven: as if the man alone generates, and not the woman (concerning which soon below),

9. Aristotle, *Generation of animals,* trans. A. L. Peck (Cambridge, MA: Harvard University Press, 1974), 175 and 401.

10. The two major works of St. Thomas Aquinas, *Summa Theologica* and *Summa Contra Gentiles,* incorporated many principles of Aristotelian philosophy in such matters as form, matter, universals, particulars, and causation into Christian theology. Accordingly, the male is the active, and therefore normative, version of the human species; any particular act of generation has the male as its intended goal, but the female is intended in a universal sense as part of nature.

11. Johannes Viguerius, *Institutiones ad Christianam Theologiam, Sacrarum literarum universaliumque Conciliorum authoritate* (Antwerp, 1558), fol. 277b: "Et licet nunc mulieres subdantur viris, propter imbecillitatem animi et defectum roboris."

12. The commentary of Thomas de Vio (Cajetan) is included in Thomas Aquinas, *Opera Omnia,* vol. 11, *Summa Theologiae Tertia Pars* (Rome, 1903), esp. 338–339. The commentary of Francesco Sylvestri, known as Ferrariensis (c. 1474–1528) on the *Summa Contra Gentiles* was included in the Venice 1524 and Rome 1570 editions of the work as well as in the above edition of Thomas's collected works. The third book of the *Summa Contra Gentiles* is volume 14, published in 1926. The other commentators mentioned by Voetius, Jerome de Medices (d. 1622) and Guevara Alagona (1549–1624), were Thomists of the Counter-Reformation era.

13. The Sentences of Peter Lombard (ca. 1100–1160) were a systematic compilation of the theological knowledge of the time, served as a textbook, and formed the basis of many medieval theological commentaries, such as those of Bonaventure (1221–1274), Giles of Rome (Aegidius Romanus, ca. 1245–1316) and Richard of Mediavilla (ca. 1249–1307).

even to the extent that in generating the particular he always intends the more perfect, i.e., the male; since he intends a human being, i.e., to generate a likeness of himself; but not this or that sex of human being and since he aims at a perfection that is of the essence and of the whole, not accidental.

This monstrous opinion is refuted from scripture and reason.

From scripture

1. From Matthew 19:4: "Have you not read that from the beginning He made them male and female?" Genesis 1:27: "And God created human beings, . . . male and female he created them." If God from the beginning through creation immediately brought forth the woman equally with the man: therefore through providence afterward he brings forth women and men mediately and indeed for their own sake according to secondary causes.

2. Since in the state of righteousness, according to the blessing in Genesis 1:28, human beings were generated both female and male in the perfection due to them by nature; and the original "Indeed, it was very good" (Genesis 1:31) would have continued among the works of God. Therefore every defect, weakening, disorder, or monstrosity was absent. For all those defects and all weaknesses entered through sin: "For the creation was subjected to futility . . . " (Romans 8:20); "creation will be set free from its bondage to decay" (8:21); "cursed is the ground because of you . . . " (Genesis 3:17); "and the sky over your head shall be bronze, and the earth . . . iron" (Deuteronomy 28:23).

3. Since in the rebirth and restitution of the world God blessed Noah and his sons, saying, "Be fruitful and multiply, and fill the earth" (Genesis 9:1); that is, so that from men and women men and women will be generated according to the order and law of nature established in the first creation (Genesis 1:28), so that no order, no law, no intention of a particular agent or generating force ought to be imagined here distinct from the law, order, and intention of the universal agent or of nature whether naturing or natured.[14]

From reason

1. Since a general definition of monster does not apply to women: therefore she is not a mistake of nature or a monster. The definition that

---

14. The terms *natura naturans* and *natura naturata*, which Voetius uses here, came from the medieval Latin translation of Aristotle's works and referred to the relationship between potency and actuality in the metaphysical scale of being.

Fortunius Lycetus (*Concerning Monsters,* book 1, chaps. 11–13) developed, explained, and approved is this: "A monster is a subcelestial being with an aberrant constitution of its members, inspiring horror and astonishment in those seeing it, coming into existence rather rarely, born out of the secondary constitution of nature on account of some impediment in the elements of its configuration."[15]

2. Since what happens normally is not an aberration of nature; and since no fewer women are born than men; on the contrary, more women are born than men. Therefore woman is not an accident, an aberration, a mistake, or monster.

3. Since if nature frequently produces women who are called "viragoes," with qualities and gifts both of mind and body more perfect than many, if not most, men, therefore those women are not mistakes or defects of nature.

4. An argument specifically against Aristotle is that whatever has been from eternity is not an accident, aberration, or mistake. But the generation of females has been with the world and the nature of things from eternity, according to Aristotle. Therefore it is not an accident or mistake of nature.

5. An argument specifically against Thomas and his followers: Since it was right that woman should be produced in the first production, part 1, qu. 92, art. 1; and since in the first constitution of nature all works were perfect and very good by the intention of God: therefore so too was the woman who was produced then. And consequently according to the order then instituted in human beings, "increase and multiply," women and men were to be continued and perpetuated equally through generation and the succession of individuals.

This is over against what is put forth by some, concerning women changed into men, from which it follows that the female is something imperfect and inferior and for that reason the male, not the female, is intended by nature when generating. That is just as valid as if you say that males are imperfect and weak by nature and for that reason not intended by her, but rather females: because males may sometimes be changed into females. But of this mutation more below.

This fiction of Cajetan in his commentary on Genesis 2 is refuted so easily and is brought forth by him without proof.[16] But Pereira says in his

---

15. Fortunius Lycetus (Licetus), *De Monstrorum Causis, Natura, et Differentiis* (Padua, 1634), 45.

16. Thomas de Vio (1468–1534), better known as Cajetan from his home town of Gaeta in Italy, was a leading defender of Thomas Aquinas and of his Dominican order but was also open to humanistic influences in his critical approach to the biblical text. For his interpretation of Genesis 2:21, which he regards as a parable of the Aristotelian view of woman's

commentary (bk. 4) on Genesis 2:23: "Hear how Cajetan, persisting in his commentary and opinions, which we explained above, interprets these words: 'Clearly,' he says, 'Moses indicates by these words the nature as well as the production of woman. For any woman, even if she is impaired man, is bone from men's bones and flesh from men's flesh. For the man's semen intends to produce a man: but when a defect intervenes so that it is not healthy enough to make a whole man, it makes an impaired man, that is, a woman: hence the woman is bone of the intended bones of the man and flesh of the intended male flesh. However, it is said with the plural *from the bones* to signify that, although the flesh of the woman may be less perfect than that of the man, nevertheless her disposition is no less fleshly: but indeed so much the more, insofar as it is joined to less strength of body.'"[17] But Pereira declares these things to be sheer nonsense and fictions of Cajetan because of the falseness and absurdity of the opinion from which they flowed, and also because their treatment is so obscure, confused, harsh, and impetuous.

Question III. Whether the woman actively cooperates in the generation of the offspring

Response: Aristotle denies this in *On the generation of animals*, book 1, chaps. 19–20, relying mainly on the argument that she has no seed and does not contribute any to generation, as he argues in chap. 20. Those who followed Aristotle include Averroes, Albertus, Durandus, Paludanus, Capreolus, Herveus, Thomas, along with Cajetan on book 3, question 32, article 4 (of Thomas Aquinas's *Summa Theologiae*).[18] Among the more recent authors, Caspar Bartholinus in the controversial subjects of the *Anatomical*

---

relation to man, see Thomas de Vio, *Opera Omnia Quotquot in Sacrae Scripturae expositionem reperiuntur* (Lyon, 1639), 22.

17. Benedictus Pererius, or Benito Pereira (1535–1610), *Commentariorum et Disputationum in Genesin* (Cologne, 1606), 155, 217. Pereira is quoting with slight modifications from Cajetan's commentary on Genesis 2:23 as found in Thomas de Vio, *Opera Omnia*, 23.

18. This list of commentators on Aristotle's *De Generatione Animalium* coincides to a great extent with that given by the Jesuits of the University of Coimbra, *Commentarii Collegii Conimbricensis Societatis Jesu: In Libros de Generatione et Corruptione Aristotelis Stagiritiae* (Mainz, 1550), 178, where the citations are more complete than in Voetius's treatment here. Averroes (1126–1198) was a Moslem Aristotelian commentator who brought Aristotle's writings to the attention of Christian thinkers, most notably Thomas Aquinas and Albertus Magnus (ca. 1200–1280). All the other commentators were Dominicans. Durandus of Saint-Pourçain (c. 1275–1334) was an independent thinker who opposed certain views of Thomas Aquinas and in turn was later attacked by John Capreolus (c. 1380–1444), whose works were limited to defenses of Thomas's theology. Both Peter of La Palu or Paludanus (c. 1277–1342) and Harvey Nedellec or Herveus Natalis (c. 1250–1323) regarded themselves as strong supporters of Thomas, and Harvey played a role in Thomas's canonization, yet they did not rigidly adopt all of Thomas's positions. Except for Averroes, this group of writers belonged to the Dominican order.

Institutes (1632) argues a middle opinion, that women indeed have seed but that it nevertheless does not actively cooperate in generation.[19]

But, taking everything into account, the affirmative is to be held, both on account of the authority of scripture and on account of reason.

As for scripture

1. It attributes generation to the woman through seed or "vim seminarium." Leviticus 12:2: "If a woman has conceived seed [*seminificaverit*] and borne a male child, she shall be unclean for seven days. She shall be unclean according to the days of separation of her menstruation."[20] Here seminification is clearly enough distinguished from giving birth and seed is distinguished from menstrual blood and its purification. Add to that Hebrews 11:11: "Sarah received strength to cast seed [*eis katabolein spermatos*]."[21]

2. From the incarnation of Christ, for the Logos was made flesh, John 1:14. "Since the children share in flesh and blood, he himself likewise partook of the same nature" (Hebrews 2:14). Therefore this occurred through generation and the seed of a woman, namely of the most holy virgin Mary, who gave birth to God and who conceived him in the uterus and bore him, so that he would be the fruit of her womb (Luke 1:31–32, 42), the fruit of the loins of David, according to the flesh (Acts 2:30), who in that respect is from the fathers (Romans 9:5) and consequently a son of David, the son of Abraham, the son of Adam (Matthew 1:1 with Luke 3:38). And to that extent he is our brother, of one flesh with us (Acts 17:26 together with Hebrews 2:11–17). These things the scholastics should have considered first of all and should not have adhered to the authority of Aristotle, who errs gravely here. Therefore, more correctly,

19. Caspar Bartholinus, *Controversiae Anatomicae et Affines Nobiliores ac Rariores* (Goslar, 1631), 251–265. This work was published together with *Institutiones Anatomicae corporis humani utriusque sexus historiam et declamationem exhibentes* (Goslar, 1632).

20. The Latin text used by Voetius clearly conveys a sense of woman's contribution to conception in a way that more modern translations, such as the Revised Standard Version ("If a woman conceives") do not. My translation borrows the closer but still ambiguous phrase "conceive seed" from the King James Version. The Leviticus passage goes on to specify that the length of time a woman is considered unclean after the birth of a daughter is twice as long as for that of a son.

21. The translation here is directly from Voetius, as no commonly used English translation conveys this sense of Sarah's active contribution. Dutch scholars of the time were well aware that the Greek text had a more active connotation than the Latin Vulgate. This was therefore a critical verse in debates on embryology and Christology with the Anabaptists. See Joyce Irwin, "The Use of Hebrews 11:11 as Embryological Proof-Text," *Harvard Theological Review* (July-October 1978): 312–316.

Scotus, Bonaventure, Ockham, Meyronnes, Bassolus, Biel, Lichetus, Major,[22] having abandoned Aristotle, embraced the affirmative; and among the more recent writers who abandoned Aristotle and Thomas are the (Jesuit) commentators at the University of Coimbra treating Aristotle's *On Generation and Corruption*, chap. 4, question 27,[23] although in the same work in a certain manner they work for the honor of Aristotle, Thomas, and their followers, saying that their opinion has great probability. Peter Wadding[24] in his *Treatise on the Incarnation* says he is removing himself for the time from the truth of this question, whether medical or philosophical, but posits for the sake of argument what many of the more recent already hold, namely that women actively cooperate. Suarez, writing on Thomas, book 3, qu. 32, art. 4, removes himself from this dispute: "I do not think," he says, "that a commentary should be joined to this article. For if we were to discuss the many philosophic matters that D. Thomas touches on in it, they would require a long disputation rather removed from our purpose."[25]

Arguments from reason for affirming the opinion are taken from the fields of physics and anatomy, from parts that are found in a woman, namely from the vessels preparing the seed, the genitals, the discharging vessels or those that carry the seed, and from their twofold direction, one of which is into the base of the uterus and the other of which is into the neck of the uterus. Concerning these things see Laurentius, or the anatomies of others after him.

Question IV. Whether a woman may truly be changed into a man

Response. It is not to be denied that some change happens contrary to experience. See the examples in Pliny, book 7, chapter 4; and Gellius, book 9, chapter 4.[26] They are also cited by the more recent authors Lusitanus, Donatus, Torquemada, Volaterranus, Fregoso, Pontano, Paré.[27] See

22. This list coincides even more closely than the above list of Aristotelians (see n. 18) with the summary of the Jesuits of Coimbra. That Voetius proceeds in this same sentence to refer to them indicates that he was relying on this work for his evaluation of these authors, all of whom wrote commentaries on Peter Lombard's *Sentences* and belonged to the Franciscan order.

23. *Commentarii Collegii Conimbricensis*, 177–181.

24. Peter Wadding (Wadingus or Wadingius), *Tractatus de Incarnatione* (Antwerp, 1636), 188.

25. Francis Suarez,*Opera Omnia* (Paris, 1866), 19:166.

26. Pliny, *Natural History* (*Historia naturalis*) vol. 2 (books 3–7), trans. H. Rackham (Cambridge: Harvard University Press, 1942), 531; Aulus Gellius, *The Attic Nights* (*Noctes Attici*), vol. 2, trans. John C. Rolfe (Cambridge: Harvard University Press, 1927), 167–169.

27. Amatus Lusitanus, *Centuriae II Priores quibus praemittitur Commentario de introitu medici ad aegrotan-*

this question as treated by Caspar Bartholinus in *Anatomical Controversies*,[28] Laurentius, *On Anatomy*, book 7, chapter 12, question 8,[29] and Fortunius Lycetus, *Concerning Monsters*, book 2, chapter 54.[30] Concerning the cause and manner of the mutation philosophers and physicians disagree. What if it is said that they were hermaphrodites and had hidden male sexual parts that afterward broke through?

Concerning hermaphrodites and the various kinds of them, see further Ambroise Paré.[31] And after all these the most complete is Caspar Bauhin's treatise devoted to the subject.[32] Whatever may be the case concerning the mode by which these women change into men (which I accept as having been explained by Laurentius, Lycetus, Bartholinus); nevertheless it is not shown to be a change of one species into another species; nor from this can one conclude that women are a defect of nature or imperfect or accidental males. Bartholinus argues this well in the place cited above. Because also from men changed into women (in Laurentius, Lycetus, Bartholinus, loc. cit.), one clearly cannot conclude that men are misbegotten women and defects of nature: thus in turn it is not possible to conclude from women changed into men that they are accidental males.

Question V. Whether man and woman were created at the same time and even as two persons joined to each other, but afterward split apart and separated by God

Response. First the affirmative: Cajetan took this story of the creation of a man and a woman as parable and allegorical description.[33] But his commentary was rejected by Pereira, Cornelius à Lapide, Marius, and other papal commentators.[34] Refutation of his theory is afforded clearly and de-

---

tem de crisi et diebus Decretoriis (Lyon, 1580), 553–554; Marcellus Donatus, *De Medica Historia Mirabili* (Venice, 1597), fol. 215b–216b (bk. 6, chap. 2); Antonio de Torquemada, *Jardin de Flores Curiosas* (Salamanca, 1570), fol. 12–13; Raphael Volaterranus (Raffaelo Maffei), *Commentariorum Urbanorum* (Paris, 1511), bk. 24, fol. 259b; Battista Fregoso (Fulgosus), *Exemplorum, hoc est, dictorum factorumque memorabilium* (Basel, 1567), 187–188; Giovanni Gioviano Pontano, *De Rebus Coelestibus*, in *Opera* (Basel, 1556–1566), 3: 2513 (bk. 11, chap. 17); Ambroise Paré (Ambrosius Pareus), *Opera Chirurgica* (Frankfurt, 1594), 728–729 (bk. 24, chap. 5).

28. Bartholinus, *Controversiae Anatomicae*, 120–128.

29. André Du Laurens (Andreas Laurentius) *Opera Omnia Anatomica et Medica* (Frankfurt, 1627), 274–275.

30. Lycetus, *De Monstrorum . . .* , 172–177.

31. Paré, *Opera Chirurgica*, 727 (bk. 24, chap. 4).

32. Caspar Bauhin, *De Hermaphroditorum monstrosorumque partuum Natura ex Theologorum, Jureconsultorum, Medicorum, Philosophorum et Rabbinorum sententia* (Oppenheim, 1614).

33. Thomas de Vio, *Opera Omnia*, 13, on Genesis 1:27.

34. Pereira, *Commentariorum et Disputationum*, 153; Cornelius à Lapide, *Commentaria in Pentateuchum*

cisively from 1 Timothy 2:13: "Adam was formed first, then Eve." And from 1 Corinthians 11:8: "For the man was not from the woman, but the woman from the man."

Next, some Rabbis hold the *affirmative,* saying that humans were created androgynous: not that both sexes would be in the same body, but in different connected bodies that would be placed so that one would be on the right, the other on the left, or so that one would be in front, the other behind. Ibn Ezra wrote in his commentary on Genesis 1:27: "And in the beginning Adam was created in two persons."[35] Among Roman Christians Franciscus Georgius not seldom grazed on Rabbinic and Cabalistic bran: "Why was it written that a helper was not found for the man? Since from the beginning they were created paired, that is, masculine and feminine? Whether perhaps (as Plato teaches) they were joined in the beginning as male, and the female was afterward cut along the back: so that they might be joined facing each other for generating offspring? And in this as in other matters, Plato himself was led by that most irreproachable philosopher, Moses. We can manifestly learn this from what the *Zohar* teaches: and from Scripture itself: where it is maintained that woman had been formed from the side or the rib cut from the Protoplast. For the word *Zelah* signifies both, that is the rib and the side. Hence (as Plato himself goes on to say) the one desires its other half. Once the cutting was done, however, the woman was the helper of the man, standing, that is, in his presence. This is just as the truth of the Hebrew text holds. Hence, the common edition reads 'like himself'" (*Problems from Sacred Scripture,* vol. I, sect. I, fol. 4–5, qu. 29).[36]

But this fiction vanishes in the reading of the text of Genesis 2:20–22 together with vss. 15–17 where, when Adam had already been created and placed in Eden, God says (v. 18), "It is not good for the man to be alone; I will make a helper for him, which will be in his presence. And the lord God made sleep fall . . ."

Question VI. Whether the woman was created in the image of God
    Response: affirmative from Genesis 1:27 and 5:1–2. *Second,* since the

Mosis (Antwerp, 1618), 68; Leonard Marius, *Commentariorum in universam S. Scripturam* (Cologne, 1621), 35–36.

35. Abraham Ibn Ezra (ca. 1092–1167), *Yesod Morah v'sod Torah,* ed. Samuel Waxman (Jerusalem, 1931), commentary on Genesis 1:27.

36. Franciscus Georgius, *In Scripturam Sacram Problemata* (Paris, 1575), fol. 4b–5a. The *Zohar,* mentioned within the citation, was the main book of Cabala, a group of mystical-theosophical writings that were most influential during the late Middle Ages and Early Modern era.

woman is a human being; and moreover a human being is in fact made in the image of God, Genesis 9:6, James 3:9. These places admit of no exception. *Third*, since women and men are recreated and renewed equally in the image of God through regeneration, Ephesians 4:24, Colossians 3:10 along with 2 Peter 1:3–4. For there are faithful women in Christ, and through Christ they are saved, 1 Timothy 2:15 along with Acts 4:12. Indeed those who are already in Christ are new creatures, 2 Corinthians 5:17.

But *in opposition* to this is 1 Corinthians 11:7, where the man is said to be the image and glory of God, yet the woman the glory of the man. *Response*: It is the fallacy of arguing from a relative statement to an absolute statement. For the man is not said to be universally and exclusively the image of God, but in some specific respect, insofar as the man was created first and the woman after and from him; and consequently to this extent the man by his preeminence, superiority, seniority over the woman bears the likeness and image of God as first and highest in primacy and superiority. This is evident from verses 8 and 9 which follow: "For the man is not from the woman, but the woman from the man. Nor was the man created because of the woman but the woman because of the man." And 1 Timothy 2:11–13, "Let a woman learn in silence with all submissiveness. I do not permit a woman to teach or to acquire authority over men, . . . for Adam was formed first, then Eve." Briefly the man is the origin and basis from which and the reason on account of which the woman was brought forth. Consequently he is the head and he has preeminence, superiority, or lordship over the woman, although both have superiority and lordship over the remaining creatures, according to Genesis 1:26–27 : "'Let us make the human being according to our image, . . . so that he may be above the fish of the sea. . . .' And God created the human according to his image, . . . male and female he created them." But the woman does not have superiority over the man as the man has superiority over the woman; and in this respect he is and is called in a particular manner the image of God and the glory of God; to this extent God wants the glory of his majesty and dominion to shine and radiate in him by a certain image. Thus interpreters commonly affirm according to Genesis 1:26–27 and 1 Corinthians 11:7 that the woman was created according to the image of God, but in this particular respect they deny that she is the image of God. Grotius in commenting on 1 Corinthians 11:7 correctly affirmed from Isidore [of Seville] that the man "was made in the likeness of God, admittedly with authority also over his wife," but he immediately subjoins this reason:

"Likewise it is not said of woman that she was created in the image of God (Genesis 1:26–27)."[37] This is a mental slip in writing. For in the place cited, Genesis 1:27, it is clearly said that she was created in the image of God.

Question VII. Whether woman was created on the sixth day

Response. Thomas denies this in part I, qu. 73, art. 1, resp. 3, asserting that she was created on the seventh day: "Nothing entirely new was afterward [after six days] made by God, but all things subsequently made had in a sense been made before in the work of the six days. Some things, indeed, had a previous existence materially, as the rib from the side of Adam out of which God formed Eve."[38] Jerome de Medices openly follows the opinion of Thomas in his formal explication of Thomas's *Summa.*[39] And Catharinus in his commentary on Genesis 2 (as noted and rejected by Suarez in chap. 11, no. 1; Arriaga on Thomas's treatise on the work of the six days; and by à Lapide on Genesis 2:18) followed the same opinion.[40] But the authors cited hold the opposite, as do Lippoman, Pereira, Marius, and à Lapide in their commentaries and Bonaventure, 2 dist. 18, qu. 2.[41] So also those of our faith generally, in notes and commentaries.

The reasons are *first* because in Genesis 1:27 it is said "male and female he created them," and in verse 28, "and God blessed them, and said, 'Be fruitful and multiply' . . . "; and *second* because God, having finished this last of the works of creation, saw "all things that he had made, and behold they were good. And there was evening and there was morning, a sixth day." And after that in chapter 2, verse 1: 'Thus the heavens and the earth were

37. Hugo Grotius (Hugo de Groot), *Opera Omnia Theologica* II/2 (Amsterdam, 1679; reprint Stuttgart, 1982), 805. Isidore of Seville (c. 560–636) was the last of the Western Latin Church Fathers.

38. Thomas Aquinas, *Summa Theologiae,* English translation in *Basic Writings,* ed. Anton C. Pegis (New York: Random House, 1945), 1:669. Voetius's work here erroneously gives "pag. I" rather than "pars I."

39. Jerome de Medices, *Explicatio formalis summae Theologicae Th. Aquinatis* (Vici, 1858).

40. Ambrosius Catharinus, *In Quinque Priora Capita Libri Geneseos* (Rome, 1552), col. 118–119; Suarez, *Commentarium ac Disputationum in primam partem divi Thomae Partis II* (Mainz, 1622), 106; Rodericus de Arriaga, *Disputationes Theologicae in Primam Partem D. Thomae* (Antwerp, 1643), 2:378 (De Opere Sex Dierum, disp. 34, sect. 2); à Lapide, *Commentaria.*

41. This list appears to have been copied from à Lapide at the place cited above, with Marius added by Voetius. See Aloysius Lippoman, *Catena in Genesin ex authoribus ecclesiasticis* (Paris, 1546); Pereira, *Commentariorum et Disputationum,* 154; Marius, *Commentariorum,* 34; à Lapide, *Commentaria,* 68; Bonaventure, *Opera Omnia* (Quarrachi, 1885), 2:437 (*Sententiarum,* bk. 2, dist. 18, art. 1, qu. 2).

finished, and all the host of them. And on the seventh day God finished his work which he had done, and he rested on the seventh day from all his work which he had done." Consider also Exodus 20:11: "For in six days the Lord made heaven and earth, the sea, and all that is in them, and rested the seventh day."

The reasoning that moves them to invent this paradox against the simple story of scripture seems to have been twofold for them.

First, that after the works of the six days are reported, finally the creation of woman is reported in Genesis 2:21–23.

Second, that it is not reasonable or conceivable that all those things that are reported in chapter 2 concerning the man alone, concerning his placement in Eden, especially concerning all the animals that were led to Adam, etc., could have taken place in such a short time.

Response to 1: Similarly it would be possible to say that in the sequence of the story, after the six days and the respite of the seventh day, finally the creation of Adam out of the earth is reported, and the blowing of the breath of life into his nostrils. Adam would therefore not have been created on the sixth day but on the seventh or on some day beyond that. It would similarly be possible to conclude that Paradise, the vapor from the earth, etc., were produced only after the six days. Which is absurd.

Response to 2: In this way infidels, atheists, or Epicureans and Libertines weigh the stories of scripture on the scales of their own reason. And they deny the *fact,* since they do not understand the *why* and *how* of it. And to that extent they think they detect the absurd, irrational, impossible, or contradictory in it. You have examples in "objections of the simple-minded" against the story of creation, which Franciscus Junius reports and refutes in his *Protoktisia.*[42] Likewise others stumble on Genesis 2:2, "and on the seventh day God finished . . . ," for which reason others have substituted "on the sixth day"; other commentators (see Jerome on Genesis)[43] have written that God finished his works on the seventh day and blessed them. See concerning this Galatinus's *Work on the secrets of Catholic truth,* book xi, chap. 10;[44] and Sixtus Senensis's *Sacred Library,* book 5, note 23.[45]

---

42. Franciscus Junius, *Protoktisia, seu Creationis a Deo Factae, et in ea prioris Adami ex Creatione integri et ex lapsa corrupti historia* ([Heidelberg], 1589).

43. The Septuagint version reads, "And God finished on the sixth day his works which he made, and he ceased on the seventh day from all his works which he made." *The Septuagint Version: Greek and English,* ed. Lancelot C. L. Brenton (Grand Rapids, MI: Zondervan Publishing House, 1970).

44. Petrus Galatinus (Pietro Colonna), *Opus de Arcanis Catholicae Veritatis* (Basel, 1550), 694–695.

45. Sixtus Senensis, *Bibliotheca Sancta* (Cologne, 1626), 421–422.

Among the more recent Jewish writers, see Menasse ben Israel's *Conciliator*, qu. 13, on Genesis.[46] And the Hebrew verb in Genesis 2:2 can be correctly translated "had completed," according to Mercerus and Drusius in their commentaries and Amama in his evaluation of the Vulgate.[47] Similar traps are woven against the stories of the flood, the plagues of Egypt, the crossing of the Red Sea and Jordan, Samson, etc.

But let us consider the objections, distinctions, exceptions that have been brought forth from whatever source on behalf of this offensive opinion, or that might be brought forth.

Objection I. It is objected that after the works of the six days and after God's rest and inactivity, finally the creation of woman is reported; therefore the woman was created after the works of the six days, namely on the seventh day or after it. *Response:* Chapter 2 contains a fuller and more detailed explanation of certain works of creation that had already been made during the six days and that were to be comprehended in chapter 1 under general titles (so to speak). Here, however, they are repeated, Genesis 2:4–5: "These are the generations of the heavens and the earth when they were created, . . . when no plant of the field . . . and no herb of the field had yet sprung up, . . ." After this recapitulation or conclusion is given by way of preface, verse 6 goes on to an explication of the works pertaining to the third day and to the sixth day. Pertaining to the third day are (1) the mist that moistened the whole earth, (2) the production of trees and plants, (3) the adorning of the garden or paradise, (4) the arranging of the rivers of paradise. Pertaining to the sixth day are (1) the formation of Adam (vs. 7), (2) his placement in the garden of Eden, (3) the bringing of the animals to Adam and his naming of them, (4) the creation of Eve (vss. 18–23), (5) the institution of marriage (vss. 23–24), (6) the commandment concerning the tree of the knowledge of good and evil. Pertaining to the fifth day are the production of the animals of the earth and of the air (vss. 19–20).

One would have to say that all these things, as well as the creation of woman, were done after the works of the six days, either on the seventh or

---

46. Menasse ben Israel, *Conciliator, sive De convenientia locorum Sacrae Scripturae, quae pugnare inter se videntur* (Amsterdam, 1633), 21.

47. Joannis Mercerus (Jean Mercier), *In Genesin Primum Mosis Librum, sic a Graecis Appelatum Commentarius* ([Geneva?], 1598), 37; Johannes Drusius, *Ad Loca Difficiliora Pentateuchi, id est Quinque Librorum Mosis Commentarius* (Franeker, 1617), 16–17; Sixtinus Amama, *Censura Vulgatae atque a Tridentinis Canonizatae Versionis Quinque Librorum Mosis* (Franeker, 1620), 3–5. For insights into these other biblical scholars at Dutch universities at the time of Voetius, see Peter T. van Rooden, *Theology, Biblical Scholarship, and Rabbinical Studies in the Seventeenth Century* (Leiden: E. J. Brill, 1989).

on some following day, because in the sequence of the sacred text they, like the creation of woman, are reported after the historical narrative of the six days of creation and the resting on the seventh day (Genesis 2:1–2). But that is absurd: therefore the other is also absurd.

Exception II. When it is said in Genesis 1:27 that they were created "male and female," that indicates only what God wanted, namely, in order that man be, that in his time he be made or rather be male and female; it does not, however, indicate that woman was formed then. Lyra in his glosses writes that this was said by "anticipation": but he assigns the anticipation not to the creation of woman (2:21–23) but to the intercourse of the male and the female in generation, which would soon be spoken of in vs. 1:28.[48]

Response 1: This is inconsistent with the text, since the will or the intention of God concerning the creation of the human being in his image is put forth in verse 26: and the work or execution according to that will in verse 27. *Next,* if the will of God in verse 27 is reported concerning only the future creation of the woman in the image of God and not the actual creation of woman or the actual work of God, why could not the same be said equally concerning Adam? "Male . . . he created them," that is, God willed concerning the man what he would be in his time, and of what sort he would be, i.e. (in order that this passage receive its true sense), from the time when God formed Adam "of dust from the ground and breathed into his nostrils the breath of life; and man became a living being" (Genesis 2:7). *Third,* because against the creation of woman within the sixth day the exception is made in regard to Genesis 1:27 that those things which had been put forth in abbreviated form are distinctly and separately narrated in Genesis 2:8, 15, 16–23: this supports our position. Therefore just as the creation of the man, which is put forth in abbreviated form in 1:27, is told in detail in 2:8, 15, etc., so also the creation of the woman is put forth in abbreviated form in 1:27 and told in detail in chapter 2. There the intention or will of God appears first (vss. 18, 20), then the execution of the same (vss. 21–23), that is, the formation of the woman and the manner in which she was formed. In addition, just as the works of the third and the fifth day are put forth in abbreviated form in chapter 1, they are then told in more extended and detailed form in chapter 2:6 concerning the mist; verses 8–16 concerning paradise, its trees, rivers, location, inhabitants; and

---

48. Nicolas of Lyra, *Glossae in universa biblia: Postilla* (Nuremberg, 1481), on Genesis 1 (pages not numbered).

verses 19–20 concerning the production of beasts of burden, beasts of the field, and birds of the air.

Response 2. Concerning the "anticipation" or *Lyranic prolepsis*, which others also think was utilized in the words of Genesis 1:27, "male and female he created them," with respect to the creation of the woman which is to follow after the sixth day, one must not move away from the literal expression and resort to a figurative meaning unless a comparison of the logical connections or of scripture compels us. But we hardly see any such necessity here—no more than in the words indicating the creation of the man within the sixth day. Further, it is to be observed from the precepts of the rhetoricians that those examples that are thought to be found in the Poets are said to be poetic prolepses (as they are distinctly called from grammar and oratory), designating by that term places or ceremonies that indeed obtained at the time when they were writing, but hardly at all at the time when those deeds were done which they make known. However, the philological authors may charge them with unequal expressions and confusion of time, or may explain with some other interpretation, without regard to prolepsis. See concerning this Vossius, *Oratorical Institutes*, book 5, chap. 11, para. 7, who says on page 399, "if I should wish to follow the practice of unequal expressions by this kind of poet, I would have the volume made from them alone."[49] And then referring to the testimony of the noted Veleius Paterculus, he wisely warns, "These things show us sufficiently that we should not excuse all things of this sort as proleptic out of reverence to the poets, but we should admit that some sins have been committed by them through anachronisms."[50] Augustine grants that in scripture proleptic anticipations can be found in place names, and he cites Exodus 19:22.[51] But in this he errs by presuming there were no priests before Aaron. More recent writers, such as Lippoman, Cajetan, Cornelius à Lapide, and Marius,[52]

49. Gerardus Johannes Vossius, *Commentariorum Rhetoricorum sive Oratoriarum Institutionum* (Leiden, 1630; reprint Kronberg, 1974), 399.

50. Vossius, ibid., quotes from Velleius Paterculus's *History of Rome* (*Historiae Romanae*) 1.3, (English translation by Frederick Shipley [Cambridge, MA, 1924], 9) where he reports that the name Thessaly was used by those writing about the Trojan War, even though the name at the time was Myrmidonum and only later became Thessaly after young Thessalus led the Pelasgians to conquer the city.

51. Aurelius Augustinus, *Quaestionum in Heptateuchum*, Corpus Christianorum Series Latina 33 (Turnholt, 1958), 191.

52. Lippoman, *Catena in Exodum ex Auctoribus ecclesiasticis* (Paris, 1550), fol. 161; Cajetan (Thomas de Vio, *Opera Omnia*); à Lapide, *Commentaria*, 474; Marius, *Commentariorum*, 495.

correctly observe and argue the contrary; and those from our own camp who take this position include Franciscus Junius, Diodati, Piscator, Willet, Christopher Cartwright, renowned in England and the Low Countries, Rivet.[53] Similarly from the Rabbis there are Ibn Ezra and Sel. Jarchi, with whom Menasse ben Israel first agrees in his *Conciliator*, question 29, on Exodus.[54] But afterward, wavering, he approves the exposition that he repeats from *Mechilta* (which is a commentary on Exodus) concerning the sons of Aaron, who were priests by virtue of their power; and here they are called priests by anticipation, a practice in scripture "by which names are imposed on this or that which they only later receive."[55] But such an exegesis hardly fits the cited text, which reads as follows: "And also let the priests who come near to the Lord sanctify themselves, lest the Lord break forth upon them."[56] Jerome, in his commentary on Ezekiel 30:15–16, says that the Hebrew word *No* is to be interpreted as Alexandria by anticipation or prolepsis.[57] But Bochart, in his *Sacred Geography*, rightly refutes this prolepsis (part I, book I, chap. 1, p. 6).[58] But whatever may be the case with regard to Jerome's naming this as prolepsis, nevertheless the example does not qualify as scriptural prolepsis. Prolepsis in scripture is thought to be found in Exodus 3:2, where Horeb is called the mountain of God, which it is afterward called, partly on account of that vision, partly on account of God descending onto that mountain to bring the law. But in Hebrew usage nothing prevents this place from being explained without prolepsis, as in Psalm 36:7, "the mountains of God"; Psalm 80:11, "the cedars of God"; Song of Solomon 8:6, "the flame of God"; Jonah 3:3, "the large city of God"; Jeremiah 2:31, "the wilderness of God"; 1 Samuel 14:15, "the trembling of God." Rabbi David Qimhi already observed in his commentary on Psalm 36:7, just as the mountains of God are the highest mountains, "so,

53. See the interpretations of Exodus 19:22 in Junius, *Libri II Mosis qui Exodus Vulgo inscribitur Analytica Explicatio* (Leiden, 1603); *La Sainte Bible*, interpreted by Jean Diodati (Geneva, 1644); Johannes Piscator, *Commentarium in Omnes Libris Veteris Testamenti I* (Herborn, 1643); Andrew Willet, *Hexapla in Exodum: That Is, a Sixfold Commentary upon the Second Booke of Moses Called Exodus* (London, 1608), 303–304; Christopher Cartwright, *Electa Thargumico-Rabbinica sive annotationes in Exodum* (London, 1653), 236; André Rivet, *Commentarii in Librum Secundum Mosis, qui Exodus apud Graecos inscribitur* in *Operum Theologicorum Tomus Primus* (Rotterdam, 1651), 1027.

54. Menasse ben Israel, *Conciliator*, 139. The reference to "Sel. Jarchi" is to Solomon ben Yitzhak (1040–1105), commonly referred to as Rashi, a widely read rabbinic commentator.

55. Ibid.

56. Exodus 19:22.

57. Jerome (Hieronymus), *Commentariorum in Hiezechielem*, Corpus Christianorum Series Latina 75 (Turnholt, 1964), 421.

58. Samuel Bochart, *Geographiae Sacrae* (Caen, 1646), 6.

by customary usage of the language, whenever something is to be emphasized, the word *el* is placed next to it."[59] In Judges 15:9 the Philistines are reported to have pitched camp in Lehi, yet the place is first named Lehi in verse 17. In this case a certain prolepsis must be admitted with Martyr and Mariana. In the same particular narrative where he reports on the deed done in that place and the name Lehi that was thenceforth given to it, he calls it Lehi at the beginning of the same narrative.

Similarly, at the beginning of the particular narrative in Judges 2:1 the place is called Bokim. But on the basis of one or the other example of prolepsis, a prolepsis ought not be fabricated for the names of whatever places and men you please, lest a prolepsis of whole propositions and assertions be fabricated; to interpret, for example, "God created woman" to mean that she nevertheless was created afterward, after the sixth day. And Genesis 2:3, "And God blessed the seventh day and made it holy": in the opinion of those alleging prolepsis, the day was in fact sanctified and instituted 2,453 years later more or less, namely when God gave the law through Moses, Exodus 20. Along with Rivet, in his dissertation on the origin of the Sabbath, we deny that examples of this sort of prolepsis occur in scripture; and with Walaeus we say "it is dangerous to compose such prolepses."[60] And when things of this sort have been found in secular writings, some have tried to justify them as prolepses, but we consider it more correct to show them to be errors, oversights, or confusion of times. See Vossius, cited above.

Objection III. But it is extremely questionable how everything could have been completed in one day:

1. Production of birds and fishes and quadrupeds in Genesis 1:24–25
2. Production of man, blessing him, and giving him the instructions concerning food, Genesis 1:26–30
3. Placing the man in Paradise, and giving instructions, Genesis 2:15–17
4. Bringing the animals to the man for him to inspect them and give them names, Genesis 2:18–20
5. Sending him into a deep, and thus doubtless a long sleep, and creating the woman from his side, vss. 21–22

59. Dawid Qimhi, *Psalmi cum Commentariis* (Isny, 1542).

60. In his collected works, Rivet's discussion of the origin of the Sabbath, together with his reply to his critics, is included after the exegesis of Exodus 20:8–11 in *Praelectiones Pleniores in Cap. XX Exodi*, in *Commentarii*. The reference to Walaeus appears on 1310. Antonius Walaeus, *Dissertatio De Sabbatho, seu vero sensu atque usu IV. praecepto*, in *Opera Omnia* (Leiden, 1647), 1:278–280.

These things are narrated separately and distinctly in Genesis 2, which previously were presented in summary fashion and indeed in such a way that they could not be seen to have been completed in the space of one day.

Response 1. From this doubt, or by reason of the doubt, it is not possible to conclude with certainty with Abulensis that Genesis 1:27 "male and female he created them" holds true from the time when the woman was produced from the side of the man, and not before.[61] For from doubt and uncertainty, nothing can properly be concluded. But if I omit "it doesn't seem" and "I doubt," who would say that he knows and believes for certain that those things were not completed or could not have been completed within the confines of a single day? Already I require for this a reason or demonstration that relies either on certain knowledge or on faith, whether from the word of God, from reason, or from both. Without these it is vain to advance anything as certain and necessary out of doubt, ignorance, falsehood, verisimilitude, or conjecture.

But if an instance be given, it would be a line of argument from the absurd consequence: already we ask again that this absurd, contradictory, and impossible argument be carefully tested. 1. The production of birds, fishes, and quadrupeds by means of creation—why could that not happen? For it was not necessary to create single individuals of species or single species in succession. What pre-vents individuals of every species (male and female, of course) from being created together in an instant of time? Indeed we would say that if not all, at least many or most species were created at the same time. Think about how many species of birds and especially fishes were created on the fifth day! One day was enough time for this. 2. The production of man and the giving of instructions does not require a long extent of time. 3. Neither does the placing of him in paradise.

But 1. bringing animals to Adam, 2. surveying them and endowing them with names, and 3. sending him into a deep and long sleep all seem to have required some time.

Response 1. Is that in fact so? Who will deny that that space of time could have been kept within the sixth day? Must one suppose that a long time was required for showing the animals to Adam, as if, namely, from all parts of the earth the footed animals had to walk or all reptiles had to crawl (as they now do), and even the tortoise taking slow steps and carrying his house, to come to Adam? Could God either immediately or

---

61. Alphonse Tostatus (Abulensis), *Opera Omnia Quotquot in Scripturae sacrae expositionem et alia, adhuc extare inventa sunt* (Cologne, 1613), 77.

through the ministry of angels have gathered those animals that were in paradise or not far from paradise and shown them for Adam's viewing?

Response 2: The sending of the deep sleep and the formation of woman did not require so much time that it could not have been done on the sixth day. I read of a "heavy and deep sleep" in the text, not of a long sleep. And so this contributes nothing toward a need for extending the time. What if someone should arouse doubts leading to denial of this story or transforming it into a fictional parable, asking how and whether the body of Adam could have been consolidated in such a short time after a new rib had been inserted with the flesh; shall we consider that this curious and silly doubt cannot be removed or rather blown apart?[62]

CHAPTER TWO

Concerning those things which pertain to the
secular and political status of women

Question I: Whether women are inferior in dignity to men

Response in the *affirmative*, based on its affirmation and the reasons advanced by the Apostle in 1 Corinthians 11 and 1 Timothy 2, which we will not repeat here. Nature, which the Apostle brings to bear on the question of women's hair in 1 Corinthians 11:13–15, dictates the same thing. So does natural law, which is written in the hearts of all; that is to say, either explicitly or implicitly. Let no one falsely restrict the law of nature, natural law, or nature to "common notions" or those practical principles of whose truth none can be ignorant or deny in their inner conscience. And let no one adduce laws held at times by some people which are contrary to various laws of nature. I shall not here recall for consideration the analogies of some stemming from that "first lie" in explanation of 1 Corinthians 11:14 and in explanation of the natural moral law. More than enough was written on this in *Sylva Quaestionum Insignium* (1650) by the noted Carolus de Maets, now deceased, but when he lived, a very close colleague of ours.[63] And before him Ames warned in his *Cases of Con-*

---

62. Voetius continues with three more sets of objections and responses, which I have omitted, as his position in support of the sixth day creation of woman seems sufficiently established.

63. In this work de Maets sided with Voetius in a controversy that had begun in 1643 over the interpretation of 1 Corinthians 11:13–15 on the question of natural law in relation to hair. Voetius's interpretation of the passage had been attacked by Godefrid Udemann under the pen name Poimenander, who argued for Christian liberty in the wearing of wigs. Voetius

science, book 1, chapter 2, paragraph 6: "To *synteresis* taken in a broader sense ought to be referred not only general conclusions concerning law which are deduced by clear consequence from natural principles . . . ." and paragraph 7: "natural consequence is that which acknowledges for law the principles of nature and the conclusions arising from them."[64] Because if somewhere by the error of some persons and by bad custom women's dignity is raised above that of men, it does not follow thereupon that what we said is not of natural law, since they have not drawn the consequences from first principles and "common notions," as for example those who approve some falsehoods (either polygamy or incest or such).

Question II. Whether women are inferior to the extent that in the state of marriage they ought to be subordinated like servants

The *response* is in the *negative* because by divine and natural law the power of the paterfamilias over his wife, children, and servants is differentiated. The divine law is supplied for us in Genesis 2:18, that "she may be with him." And Genesis 1:24, "that they may be one flesh," together with Ephesians 5:28–31. The natural law extends from this, because they are co-causes not only in the work pertaining to the proper administration of the family and family affairs, but also in procreating children, where there can be neither the man without the woman nor the woman without the man. Civil law makes distinctions, for which the words of Ulpian, *de testam. de injur.*, book 1, are cited: "The son still in the household is in the complete power (*potestas*) of the father, the wife in his tutelage (*manus*), the servant in his possession (*mancipium*)."[65] Add to that what is accounted as a

---

was a Precisianist who believed that nearly all facets of human behavior, no matter how inconsequential they might seem, fell under the moral law. Voetius narrated the course of the controversy and offered additional supporting quotations from many theological authorities in "De Excelsis Mundi," *Selectarum Disputationum Theologicarum* (Amsterdam, 1667), 4:463–492.

64. William Ames, *De Conscientia et eius Jure vel Casibus* (Amsterdam, [1650]), 6. English translation: *Conscience, with the Power and Cases Thereof* (London, 1643), 4. The completion of the sentence in paragraph 6 is "but likewise all practical truths to which we give firm assent through the revelation we have by faith." Ames defines the *synteresis*, a commonly used term in medieval theology, as "a habit of understanding by which we assent unto the principles of moral actions, that is, such actions as are our duty because God hath willed or commanded them."

65. The *Corpus Iuris Civilis*, to which Voetius refers, is composed of the Institutions, a concise summary of the law by emperor Justinian, the Digest, in which the writings of Roman jurists such as Ulpian (d. 228) are extracted and codified, the Code of Justinian, a collection of imperial ordinances or constitutions including those of Justinian up to 534, and the Novels, or the legal work of Justinian between 534 and 565. The modern critical edition was edited by Theodor Mommsen and others in the nineteenth century and has undergone numerous editions. On Roman family law, see W. W. Buckland, *A Textbook of Roman Law from Augustus to Justinian*, 3d ed. rev. by Peter Stein (Cambridge: Cambridge University Press, 1975), esp. 118:

person, *Novell.* 22, para. *quae vero.* And that the authority which the husband uses toward the wife they describe as "like that of a father and guardian," according to Cujacius, *Observations*, book 16, chap. 33; & book 7, chap. 11[66] (hence Aristotle deservedly reproves the barbarians, who used their wives for whatever servile functions they wished), so that they be a co-cause, that is, an instrument as the Delphic sword is an instrument. Therefore the harsh statement of Augustine in the fifth book of questions on Deuteronomy, chap. 33, "women are subject to their husbands according to the law almost as servants."[67] Filesacus in book 2 of selected topics, chap. 6, on "a proper wife," cites the passage in Augustine's *Questions on Genesis*, chap. 153, which states, "It is the natural order among human beings that women should serve men and sons their parents, since it is not just that the greater should serve the lesser." He then explains and excuses Augustine in this way: "because the word of serving which he uses is not according to the usage of the jurists but in the sense of gratifying and pleasing."[68] But perhaps Augustine can be excused otherwise by correlating this passage from chap. 39 of the work cited on Genesis, "because by the decree of God the woman deserved from her guilt that she be under the man in some sort of way in a servile condition,"[69] since, namely, that subjection to the man and the aid to be offered him is with discomfort, which would not have been the case in the state of innocence, if in fact man had remained in that state, just as he would have cultivated the land (Genesis 1:28 & 2:15) but not with discomfort as after the entry of sin (Genesis 4:17).

Question III. Whether the superiority of a man over his wife extends to beatings

   Response: This question we treated above in part 1, book 3, treatise 1, section 3, chapter 3.[70] We will not repeat it here, but only add to the ju-

---

"Manus placed the wife *filiae loco* and made her the sister of her own children. . . . In the time of Augustus it was in decay and it seems to have died out altogether not long after Gaius [second century]." On the status of women according to Roman law, see Sarah B. Pomeroy, *Goddesses, Whores, Wives, and Slaves: Women in Classical Antiquity* (New York: Schocken Books, 1984), chap. 8.

66. Jacob Cujacius (Jacques Cujas), *Observantium et Emendationum Libri XXVIII* (Cologne, 1598), 277–278, 784–785.

67. Augustine, *Quaestionum in Heptateuchum* (Turnholt, 1958), 293, on Deuteronomy 22:13–21.

68. Jean Filesac, *Selectorum Liber Secundus* (Paris, 1631), 308: "Interim serviendi verbum, quo S. Augustinus usus, non ex Iurisconsultorum regulis explicandum est, sed pro morem gerere & obsequi usurpavit, quemadmodum Apostolus, dum Christianos adolescentulas matrimonio copulatas, viris suis subditas esse praecipit.

69. Augustine, *Quaestiones in Heptateuchum*, 59.

70. Gisbertus Voetius, *Politica Ecclesiastica*, vol. 1 (Amsterdam, 1663).

ridical authors on the affirmative side Farinacius and his *On Crimes of the Flesh*, question 143, no. 148ff [*sic*];[71] and Althusius, who cites Farinacius with approval in his *Decalogue*, book 1, chap. 29. Agreeing with these opinions is the law of Mohammed, chap. 9 of the Koran, where he decrees that if wives do not obey the precepts of the husband, "they should be detained at home or in bed and beaten."[72] And to the authorities cited in the same place on the negative side, add from the theologians Theodore Thummius, *Decalogue*, p. 431; and Forbes, *Theological-Historical Instruction*, book 4, chap. 12, who supports his opinion with various arguments.[73]

Add from the jurists George Viviennius's treatise on the mistress of a household and Conrad Rittershusius's third book of sacred readings, chapter 2.[74] Above all, add here Chrysostom, who in his 26th homily on the First Letter to the Corinthians most vehemently disapproves of beating.[75]

Question IV: Whether a husband has the power of life and death over his wife

The *response* is in the *negative* because the right of the sword is assigned only to the public authority or magistrate, not to the domestic authority whether of the husband or the father or the master or mistress.

This is proved first from Romans 13:4, "for [the authority] is God's servant . . . for the authority does not bear the sword in vain. He is the servant of God to execute wrath on the wrongdoer." Compare the passages in Deuteronomy 21:1–2 and 22:15–20. Second, since if that right

71. Prosper Farinacci (Farinacius), *Operum Criminalium Pars Quinta*, 2d ed. (Nuremberg, 1676), 656–657. The correct number for the reference, 184, is given by Johannes Althusius, *Dicaeologicae* (Frankfurt, 1618), in his chapter on a husband's rights and powers.

72. *The Message of the Qurán*, trans. Muhammad Asad (Gibraltar: Dar Al-Andalus, 1980), 109–110 (Fourth Surah, para. 34): "Men shall take full care of women with the bounties which God has bestowed more abundantly on the former than on the latter. . . . And as for those women whose ill-will you have reason to fear, admonish them [first]; then leave them alone in bed; then beat them; and if thereupon they pay you heed, do not seek to harm them."

73. Theodor Thummius, *Decalogus, in quo Virtutes et Vitia ex Verbo Dei et Pia Antiquitate* (Tübingen, 1626), 431. Thummius cites the homily of Chrysostom which Voetius quotes regarding wife-beating. John Forbes, *Instructiones Historico-Theologicae de Doctrina Christiana* (Geneva, 1699), 198.

74. Georgius Viviennius, *De Officio Probae Matrisfamilias* (Antwerp, 1563); German trans.: *Weiberspiegel* (1565). Conrad Rittershusius, *Sacrarum Lectionum Libri Octo Quibus multa ad Jus Civile & ad Historias pertinentia* (Nuremberg, 1693), 148–151.

75. St. John Chrysostom, *Homilies on the Epistle of Paul to the Corinthians*, in Philip Schaff, *A Select Library of the Nicene and Post-Nicene Fathers of the Christian Church* (reprint Grand Rapids: Wm. B. Eerdmans Publ. Co., 1989), 12:155–156. I omit the lengthy citation from this text which Voetius presents.

does not fall to the power of the father, therefore much less does it fall to the power of the husband. But it does not fall to the power of the father. Therefore. . . The consequence of the major premise is proved, since the authority of the father over children is greater than that of the husband over a wife. In *Politics*, book 8,[76] the philosopher compares the former to monarchical authority, the latter to civil or aristocratic authority. Add from the preceding question that if the husband does not have the right of punishment through beating, much less does he have the right of killing the wife.

The minor premise is proved from Deuteronomy 21:17ff, where a rebellious son is commanded to be handed over to the magistrate, who punishes him by death. Formerly among some tribes and Celts (according to Aristotle in the previously cited passage) that right was assigned to the husband; also among the Romans through the ancient law of Romulus. Dionysius Halicarnassus reports, "If a wife had committed some wrong, she was punished by the judgment of the offended husband; the relatives decided with him concerning crimes of this sort."[77] The law of the Gauls was nearly the same, as Julius Caesar testifies in book 6 of his commentaries.[78] King Theodoricus (according to Cassiodorus in book 1, letter 37, of his *Variarum*) decrees that a husband whose wife has committed adultery is to be permitted to murder the adulterer.[79] This permission is restricted in the section on adultery in the Julian law:[80] "It is permitted for a husband to kill an adulterer of his wife, but not just anyone he wills." Concerning the ancient law of the Romans on killing wives caught in adultery, Gellius, in his *Attic Nights*, book 10, chap. 23, quotes from a certain oration of Cato: "If you should take your wife in adultery, you may with impunity put her to death without a trial; but if you should commit adultery or indecency, she must not presume to lay a finger on you, nor does the law allow it."[81]

---

76. Aristotle, *Politics* 1.12, 1259b. The reference fits book 1, not book 8.

77. Dionysius Halicarnassus, *The Roman Antiquities*, trans. Earnest Cary (Cambridge, MA, 1937), 382–385. The seventeenth-century edition, *Antiquitatem sive originum Romanarum in Scripta quae extant omnia, Historica & Rhetoricae* (Hanoviae, 1615), 93, coincides better with Voetius's citation.

78. "[Among the Gauls] men have the power of life and death over their wives, as over their children." Julius Caesar, *The Gallic War*, trans. H. J. Edwards (Cambridge, MA: Harvard University Press, 1917), 343–345.

79. Magnus Aurelius Cassiodorus, *Variarum Libri XII*, ed. A. J. Fridh, in *Opera I*, Corpus Christianorum Series Latina 96 (Turnholt, 1973), 43. A lengthy citation that Voetius includes is omitted here.

80. The Julian law concerning adultery is the focus of book 9.9 of the Codex and book 48.5 of the Digests. See also Pomeroy, *Goddesses, Whores, Wives, and Slaves*, chap. 8.

81. Gellius, *Attic Nights*, 2.279 (bk. 10, chap. 23).

Among the ancient Germans the husband expelled the adulteress from the house with her hair shorn and punished her by whipping her naked through the entire town. But whatever custom, whatever human law is put forward as a pretext, we must hold firmly to the proposition that in these and other crimes punishment is not to be inflicted by those who have an interest in the matter or by the husband, but by those who possess the public power.

Question V. Whether women are to be engaged in public office and governance

Response: This is debated by the political writers Bodin, Tholosanus, Arnisaeus, Canoniero, Besold, whose works may be consulted.[82]

For our part, since against the rule of women over men it is customary to assert reasons based on divine law (Genesis 2, 1 Corinthians 11, 1 Timothy 2), we respond briefly that women are not ordinarily to be appointed to office in a polyarchic government; still less are they to be preferred over men. In a case of extreme necessity and when some woman is found who is superior to men of that place in prudence, courage, and a gift for counsel, I think such women are certainly to be called in quite temporarily for consultation or direction. Thus Deborah became and was said to be politically a "mother in Israel" (Judges 5:7). And the city of Abel, in a case of necessity, made use of the counsel of a wise woman, using her also as a kind of legate to Joab to speak to and negotiate with him about ending the war (2 Samuel 20:15–22). For if the work and counsel of a poor and wise man, who in a case of necessity could rescue the city, is to be used (Ecclesiastes 9:14–15), why not that of a wise woman in a similar case? In a state where the monarch is chosen or elected it does not seem that the office should be diverted toward the female sex, since it cannot happen that in the entire realm or among the neighbors and allies men could not be found who are abundantly equipped with gifts and prerequi-

---

82. These political theorists of the late sixteenth and early seventeenth centuries included in their comprehensive works a discussion of the legitimacy of female rule. Their conclusions ranged from the strongly negative opinion of Canoniero, who argued from natural law, divine law, and a variety of points best designated as folklore and prejudice, to the neutral position of Pierre Gregoire (Tholosanus), who thoroughly summarized arguments and evidence from both sides and concluded that it was an adiaphoron, a matter neither commanded nor forbidden. The others came to a negative conclusion, using a variety of reasoning from nature, scripture, and historical experience to show that women were not well suited to govern. See Jean Bodin, *Six livres de la Republique*, bk. 6, chap. 5; Pierre Gregoire (Tholosanus), *De Republica* (1597), bk. 7, chap. 11 (443–479); Henning Arnisaeus, *Doctrina Politica*, in *Opera Politica Omnia I* (Strasbourg, 1648), chap. 11, 91–96; Pietro Andrea Canoniero, *Dell' Introduzzione alla Politica alla Ragion di Stato et Pratica del buon Governo* (Antwerp, 1614), bk. 8, chap. 2, 405ff.; Christopher Besold, *Collegii Politici Classis Prima; Reipublicae Naturam et Constitutionem XII* (Tübingen, 1614), disp. 6.35, p. 17.

sites for that office. In a state where the monarchy is by succession, particular arguments could recommend whether in any given state a law or statute should be written concerning succession of the next heir, and even of a woman, assuming that no masculine offspring from the departing king had been left. Nor do we think that England offended divine or natural law when Mary and Elizabeth ruled as queens, not to speak of widowed queens and princesses constituted as governors by the will as much of the dead king or prince as of the nobility or the estates of the kingdom or principality. In the kingdom of France, where women are said to be excluded from succession, Hotman in *Franco-Gallia* (4th ed.), chap. 36, and Matharel in *Hotman's Franco-Gallia*, chap. 10, p. 132, debate among themselves whether such can happen.[83]

Question VI. Whether women should bear arms and fight wars

Response: We distinguish between waging war, bearing arms (i.e., serving as a soldier), and accompanying the military. The former is in general not only permitted to women and princesses whether ruling legitimately or governing temporarily by some chance and acting as a proxy (as was formerly Margaret of Parma in the Low Countries[84] and as is today the most serene queen of Spain),[85] but, given their position,

---

83. Francis Hotman (Hotomannus), *Franco-Gallia*, 4th ed. (Frankfurt, 1586), chap. x (pp. 75–79). (Note: as there are only 27 chapters in the book, Voetius's citation is unclear.) Hotman traced the development of the Salic law from the original intent of preventing women from inheriting land through the 1328 succession struggle, when it began to be referred to in relation to women inheriting the throne, up to his own time, arguing that there was no legal basis for excluding women from the line of inheritance but that it had become custom. This was part of Hotman's larger argument that the monarchy had not originally been hereditary but rather that kings had been elected by councils of the nobles. Hotman, a Reformed jurist, was opposed by the monarchists such as Antonius Matharellus (Antoine Matharel), who in *Ad Franc. Hotomani Franco-Galliam Responsio* (Paris, 1575), 69, referred to the Salic law on exclusion of women from the throne as a "very ancient and holy institution observed for nearly 1200 years" and one of the reasons for the strength of the French kingdom. Though Hotman was the better historian, he was forced to leave France during the St. Bartholomew's Day massacre of 1572, and the tradition of excluding women from rule was recognized as law in 1593.

84. Margaret of Parma, daughter of Emperor Charles V, was regent in the Netherlands from 1559 until 1567 and tried to reconcile the conflicting ambitions of the Dutch nobility and the Hapsburg rulers until the Duke of Alva entered the country with his army and took over her position. See the pamphlet written when she was reappointed regent in 1580 praising her love of God and sincere desire for peace: "The return of harmony in the Netherlands by the return of Madame, 1580," in *Texts concerning the Revolt of the Netherlands*, ed. E. H. Kossman and A. F. Mellink (Cambridge: Cambridge University Press, 1974), 203–206. Nevertheless, her son Alexander prevented her from exercising any influence.

85. Mariana of Austria was regent in Spain from 1665 until 1675, when her son, Charles II, came of age and assumed the throne.

necessary since by divine, natural, and human law they are obligated to defend the republic and to guard the subjects with just arms. And thus the most serene queen of England and Ireland fought wars with the king of Spain Philip II and with the Irish. She had as an example Deborah, who in Judges 4 even undertook an expedition with Barak. But the difficulty is whether it is fitting for women to serve as a soldier and take part in expeditions of war, sieges, assaults, battles, and attacks.

We distinguish: it is not becoming nor is it suitable for preserving chastity and modesty if women pass their time within the eyesight of men; they are mixed with men by day and night on stations, vigils, clandestine attacks, ambushes, battles, when they do such things with men. Nevertheless we do not disapprove if in a case of extreme necessity of the state and the lack of men they should repel and turn back an attacking enemy with hurled rocks, firebrands smeared with pitch, and other instruments; further if they should aid the soldiers by gathering rocks, and carrying gunpowder, ammunition, arms, and other weapons necessary for defense or offense. At the year-long siege of Haarlem in the Dutch war and also in the year-long siege of Maastricht, women performed extraordinary military service.[86] As a result, a great many women were killed when the Spanish took Maastricht. And this is the opinion of Martyr in his *Loci*, classis 4, chap. 16, para. 13.[87] Scharpius followed him in his *Symphony of Prophets and Apostles*, question 40, p. 241.[88] Hence we seem to have to condemn the warlike Amazons, about whom wrote Pliny, Stephanus, Strabo, and other geographers and Nieremberg in his *Natural History*,[89] commenting on Virgil's *Aeneid* from book I:

86. See John Lothrop Motley, *The Rise of the Dutch Republic* (New York: Harper, 1900), 3:353 and 5:141. Referring to the siege of Maastricht in 1579, Motley writes, "The tried veterans of Spain, Italy and Burgundy were met face to face by the burghers of Maestricht, together with their wives and children. All were armed to the teeth and fought with what seemed superhuman valor. The women, fierce as tigresses defending their young, swarmed to the walls, and fought in the foremost rank. They threw pails of boiling water on the besiegers, they hurled firebrands in their faces, they quoited blazing pitch-hoops with unerring dexterity about their necks."

87. Peter Martyr Vermigli, *Loci Communes* (Zurich, 1582), 940. Martyr, a Reformed theologian, criticized Plato for proposing that women be trained militarily with men. The word of God, as he understood it, did not permit this. Only in cases of emergency should women be asked to aid in the defense of their country in such support tasks as carrying rocks, for example.

88. Johann Scharpius, *Symphonia Prophetarum & Apostolorum* (Geneva, 1625).

89. Pliny, *Natural History*, vol. 2 (Cambridge: Harvard University Press, 1969), bk. 7.201 (pp. 640–641). Stephanus Byzantinus, *Peri Poleon Kai Demon/De Urbibus et Populis*, ed. Abraham Berkelius (Leiden, 1694), 365–366. Strabo, *The Geography*, trans. Horace Leonard Jones (Cambridge, 1928), 5:237 (bk. 11.5.3); Joannis Eusebius Nieremberg, *Historia Naturae* (Antwerp, 1635), 135.

Penthesilea in her fury leads the ranks of crescent-shielded Amazons

and from book XI:

> *a band just like the Thracian Amazons when they ride hard upon*
> *Thermodon's shores and fight in gilded armor.*[90]

Also the Bohemian women who under the leadership of Valasca held the princedom with arms for seven years, as witnesses Aeneas Sylvius in his *History of Bohemia*, chap. 7, who there and in chap. 5 mentions Libussa the virgin daughter of Crocis, second duke of the Bohemians, who for many years ruled Bohemia.[91] The same author adds in his description of Asia, chap. 20,[92] after citations from authors who reported on the Amazons, that Maria ruled like a man[93] in Hungary and that in the kingdom of Naples the two Joannas ruled the state. Concerning Maria who was elevated by the Hungarians to the highest position in the kingdom so that they might pronounce and greet her not only as queen but as king, see Bonfinium's *Decades*, no. 3, book I, p. 355.[94] Nor do we approve what Plato wants in the *Republic*, dialogue 5, and in the *Laws*, dialogue 7,[95] namely that women should have their studies in common with men, especially military studies, and that they should train in the nude. This last injunction, Bessarion says in *Against Plato's Calumniator*, book 4, chap. 5, was introduced not first and exclusively by Plato, but already earlier by Minos and Lycurgus.[96] As for the warlike girl Joan of Arc, called the Maid of Orleans, who was accused by her enemies of armed exploits and of having assumed the clothing of a man, we discussed her in *Selected Disputations II*, "On Miracles," pp. 1031–1136.[97]

---

90. *The Aeneid of Virgil*, trans. Allen Mandelbaum (Berkeley: University of California Press, 1971), 18 (1.490–491) and 306 (11.659–660).

91. Aeneas Sylvius Senensis (Pope Pius II), *De Bohemorum origine, ac gestis historia, variarum rerum narrationem complectens* (Salingiaci, 1538), 14, 11.

92. Aeneas Sylvius, *Asiae Europaeque elegantiss. descriptio* (N.p., 1531), 43–49 (chap. 20).

93. Voetius's printed text has here *civiliter*, "like a citizen," but the original source he is citing has *viriliter*, "like a man, manfully," which also fits the context better.

94. Antonius de Bonfinis, *Rerum Ungaricarum Decades*, ed. I Fógel et alia, Bibliotheca Scriptorum Medii Recentisque Aevorum (Leipzig, 1936), 3.24.

95. *The Collected Dialogues of Plato*, ed. Edith Hamilton and Huntington Cairns (Princeton: Princeton University Press, 1961), 690–691 (*Republic* 5.451e–452e); 1376 (*Laws* 804e–805a).

96. Cardinal Bessarion, *In Calumniatorem Platonis*, ed. L. Mohler (Paderborn, 1927; repr. Paderborn, 1967), 525.

97. Voetius, *Disputationes Theologicae Selectae* II (Utrecht, 1655), 1031–1036.

Question VII. Whether the studies of wisdom and of letters are fitting for women

Response in the *affirmative* for those, that is to say, to whom God gives this leisure and whose mind, bodily temperament, and solitary status permit this. I apply no arguments except those which the most noble and learned maiden Anna Maria van Schurman collected in 1638, which were included in her edited works. Examples of literary women were gathered by Beverovicius in his *On the Excellence of the Female Sex*, book 2, chapter 2.[98] The distinguished Hottinger presents something of a catalogue of the same in his dedicatory letter to part 5 ("The Sixteenth Century") of his *Ecclesiastical History.*[99] I refer the reader to these. To be added to the catalogues of Beverovicius and Hottinger are:

Proba Falconia, a Roman whose *Centones Virgiliani* still exist, in which she cleverly describes deeds of the Old and New Testaments. Concerning her see Baronius on year 395, para. 2; and 410, para. 4;[100] Sixtus Senensis, in *Bibliotheca*, book 4, p. 368. Gesner in *Bibliotheca* and Vossius in his book *On Latin Poets*, p. 60, write that she was the wife of Adelphus, a proconsul.[101] There exist the *Centones Homerici* in which the life and deeds of Christ are described, which were published in octavo in Frankfurt in 1541 together with Proba's *Centones Virgiliani* and Nonnus's *Paraphrase of John.*[102]

Eudocia, the wife of Theodocius the younger, was quite learned. Fulgosus in his *Collected Sources* and Gesner in his *Bibliotheca* ascribe the Homeric centones to her under the name *Eudoxia* (it should read *Eudocia*, for Eudoxia was the daughter of Eudocia and was married to Valentinian III);[103] yet the editions of Manutius and H. Stephanus attribute them to an unknown author.[104] Concerning the education and writings of this Eudo-

---

98. Jan van Beverwyck (Beverovicius), *Van de Uitnementheyt des vrouwelicken Geslachts* (Dordrecht, 1639).

99. Joh. Heinrich Hottinger, *Historiae Ecclesiasticae, Novi Testamenti, Seculum XVI seu Pars Quinta* (Zurich, 1655), fol. a2–a5. Hottinger dedicates this volume to Princess Elizabeth of the Palatinate and praises her and "that other prodigy" in Utrecht.

100. Caesar Baronius, *Annales Ecclesiastici* (Cologne, 1624), vol. 4, col . 779; and vol. 5, col. 327. Paragraph numbers in these volumes do not coincide with those given by Voetius.

101. Sixtus Senensis, *Bibliotheca Sancta* (Cologne, 1626), bk. 4.368; Conrad Gesner, *Bibliotheca Universalis, sive Catalogus omnium scriptorum locupletissimus, in tribus linguis, Latina, Graeca, & Hebraica* (Zurich, 1545), fol. 570b; Gerardus Johannes Vossius, *Veterum Poetarum Temporibus*, vol. 2, *De Poetis Latinis* (Amsterdam, 1662), 60.

102. Nonnus of Panopolis (c. 400) is said to be the author of the Greek poem known as the *Paraphrase of the Fourth Gospel*. Little else is known about him.

103. Fregoso, *De dictis factisque memorabilibus collectanea* (Milan, 1508); Gesner, fol. 227b. I have altered the last reference to the name; Voetius's text has Eudoxia as the daughter of Eudoxia.

104. Aldus Manutius, an important editor and printer in Venice in the early 16th century, and Henricus Stephanus, patriarch of an important printing house in Paris, produced editions of

cia, see Socrates's *Ecclesiastical History*, book 7, chap. 22; and Photius's *Biblio-theca*, codex 183ff.[105]

Elpis the wife of Boethius was lettered and a lover of poetry.[106] Heloise or Eloise the wife of Peter Abelard, was "in knowledge by no means unequal" to her husband; these are the words of Baronius on the year 1140, para. 12.[107] In para. 10 he cites the letters of Peter of Cluny. Stephanus Paschasius in his *Investigations*, book 6, chap. 17, quite accurately describes the life of Abelard, the love between him and Heloise, and the extraordinary "married unmarried man."[108] His paradoxical and heretical teachings and the opposition both of private persons and of councils are reviewed in Baronius, loc. cit.

Maria Cunitia of Pitschen in Silesia is still alive today, if I am not mistaken; she displays her knowledge in languages and in theoretical sciences more than sufficiently in publishing *Urania propitia* or *Astronomical Tables . . .* in Latin and German, 1650.[109]

Maria Lansberg, the sister of Francis and Philipp Lansberg, famous preachers in the Netherlands at Rotterdam and Goes, the latter of whom became known to the world through various published writings in mathematics and chronology. She was versed in Latin and Greek letters and quite productive in poetry, as I remember having gathered from several of her Latin letters and various epigrams (some of which were to the most noble Queen Elizabeth of England) inscribed in some book that her son Johannes Leur or Leurius (for that was the name of the man whom

---

many Greek and Roman classics. Stephanus's edition of the *Homerici Centones* along with Proba Falconia's *Centones Virgilianos* & Nonnus's *Paraphrasis* appeared in 1578 with his comment in the preface that "some ascribe this work to Eudoxia."

105. Socrates Scholasticus, *Historia Ecclesiastica* 7, *Patrologia Graeca* [hereafter abbreviated *PG*] 67.783; Photius, *Myriobiblon sive Bibliotheca*, in *Opera Omnia* 7, *PG* 103.535, 538.

106. Elpis was a noblewoman of Sicily who wrote hymns, but the report that she was married to the famous philosopher Boethius is found in only one source and contradicts other sources according to which he was married to Rusticana, daughter of Symmachus. See *Nouvelle Biographie Universelle* (Paris, 1853), 6:333.

107. *Annales Ecclesiastici* 12, col. 303.

108. Estienne Pasquier (Stephanus Paschasius), *Les Recherches de la France* (Paris, 1643), 507–513 (bk. 6, chap. 17).

109. Maria Kunitzin (Cunitia) was the daughter of noted physician Heinrich Kunitzin and the wife of mathematician and physican Elias von Löwen. Skilled in music, painting, and languages, she devoted herself primarily to astronomy. Her astronomical tables were first conceived on a smaller scale, but when she and her husband were driven from Silesia to a cloister in Poland during the Thirty Year's War, she expanded the project to include the course of all the planets for all time, past, present, and future. Johann Heinrich Zedler, *Grosses Vollständiges Universal-Lexikon* (Halle, 1737; repr. Graz, 1961), 15:2134–35.

Maria had married), then our fellow student at Leiden some sixty years ago more or less, gave me to examine. For the purposes of the review, I read out loud some of the poems in the book and he read out some of them. What happened to that book and in whose hands it now lies hidden, I do not know. Its possessor, Johannes Leurius, spent several years as preacher in the fortress of Saint Andrew in the territory and district of Bommel; from there through the change of affairs that occurred in 1619[110] he either left or was let go because he had ministered for some time in private, that is to say, in clandestine Remonstrant conventicles, and then he passed away. Whether any of his heirs remain and who they are (I know for certain that he was married), and among whom this monument to Dutch women's learning might be sought, I am not at present able to investigate.

Question VIII: Whether women ought to be distinguished externally from men and how

Response: There is no doubt that there should be differences and they should be distinguishable in people's behavior. But to know how they may be distinguished we must ask whether it is through signs prescribed by divine and natural law, or whether it is through signs arising from human choice or local custom; and through what signs?

We arrive at these conclusions:

1. Any individual person is distinguished from others naturally by the shape and form of the face, which God grants to each as his or her own. This is the primary sign for discernment; the secondary ones are the voice, gait, and posture.

This does not prevent that sometimes with certain people the face, voice, etc., are so similar that other people can scarcely distinguish between them. But although they cannot be thus distinguished on the spur of the moment and at first glance, nevertheless when you look more carefully and attentively, not only at the shape and form of the face but also at the voice, gait, and posture, the outward appearance of the body and of all parts of the body, height, width, and figure, you cannot but distinguish him from anyone else alive in the world. One must marvel at the power and providence of God in that distinction of innumerable persons through the diversity of faces, voices, and gaits. This can be put forth as an objection to Epicureans and atheists among others, against whom we warned in part I of *Selected Disputations,* "Concerning Atheists," part 4, p. 212, where we note that this consideration is stressed by Marin

110. At the synod of Dort in 1618, the Remonstrant struggle for broader interpretation of points in the Heidelberg Catechism such as predestination was decisively crushed, and Remonstrant pastors were removed from their posts.

Mersenne in his commentary on some chapters of Genesis.[111] Now I add, from Pedro Mejía's Lessons, part 1, chap. 38, that this can be called one of the great secrets and miracles of nature;[112] in this work he collected examples of persons so similar that they could not consistently be distinguished, such as the Artemides (from Pliny and Solinus), the Semiramides and the sons of Ninus (from Justin), the Biblii and the Publicii (from Pliny),[113] etc. Some more recent examples may be read in the same work.

2. Men and women are distinguished by certain outward members, but in ordinary conduct they ought not to be differentiated through these signs; that is, men and women ought not to walk nude, and no human law or custom can grant liberty in this area. Concerning this, see above part 1, book 2, treatise 2, section 3, p. 684ff; and Selected Disputations IV, "On the Lofty of the World," part 4, p. 404.[114]

3. They ought to be distinguished outwardly by certain external signs. External signs are established either by divine and natural law or by human choice. These are clothing and hair. We dealt with clothing in "On the Lofty of the World," p. 417ff. Concerning women's hair and on distinguishing women from men by their head covering, see the same, part 5:3f.[115] What I have said there I will not repeat except for one point, namely, that an exception be made for a case of necessity for an honorable purpose so that a woman may appear in the fashion of a man and a man in the fashion of a woman, and a woman's hair may be clipped, even shaved. Distinctive outward signs may vary out of human laws in accordance with the variety of peoples, places, and times.

---

111. Voetius, Disputationes Theologicae Selectae, part 1 (Utrecht, 1648). The disputation "De Atheismo," comprising pp. 114–226, was held on June 22, 1639, with Walter de Bruyn as respondent. Marin Mersenne's Quaestiones Celeberrimae in Genesim (Paris, 1623), was not a biblical commentary in the usual sense but a work of natural philosophy directed against those whom he regarded as atheists. In his commentary on Genesis 2:7 (cols. 1115–1134), Mersenne argues that "the wisdom, goodness, power and providence of God" (col. 1134) are evident throughout the parts of the human body.

112. Pedro Mejía, Les Diverses Leçons, contenans la lecture de variable histoires et autres choses memorable, trans. Claude Gruget (Paris, 1561). Original, in Spanish: Silva de varia lección (Seville, 1545).

113. Pliny, Natural History, 2.541 (bk. 7, para. 53).

114. Voetius, Politica Ecclesiastica 1 (Amsterdam, 1663), 683–689, explores whether in early sects, namely the Adamites, women were baptized in the nude. In "De Excelsis Mundi," Disputationes Theologicae Selectae, part 4 (Amsterdam, 1667), 404–406, Voetius writes more broadly of various reasons for either clothing or nudity, categorizing the nudity practiced by some Anabaptists as "superstitious."

115. "De Excelsis Mundi," 453–492.

CHAPTER THREE

Some matters are explicated pertaining to the spiritual
and ecclesiastical status of women

Question I: Whether there is a distinction between men and women in respect to
ecclesiastical status

The *response* is *negative* if you understand by this the mystical church, and according to the inward and invisible union, communion, and relationship of the members to Christ, you would institute a common status for them, since in Christ nothing counts except faith acting in love, Galatians 5[:6]. And all have obtained faith equally, 2 Peter 1[:1]. "There is neither male nor female . . . ," Galatians 3:28.

Conclusion 2: If by church you mean the institutional church, external and visible, there is a distinction since it is not permitted for a woman to speak or preside in church. About which more below.

Question II: Whether women are more religious than men

Response in the *affirmative:* Filesacus in *Selected Works,* book 3, p. 251. And he proves this from Exodus 38:8, 1 Samuel 2:21, and Luke 2:22, where he adds that "I see no men who did anything similar among the Hebrew people."[116] To which examples he appends the saying of Iamblichus, *On the Life of Pythagoras,* chap. 11, "Since the female sex is extremely fervent in devotion."[117] Next he adds the example of certain Gentile women from Polybius and Mamertinus.[118] Then he introduces Julian in *Misopogon* saying that old women (Christian women, of course) frequently gathered at the sepulchers of martyrs.[119] Then, to clinch the case, after adducing the example of the women setting out for the tomb of Christ with spices, he says that the clearest argument for this behavior is that that second sex, on

116. Jean Filesac, *Selectorum Liber Tertius* (Paris, 1638).

117. Iamblichus Chalcidensis, *De Vita Pythagorae,* ed. Johannis Arcerius Theodoretus (1598), 62.

118. Polybius (c. 200–c. 118 B.C.) was a Greek who wrote the history of Rome from 220 to 146 B.C. See *The Histories,* 1–6, trans. W. R. Paton (London: William Heinemann, 1922–27). Claudius Mamertinus served as consul under Emperor Julian and eulogized him in a panegyric in 361. See Samuel N. C. Lieu, *The Emperor Julian: Panegyric and Polemic* (Liverpool: Liverpool University Press, 1986).

119. Julian, Roman emperor 361–363, known as the Apostate, sought to reintroduce paganism into the empire, which had been Christian for about forty years. While in Antioch on a campaign to the East in 362, Julian encountered resistance to this attempt. His *Misopogon* is a satire on himself which details his complaints against the Antiochenes. See *The Works of the Emperor Julian,* trans. Wilmer Cave Wright (London: William Heinemann, 1913), 2:439.

account of the weakness conferred on it by nature, lacks many protections and supports and consequently, when evils assail it, takes refuge in God more easily and quickly.

For my proof of this thesis I would (a) consult general experience; (b) apply by analogy the saying of the Apostle in 1 Corinthians 1:26–30: "For you see your calling, . . . God chose what is foolish in the world, . . . and God chose what is weak in the world, . . . that no flesh should glory in his presence"; (c)[argue that] that particular school of the cross assigned to women in Genesis 3:16 is for them a school of light, that is, that for them, together with so many liberations by God from so many and such great causes of death (namely pregnancies and births), it is an occasion for devout prayers, celebrations, promises, preparations for death.

As far as today's experience is concerned, a large part of the churches in the Low Countries have more members of the feminine sex than the male; more sermons and other public or semipublic devotional exercises are frequented by them; in greater number and earlier than men, women have shown zeal for orthodoxy and devotion in difficult times and still do so today. In the ancient church, when persecution was raging, women similarly had prevailed both in numbers and zeal, as the reproaches of the pagans seem to show. Minutius says, they "gather together illiterates from the dregs of the populace and credulous women with the instability natural to their sex."[120] Thus Julian the Apostate (according to Nazianzus's second oration on Julian, and Cyril of Alexandria's sixth book against Julian)[121] laughed at Christians, because they frequented churches with children and decrepit little women and sang psalms together, etc. Celsus, in Origen's third book against Celsus, says, "By the fact that they themselves admit that these people are worthy of their God, they show that they want and are able to convince only the foolish, dishonourable and stupid, and only slaves, women and little children."[122] In Prudentius's *Crowns of Martyrdom*, in the hymn in honor of Fructuosus, bishop of the church of Tarraco, the judge Aemilian accuses Fructuosus[123] thus:

> "You," he said, "who are the teacher and propagator of this modern falsehood, seeking to make light-minded girls desert the sacred

120. Minutius Felix, *Octavius*, trans. Gerald H. Rendall (Cambridge, 1931), 335 (8.4).

121. Gregory Nazianzus, *Oratio V, Contra Julianum II* (PG 35.665–719); Cyril of Alexandria, *Adversus Julianum Imperatorem* (PG 76.559).

122. Origen, *Contra Celsum*, trans. Henry Chadwick (Cambridge: Cambridge University Press, 1965), 158 (PG 11.978).

123. Voetius's text has "Formosum" rather than "Fructuosum," presumably a printer's error.

groves and abandon Jupiter, if you are sensible you will condemn your old wives' teaching. It is commanded by the mouth of Caesar Gallienus that we shall all worship what the sovereign worships."[124]

Tertullian himself in his book against Praxeas: "The simple, unwise and unlearned always constitute the majority of believers."[125] Isidor of Pelusium, after relating the deed of Zipporah in Exodus 4, adds this common saying (bk. 1, letter 125): "since women are accustomed, when necessity demands, to use artifices more diligently than men and to take refuge in God more sincerely."[126]

Question III. Whether women are more inclined to superstition

Response: This is commonly *affirmed.* Strabo calls them "leaders of superstition" in book 7, whence the proverbial phrase "old wives' superstition," by which epithet the pagans described the Christian religion, according to Minutius in *Octavius;* according to Lactantius in book 5, chapter 1, they proclaim it to be "old wives' tales," and in Prudentius, cited above, "old wives' teachings."[127] That which the Apostle teaches us to avoid in 1 Timothy 4:7 is "old wives' tales." We read that charms, amulets, and lustrations were often prepared and applied by little old women. Since, however, underneath superstition are contained empty ritual, idolatry, and magic, it remains to be seen whether women may be said to be more inclined to any one of these particular species of superstition.

As far as the first is concerned, common experience regarding this does not leave room for doubt. Concerning the second, it seems it must likewise be affirmed if we consult religious history—both ecclesiastical and pagan—and experience. Concerning the third, if we are to lend credence to history and the frequent decrees of judges brought against prophetesses

---

124. Aurelius Prudentius Clemens, *Peristephanon Liber*, trans. H. J. Thomson (Cambridge: Harvard University Press, 1953), 205–206.

125. Tertullian, *Liber Adversus Praxeam* (*Patrologia Latina* [hereafter abbreviated *PL*] 2.180). Voetius does not quote Tertullian completely accurately. The modern English translation more accurately reads, "The simple, indeed (I will not call them unwise and unlearned), who always constitute the majority of believers." *Against Praxeas*, in *The Ante-Nicene Fathers*, ed. Alexander Roberts and James Donaldson (repr. Grand Rapids, MI: Wm. B. Eerdmans Publishing Co., 1993), 3:598.

126. Isidor of Pelusium, *Epistolarum* 1.125 (*PG* 78.266).

127. Strabo, *Geography* 3.182–183 (bk. 7.3.4) (Horace Jones translates the phrase as "chief founders of religion," but Voetius gives both Latin and Greek, allowing us to verify his pejorative understanding of the phrase); Minutius, *Octavius;* Caelus Firmianus Lactantius, *Divinae Institutiones et Epitome Divinarum Institutionem*, ed. Samuel Brandt, Corpus Scriptorum Ecclesiasticarum Latinorum 19 (Prague, 1890), bk. 5.1.403.

(concerning which we will not inquire here), women seem indeed to be more inclined toward that odious superstition. As far as prophetic magic is concerned, it is apparent from pagan histories that the devil promoted this through Pythian women and Sibylline prophetesses far more frequently than through men. Add to these the sacred story of the Pythian woman in Endor (1 Samuel 28) and the fortune-telling girl in Acts 16. It is not without cause that in Exodus 22:[18] a law is decreed against female sorcerers.

Question IV: Whether women are more inclined to heresies

The *response* is in the *negative*, as common experience and the histories and catalogues of heresies testify. It is indeed true that some women have not so much founded as spread and promoted heresies: but if they are compared to men as founders, promoters, patrons, and followers of heresies, they are far fewer in number. Concerning Jezebel, so named, you have Revelation 2:20, and concerning the women called devout you have Acts 13:50. Concerning silly women led captive, 2 Timothy 3:6–7; concerning women who deceive, see Ezekiel 13. On Helena (who is also called Selene) of Simon Magus see Eusebius, book 2, chap. 13;[128] and Irenaeus, book 1, chap. 23;[129] on Marcellina the follower of Carpocrates and the Gnostics, see Epiphanius, *Against Eighty Heresies*, 27; and Augustine, *On Heresies*, chap. 7.[130] On the seven hundred virgins who had been led astray by Arius and were promoting his heresies, see Epiphanius, *Against Eighty Heresies*, 69; along with Theodoret, book 1, chap. 4, where Alexander in his circular letter pronounces them "lawless little women," that is, "unclean foolish women" (as the Latin interpreter translates); and a little later he calls them "girlies," which the Latin interpreter translates as "soft harlots";[131] Baronius presents them thus in his history of year 318, para. 71.[132] But this paraphrase is preferable to the strict translation of the word.

---

128. Eusebius Pamphili, *Ecclesiastical History*, trans. Roy J. Deferrari (New York: Fathers of the Church, 1953), 106–107. Eusebius reports that Simon Magus was regarded as the "first author of all heresy." Helena, who traveled with him, had formerly lived in a brothel, but in Gnostic thought was called the "first Idea from him." This belief merged with the worship of the moon goddess Selene in Syria and other parts of the Middle East. For more information, see the article "Simon Magus" in James Hastings, *Encyclopedia of Religion and Ethics* (New York: Charles Scribner's Sons, 1921), 11:518ff.

129. Irenaeus, *Contra Haereses* (PG 7.1.671).

130. Epiphanius, *Adversus Octoginta Haereses* 27.6 (PG 41.371–375); Augustine, *De Haeresibus*, in *Opera Omnia* 12.2, Corpus Christianorum Series Latina 46 (Turnholt, 1969), 293.

131. Epiphanius, 69.3 (PG 42.207); Theodoret, *Ecclesiasticae Historiae* (PG 82.887ff.).

132. Caesar Baronius, *Annales Ecclesiastici* 3 (Antwerp, 1598).

Jerome portrays many more female promoters of heresies in his letter to Ctesiphont, vol. 3, fol. 115, of his works edited by Erasmus and published by Frobenius in Basel.[133]

Those current-day women who go around gossiping (against them, see 1 Timothy 5:13), who are called *cloppen queselen*, may justifiably be compared with these female accomplices of heretics; swarms of them are inundating not only papal but also Protestant lands, and we have said several things about them elsewhere. Here I shall only recall the complaint of the Jansenists or Louvain clerics concerning this kind of woman in an anonymous pamphlet in French entitled *Response of a Cleric of Louvain*,[134] where they charge the Jesuits with spreading their opinions by means of the said women, who are said to flit about among the whole populace.

Question V: Whether women should be admitted equally with men to religious exercises—public, private, and semiprivate

The *response* is in the *affirmative* since all those things are theirs and they are Christ's. And communion of the members with Christ, their head, and with each other belongs to women no less than to men. "There is neither Jew nor Greek, there is neither slave nor free, there is neither male nor female, for you are all one in Christ Jesus" (Galatians 3:28). There is only the exception that they may not speak in church (1 Timothy 2:12 and 1 Corinthians 15:34), that is, they may not perform a public office of teaching; nor may they cast votes together with men in the exercise of government and discipline in the church. The fact that God in extraordinary circumstances made use of the deeds of certain women (such as Deborah, Hulda, et al., about whom see below, book 2, treatise 2), does not make this a rule or order, nor is it for anyone to imitate. At the same time, as overseers and mothers, women are not only permitted within their own family to teach their children, maid-servants, and other domestics and to lead them in prayers and other household devotional exercises, they are also required to do this in cases where the father of the family is either absent or clearly unsuited for such tasks or estranged from the true religion or the practice of piety. Not only in their homes but also elsewhere in gatherings and occasional religious or devotional exercises or in private discussions and deliberations, where a certain woman excels by virtue of

---

133. Jerome, *Adversus Pelagium ad Ctesiphontem*, in *Opera* 3 (Epistolarum) (Basel, 1516). Voetius's extensive quotation from this letter is omitted here.

134. *Responce d'un ecclesiastique du Louvain* (1649), 96 in quarto, listed in Leopold Willaert, *Bibliotheca Janseniana Belgica* 1 (Namur, 1949), no. 2530.

learning and capacity for interpretation, she may lead in a women's meeting if the subject and the occasion comes about in this way. These kinds of private discussions, deliberations, and gatherings of the faithful for religious exercises are treated here and there, in 1 Thessalonians 4:11–14, Romans 15:14, Hebrews 3:13, Acts 12:12 and 16:13, and Matthew 18:20. Concerning private gatherings and exercises of certain women who are friends or members of the same household or fellow spirits, see above, part 1, book 2, treatise 3, chapter 1, question 10.[135]

Someone may perhaps object that women have presided over the public governance of the church among Protestants: as the papists often charge us. Supremacy was attributed to Queen Elizabeth; that is to say, she was said to be the supreme head under Christ and governor of the Anglican church. *Response:* What was attributed to her and what she claimed was not formally ecclesiastical power but political power that also had to do with the church and ecclesiastical matters. And such power is fitting for every legitimate magistrate, not only supreme but also subaltern, of whichever sex, such that, if the fortunes of the whole state belong to a woman, power with regard to the church and ecclesiastical matters must not be denied the same. But that a woman may call or choose ministers of the word, administer the keys to the kingdom of heaven, exercise discipline, and thus teach in the church, neither the word of God nor the order of reformed churches permits. See book 1, treatise 2, chapters 2 & 3, where I respond also to the charges concerning the head of the Anglican church, and I explain that title in accordance with the thinking of Anglican theologians.[136] If anyone explains otherwise or wants something to be understood otherwise, this is not to be imputed to reformed church and teaching, which holds with the Apostle in 1 Timothy 2:12 that it is not permitted for a woman to teach in church or administer sacraments. Nor does it recognize bishops of bishops, either male or female, or actual or analogical popes, either male or female. Cf. below book 2, treatise 1.[137]

And also let me add these things concerning women: authors who have pursued the praise and criticism of women or who have woven together stories of famous or remarkable women are Philipp Bergomas,[138]

135. Voetius, *Politica Ecclesiastica* 1 (Amsterdam, 1663), 859–862. Voetius answers affirmatively to the question whether women, especially celibate women, might usefully be trained beyond elementary competence in catechism.

136. Ibid., 124–182.

137. Ibid., 343–481. This treatise, "De Formulariis, seu Liturgiis, & Ritibus," is the first of four treatises "De Rebus, seu Agendis & Exercitiis Ecclesiasticis."

138. Jacob Philipp Bergomas, *De Claris Selectisque Plurimas Mulieribus* (Ferrara, 1492).

Marconville in French and Dutch,[139] Beverwyck in Dutch,[140] Ludovicus Jacobus à S. Carolo the Carmelite in his *Library of Famous Women*, and Joh. Irenaeus in *Apology for the Feminine Sex* (1544).[141] Those who touch on these matters in other works include commentators on Ecclesiastes 7:28, of whom Lorinus, Pineda, and à Lapide are from the papal camp; and Lavater, Fayus, and Geier from ours.[142] Commentators on Proverbs 22:14 include above all à Lapide in Syracide chaps. 26 and 42; Levinus Lemnius, *On the Miracles of Nature*, book 4, chap. 13;[143] and Bongo, *On the Mystery of Numbers*, no. xi, where women are spoken of quite contemptuously and absurdly.[144]

More authors denouncing women are cited by Hotman in his *Admonition* for his *Franco-Gallia*, pp. 214 and 242;[145] and in Canoniero, *Politics*, book 8, chap. 2.[146] Cf. *Selected Disputations*, part 1, "Supplement on Creation," part 10, p. 807.[147] Add to these Majolus's *Days of the Dog-Star*, colloquium 3;[148] *Alphabet of the imperfections of women*,[149] Vivaldo's *Golden Candelabra*,

139. Jean de Marconville, *De la Bonté et Mauvaistié des Femmes* (Rouen, 1573), in Dutch translation *Der Vrouwen Lof ende Lasteringhe* (Hague, 1609).

140. Jan van Beverwyck, *Van de Uitnementheyt des vrouwelicken Geslachts* (Dordrecht, 1639).

141. Johann Freder (Irenaeus), *Apologia pro Sexu Foemineo* (Frankfurt, 1574).

142. Joannis Lorinus, *Commentarii in Ecclesiasten* (Cologne, 1624), 150–152; Joannis de Pineda, *Commentarii in Ecclesiasten* (Antwerp, 1620), 648–654; à Lapide, *Commentarii in Ecclesiasten* (Antwerp, 1638), 239. Ludwig Lavater, *In Librum Solomonis qui Ecclesiastes inscribitur* (Zurich, 1584), fol. 106–107; Antonius Fayus, *In Librum Salomonis qui inscribitur Ecclesiastes* (Geneva, 1608), 196; Martin Geier, *In Salomonis Regis Israel Ecclesiasten Commentarius* (Leipzig, 1647), 273.

143. Levinus Lemnius, *De Miraculis Occultis Naturae* (Antwerp, 1574), 408–417.

144. Petrus Bungus, *Numerorum Mysteria* (Bergamo, 1599; repr. Hildesheim, 1983), 378–380, 153–154. I omit from this translation the long citation that Voetius includes from this work.

145. Hotman [pseud. Matagonis de Matagonibus], *Monitoriale Adversus Italogalliam sive Antifrancogalliam Antonii Matharelli Alvernogerni* (N.p., 1593). This is a reissue of the 1575 edition (where the pages Voetius cites correspond to 34 and 64) and is Hotman's continuation of the debate discussed in chap. II, n. 21 above.

146. Canoniero, *Dell' Introduzzione alla Politica*, chap. 2.

147. Voetius, *Disputationes Theologicae Selectae* 1 (Utrecht, 1648), 807. Works cited here but not in this text include Hippocrates's *Aphorisms*, Joannes Libaut's *Thesauro remediorum contra morbos foeminarum* (Paris, 1597), Cornelius Agrippa's *In declamatione de foeminis*, Caspar Stiblin's *Coropaedia, sive de Moribus et vita virginum* (Basel, 1555), and Erasmus's *De vidua Christiana* (Basel, 1529).

148. Simon Majolus, *Dies Caniculares, Hoc est, Colloquia Physica Nova et admiranda*, 3d ed. (Mainz, 1614). Colloquium 3 on women, a conversation among a philosopher, a theologian, and an eques deals with many of the issues that captured the imagination of other writers of the age—monster births, hermaphrodites, women changing into men—but also chastity, marriage without cohabitation, and the question whether Pope John VIII was a woman.

149. *Alphabet de l'imperfection et malice des femmes* (Paris, 1617), attributed to Jacques Olivier, bears the inscription from Ecclesiastes 7:28: "De mil hommes i'en ay trouvé un bon, & de toutes les

p. 621;[150] Heidfeld's *Sphinx Theologico-Philosophica,* chap. 17;[151] *Commentaries on the Affections of Women from the Greeks, Latins, and Barbarians.*[152] Finally, Belon, Corbey, Roderigo à Castro, and Ranchin's treatise specifically on women's illnesses.[153]

---

femmes pas une." The work evoked a series of responses and counterresponses as one stage in the *querelle des femmes*.

150. Martin Alfonso Vivaldo, *Candelabrum auream Eccl. S. Dei* (Venice, 1602).

151. Johannes Heidfeld, *Sphinx Theologico-Philosophica* (Herborn, 1621), 481–545. This book, written in question-and-answer format (ask the sphinx!), transmits much common lore about women, supported by many biblical and classical citations.

152. *Gynaeciorum sive de Mulierum Affectibus Commentarii Graecorum, Latinorum, Barbarorum, iam olim & nunc recens editorum,* 3 vols. (Basil, 1586). A fourth volume was added in 1588. This is a collection of medical writings from Hippocrates to the sixteenth century relating to gynecology and illnesses thought to be specific to women.

153. The Belon citation is obscure; Pierre Belon wrote *Pourtraicts d'oyseaux animaux, serpens, herbes, arbres, hommes et femmes d'Arabie et d'Egypte* (Paris, 1557). Hermann Corbey (Corbeius), *Gynaeceium, cum oratione de vulneribus lethalibus & non lethalibus* (1620). Rodrigo à Castro, *De Universa Muliebrum Mororum Medicina,* 2d ed. (Hamburg, 1617). Divided into a theoretical first part and a practical second part, the work professes to provide the practicing physician with all the knowledge necessary for treating women. Typical of the day, Castro relies heavily on classical authorities and seeks to reconcile differences and explain difficult passages within ancient thought. François Ranchin, *Tractatus Duo Posthumi: I. De Morbis ante partum, in partu & post partum; II. De purificatione rerum infectarum post pestilentiam* (Leiden, 1645). Also representative of the day, Ranchin relies heavily on the theory of the humors to explain women's illnesses. For a general discussion of the state of Renaissance medical thought in regard to women, see Maclean, chap. 3.

BIBLIOGRAPHY

EDITORS' INTRODUCTION

Primary Works

Alberti, Leon Battista (1404–1472). *The Family in Renaissance Florence.* Trans. Renée Neu Watkins. Columbia: University of South Carolina Press, 1969.

Ariosto, Ludovico (1474–1533). *Orlando Furioso.* Trans. Barbara Reynolds. 2 vols. New York: Penguin Books, 1975, 1977.

Astell, Mary (1666–1731). *The First English Feminist: Reflections on Marriage and Other Writings.* Ed. and intro. Bridget Hill. New York: St. Martin's Press, 1986.

Barbaro, Francesco (1390–1454). *On Wifely Duties.* Trans. Benjamin Kohl, in Kohl and R. G. Witt, eds., *The Earthly Republic.* Philadelphia: University of Pennsylvania Press, 1978, 179–228. Translation of the preface and book 2.

Boccaccio, Giovanni (1313–1375). *Concerning Famous Women.* Trans. Guido A. Guarino. New Brunswick, NJ: Rutgers University Press, 1963.

———. *Corbaccio or The Labyrinth of Love.* Trans. Anthony K. Cassell. 2d rev. ed. Binghamton, NY: Medieval and Renaissance Texts and Studies, 1993.

Bruni, Leonardo (1370–1444). "On the Study of Literature (1405) to Lady Battista Malatesta of Montefeltro," in *The Humanism of Leonardo Bruni: Selected Texts.* Trans. and intro. Gordon Griffiths, James Hankins, and David Thompson. Binghamton: Medieval and Renaissance Texts and Studies, 1987, 240–251.

Castiglione, Baldassare (1478–1529). *The Courtier.* Trans. George Bull. New York: Viking Penguin, 1967.

Elyot, Thomas (1490–1536). "Courtship," "The Girl with no Interest in Marriage," "The Repentant Girl," "Marriage," "The Abbot and the Learned Lady," and "The New Mother," in *The Colloquies of Erasmus.* Trans. Craig R. Thompson. Chicago: University of Chicago Press, 1965, 86–98, 99–111, 111–114, 114–127, 217–223.

Kempe, Margery (1373–1439). *The Book of Margery Kempe.* Trans. Barry Windsett. New York: Viking Penguin, 1986.

King, Margaret L., and Albert Rabil, Jr., eds. *Her Immaculate Hand: Selected Works by and about the Women Humanists of Quattrocento Italy.* Binghamton: Medieval and Renaissance Texts and Studies, 1983; 2d rev. paper ed., 1991.

Klein, Joan Larsen, ed. *Daughters, Wives, and Widows: Writings by Men about Women and Marriage in England, 1500–1640.* Urbana: University of Illinois Press, 1992.

Knox, John (1505–1572). *The Political Writings of John Knox: The First Blast of the Trumpet against the Monstrous Regiment of Women and Other Selected Works.* Ed. Marvin A. Breslow. Washington: Folger Shakespeare Library, 1985.

Kors, Alan C., and Edward Peters, eds. *Witchcraft in Europe, 1100–1700: A Documentary History.* Philadelphia: University of Pennsylvania Press, 1972.

Krämer, Heinrich, and Jacob Sprenger. *Malleus Maleficarum* (ca. 1487). Trans. Montague Summers. London: Pushkin Press, 1928; repr. New York: Dover, 1971. The "Hammer of Witches," a convenient source for all the misogynistic commonplaces on the eve of the sixteenth century, and an important text in the witch craze of the following centuries.

de Lorris, William, and Jean de Meun. *The Romance of the Rose.* Trans. Charles Dahlbert. Princeton: Princeton University Press, 1971; repr. Hanover, NH: University Press of New England, 1983.

de Navarre, Marguerite (1492–1549). *The Heptameron.* Trans. P. A. Chilton. New York: Viking Penguin, 1984.

de Pizan, Christine (1365–1431). *The Book of the City of Ladies.* Trans. Earl Jeffrey Richards. Foreword Marina Warner. New York: Persea Books, 1982.

_____. *The Treasury of the City of Ladies.* Trans. Sarah Lawson. New York: Viking Penguin, 1985. Also trans. and intro. Charity Cannon Willard; ed. and intro. Madeleine P. Cosman. New York: Persea Book, 1989.

Spenser, Edmund (1552–1599). *The Faerie Queene.* Ed. Thomas P. Roche, Jr. with the assistance of C. Patrick O'Donnell, Jr. New Haven: Yale University Press, 1978.

Teresa of Avila, Saint (1515–1582). *The Life of Saint Teresa of Avila by Herself.* Trans. J. M. Cohen. New York: Viking Penguin, 1957.

Vives, Juan Luis (1492–1540). *The Instruction of the Christian Woman.* Trans. Rycharde Hyrde. London, 1524, 1557.

Weyer, Johann (1515–1588). *Witches, Devils, and Doctors in the Renaissance: Johann Weyer, De praestigiis daemonum.* Ed. George Mora with Benjamin G. Kohl, Erik Midelfort, and Helen Bacon. Trans. John Shea. Binghamton: Medieval and Renaissance Texts and Studies, 1991.

Wilson, Katharina M., ed. *Medieval Women Writers.* Athens: University of Georgia Press, 1984.

_____. *Women Writers of the Renaissance and Reformation.* Athens: University of Georgia Press, 1987.

Wilson, Katharina M., and Frank J. Warnke, eds. *Women Writers of the Seventeenth Century.* Athens: University of Georgia Press, 1989.

Secondary Works: The Misogynist Tradition

Bloch, R. Howard. *Medieval Misogyny and the Invention of Western Romantic Love.* Chicago: University of Chicago Press, 1991.

Clark, Elizabeth A. *Ascetic Piety and Women's Faith: Essays on Late Ancient Christianity.* Lewiston, NY: Edwin Mellen Press, 1986.

Dixon, Suzanne. *The Roman Family.* Baltimore: Johns Hopkins University Press, 1992.

Gardner, Jane F. *Women in Roman Law and Society.* Bloomington: Indiana University Press, 1986.

Horowitz, Maryanne Cline. "Aristotle and Woman," *Journal of the History of Biology,* 9 (1976): 183–213.

Lochrie, Karma. *Margery Kempe and Translations of the Flesh.* Philadelphia: University of Pennsylvania Press, 1992.

Maclean, Ian. *The Renaissance Notion of Woman: A Study of the Fortunes of Scholasticism and Medical Science in European Intellectual Life.* Cambridge: Cambridge University Press, 1980.

Okin, Susan Moller. *Women in Western Political Thought.* Princeton: Princeton University Press, 1979.

Pagels, Elaine. *Adam, Eve, and the Serpent.* New York: HarperCollins, 1988.

Pomeroy, Sarah B. *Goddesses, Whores, Wives, and Slaves: Women in Classical Antiquity.* New York: Schocken Books, 1976.

Tetel, Marcel. *Marguerite de Navarre's Heptameron: Themes, Languages, and Structure.* Durham, NC: Duke University Press, 1973.

Treggiari, Susan. *Roman Marriage: Iusti Coniuges from the Time of Cicero to the Time of Ulpian.* Oxford: Oxford University Press, 1991.

Walsh, William T. *St. Teresa of Avila: A Biography.* Rockford, IL: TAN Books & Publications, 1987.

Warner, Marina. *Alone of All Her Sex: The Myth and the Cult of the Virgin Mary.* New York: Knopf, 1976.

Secondary Works: The Other Voice

Beilin, Elaine V. *Redeeming Eve: Women Writers of the English Renaissance.* Princeton: Princeton University Press, 1987.

Benson, Pamela Joseph. *The Invention of Renaissance Woman: The Challenge of Female Independence in the Literature and Thought of Italy and England.* University Park: Pennsylvania State University Press, 1992.

Davis, Natalie Zemon. *Society and Culture in Early Modern France.* Stanford: Stanford University Press, 1975. Especially chapters 3 and 5.

Ferguson, Margaret W., Maureen Quilligan, and Nancy J. Vickers, eds. *Rewriting the Renaissance: The Discourses of Sexual Difference in Early Modern Europe.* Chicago: University of Chicago Press, 1987.

A History of Women in the West. Vol. 1: *From Ancient Goddesses to Christian Saints.* Ed. Pauline Schmitt Pantel. Cambridge, MA: Harvard University Press, 1992. Vol. 2: *Silence of the Middle Ages.* Ed. Christiane Klapisch-Zuber. Cambridge: Harvard University Press, 1992. Vol. 3: *Renaissance and Enlightenment Paradoxes.* Ed. Natalie Zemon Davis and Arlette Farge. Cambridge: Harvard University Press, 1993.

Herlihy, David. "Did Women Have a Renaissance? A Reconsideration," *Medievalia et Humanistica,* n.s. 13 (1985): 1–22.

Hull, Suzanne W. *Chaste, Silent, and Obedient: English Books for Women, 1475–1640.* San Marino, CA: Huntington Library, 1982.

Jordan, Constance. *Renaissance Feminism: Literary Texts and Political Models.* Ithaca: Cornell University Press, 1990.

Kelly, Joan. "Did Women Have a Renaissance?" in her *Women, History and Theory.* Chicago: University of Chicago Press, 1984. Also in Renate Bridenthal, Claudia Koonz, and Susan M. Stuard, eds. *Becoming Visible: Women in European History.* 2d ed. Boston: Houghton Mifflin, 1987, 175–202.

_____. "Early Feminist Theory and the Querelle des Femmes," in *Women, History, and Theory.*

Kelso, Ruth. *Doctrine for the Lady of the Renaissance.* Foreword by Katharine M. Rogers. Urbana: University of Illinois Press, 1956, 1978.

King, Margaret L. *Women of the Renaissance.* Foreword by Catharine R. Stimpson. Chicago: University of Chicago Press, 1991.

Laqueur, Thomas. *Making Sex: Body and Gender from the Greeks to Freud.* Cambridge, MA: Harvard University Press, 1990.

Lerner, Gerda. *Creation of Feminist Consciousness, 1000–1870.* New York: Oxford University Press, 1994.

Maclean, Ian. *Woman Triumphant: Feminism in French Literature, 1610–1652.* Oxford: Clarendon Press, 1977.

Matter, E. Ann, and John Coakley, eds. *Creative Women in Medieval and Early Modern Italy.* Philadelphia: University of Pennsylvania Press, 1994. (Sequel to the Monson collection, immediately below)

Monson, Craig A., ed. *The Crannied Wall: Women, Religion, and the Arts in Early Modern Europe.* Ann Arbor: University of Michigan Press, 1992.

Rose, Mary Beth, ed. *Women in the Middle Ages and the Renaissance: Literary and Historical Perspectives.* Syracuse: Syracuse University Press, 1986.

Stuard, Susan M., "The Dominion of Gender: Women's Fortunes in the High Middle Ages." In Renate Bridenthal, Claudia Koonz, and Susan M. Stuard, eds., *Becoming Visible: Women in European History.* 2d ed. Boston: Houghton Mifflin, 1987, 153–172.

Wiesner, Merry E. *Women and Gender in Early Modern Europe.* Cambridge: Cambridge University Press, 1993.

Willard, Charity Cannon. *Christine de Pizan: Her Life and Works.* New York: Persea Books, 1984.

Wilson, Katharina, ed. *An Encyclopedia of Continental Women Writers.* New York: Garland, 1991.

ANNA MARIA VAN SCHURMAN

Baar, Mirjam de, et al. *Choosing the Better Part: Anna Maria van Schurman (1607–1678).* Dordrecht: Kluwer Academic Publishers, 1996. Originally published in Dutch as *Anna Maria van Schurman (1607–1678): Een uitzonderlijk geleerde vrouw.* Zutphen: Walburg Pers, 1992.

Beek, Pieta van. *Verbastert Christendom: Nederlandse gedichten van Anna Maria van Schurman (1607–1678).* Houten: Den Hertog, 1992.

Birch, Una [Constance Pope-Hennessy]. *Anna Maria van Schurman: Artist, Scholar, Saint.* London, 1909.

Bovenschen, Silvia. *Die imaginierte Weiblichkeit.* Frankfurt/M: Suhrkamp Verlag, 1979.

Douma, Anna M. H. *Anna Maria van Schurman en de studie der vrouw.* Amsterdam, 1924.

Gössmann, Elisabeth, ed. *Das Wohlgelahrte Frauenzimmer.* Archiv für philosophie- und theologiegeschichtliche Frauenforschung, 1. Munich, 1984.

Irwin, Joyce. "Anna Maria van Schurman: From Feminism to Pietism." *Church History* 46 (1977): 48–62.

_____. "Anna Maria van Schurman. The Star of Utrecht (1607–1678)," in J. R. Brink, ed., *Female Scholars: A Tradition of Learned Women before 1800.* Montreal: Eden Press, 1980, 68–85.

_____. "Anna Maria van Schurman: The Learned Maid," in Katharina M. Wilson, ed., *Women Writers of the Seventeenth Century.* Athens: University of Georgia Press, 1989, 164–185.

_____. "Anna Maria van Schurman and Antoinette Bourignon: Contrasting Examples of Seventeenth-Century Pietism." *Church History* 60 (September 1991): 301–315.

Linde, S. van der. "Anna Maria van Schurman en haar Eucleria." *Theologia Reformata* 21 (1978): 117–145.

Mülhaupt, Erwin. "Anna Maria von Schürmann, eine Rheinländerin zwischen zwei Frauenleitbildern." *Monatshefte für evangelische Kirchengeschichte des Rheinlandes* 19 (1970): 149–161.

Saxby, Trevor J. *The Quest for the New Jerusalem: Jean de Labadie and the Labadists, 1610–1744.* Dordrecht: Martinus Nijhoff, 1987.

Schotel, G. D. J. *Anna Maria van Schurman.* 's-Hertogenbosch, 1853.

Schurman, Anna Maria van. *Amica Dissertatio inter Annam Mariam Schurmanniam et Andr. Rivetum de capacitate ingenii muliebris ad scientias.* Paris, 1638. French translation: *Question célèbre, s'il est nécessaire ou non que les filles soient scavantes?* Paris, 1646. English translation: *The Learned Maid, Or, Whether a Maid May Be a Scholar?* Leiden, 1639.

_____. *De vitae termino.* Leiden, 1639. Dutch version: *Paelsteen van den tijt onzes levens.* Dordrecht, 1639.

_____. *Opuscula hebraea, graeca, latina, gallica, prosaica et metrica.* Leiden, 1648.

_____. *Eukleria, seu melioris partis electio.* Pt. 1: Altona, 1673; pt. 2: Amsterdam, 1685. Dutch translation: *Eucleria of Uitkiezing van het Beste Deel.* Amsterdam, 1684 (pts. 1 and 2).

Stighelen, Katlijne Van der. *Anna Maria van Schurman (1607–1678) of 'Hoe hooge dat een maeght kan in de konsten stijgen.'* Leuven: Universitaire Pers, 1987.

Wallmann, Johannes. *Philipp Jakob Spener und die Anfänge des Pietismus.* 2d ed. Tübingen: J. C. B. Mohr [Paul Siebeck], 1986. Originally published Tübingen, 1970.

Winsemius, Dieuwke. *Het grote geheim van Anna Maria van Schuurman.* Kampen, 1978.

INDEX

Accaiuoli, Andrea, xxi
Adam; degree of responsibility for the
    Fall, xii, xxiv; implications of crea-
    tion prior to Eve, xi–xii; in *Querelle
    des Femmes,* xix
Agrippa, Henricus Cornelius, xix, xx;
    *On the Nobility and Preeminence of the
    Female Sex,* xix, xxi
Alberti, Leon Battista, *On the Family,* xix
Albina, 52
Alexander the Great, 57
Alva, Duke of, 4, 123n
Amazons, xxiii. *See also* women
Ames, William, 4
ancient Rome: legal position of women
    in, x–xi
androgynous creation, theory of,
    106–7
Ann, Princess of Denmark, xxi
Anne of Brittany, Queen of France, xxi
Aristotelianism, 6, 11, 16, 18, 100n
Aristotle, viii–ix, 16, 18, 28, 30, 32, 33,
    45, 67, 83, 90, 100, 101, 103, 105,
    119, 121
Arnold, Gottfried, 15
arts and sciences. *See* humanistic edu-
    cation
arts, creative, 5–6, 27, 70, 82–84,
    86–87
Astell, Mary, xxii, xxiv; *Serious Proposal
    to the Ladies for the Advancement of Their
    True and Greatest Interest,* xxi

astrology, 59
Augustine, St., xii, 14, 59, 67, 78, 93,
    113, 119, 133
Averroes, 103

Barbaro, Francesco, *On Marriage,*
    xviii–xix, xxiv
Basil the Great, 31, 43
Beverwyck, Jan van (Beverovicius),
    5–6, 18, 20, 126, 136
Boccaccio, Giovanni, xxi
Bodin, Jean, xx
Bonaventure, 100, 100n, 105, 109
Bourignon, Antoinette, 15
Bruni, Leonardo, xxiv
Buxtorf, Johannes, 8

Cajetan (Thomas de Vio), 100, 102–3,
    103, 106, 113
Calvin, John, 3, 4, 21n
Calvinism, 3, 8, 9, 16–19
Capra, Galeazzo Flavio, *On the Excel-
    lence and Dignity of Women,* xix
Cassandra, 52
Castiglione, Baldassare, *Book of the
    Courtier;* and *Querelle des Femmes,* xviii
catalogues of women. *See* women,
    notable
Catherine de' Medici, xxiii
Catherine of Aragon, wife of Henry
    VIII, xxi
Cats, Jacob, 5, 20

Cereta, Laura, xxi
Christine, Queen, 7
Chrysostom, St. John, 120
Cicero, 43
civic affairs. *See* public affairs
Clement of Alexandria, 31
Cleobulina, 52
Cocceius, Johannes, 17
Col, Gontier, and the *Querelle des
    Femmes,* xviii
Cornelia, 52
creation myth, xi–xii. *See also* Adam,
    Eve
Cunitia, Maria, 127

Deborah, 53, 122, 124, 134
Descartes, René, 6–7, 16–17, 20–21
d'Este, Ercole I, duke of Ferrara, xxi
d'Ewes, Sir Simonds, 13, 68n, 69n
domestic affairs, 12, 25, 36, 43–44, 50,
    51, 68, 120–21
Dort, Synod of, 2, 15, 128n
DuLignon, Pierre, 9, 73
Dutch Reformed Church, 2, 3, 4, 8, 19

ecclesiastical status of women, 130,
    134–35. *See also* public affairs
education of women, 3, 6, 9–12,
    25–58, 126–28; by private tutor,
    35, 53, 81; in public schools, 3; in
    women's colleges, 35, 53
Eleanora of Aragon, wife of Ercole I
    d'Este, duke of Ferrara, xxi
Elizabeth of the Palatinate, Princess, 7,
    9, 12, 41, 57, 66, 69, 126n
Elizabeth, Queen of England, xxiii, 58,
    60, 68, 80n, 123–24, 131, 135
Elpis, 127
Elyot, Sir Thomas, *Defence of Good
    Women,* xxiii
Enonia, 52
Equicola, Mario, *On Women,* xix, xxi
Erasmus, xix, 28, 33, 44, 80, 134
Eudocia, 52, 126
Eve: degree of responsibility for Fall,
    xii, xxiv; implications of creation
    subsequent to Adam, xi–xii; in
    Querelle des Femmes, xix

exempla: of women famed for learning
    or virtue, xvii–xviii

Fedele, Cassandra, xx–xxi
Fonte, Moderata [Modesta da Pozzo],
    xxii
Francke, August Hermann, 14

Goggio, Bartolomeo, *In Praise of Women,*
    xix, xxi
Gournay, Marie le Jars de, xxiv, 13, 44,
    51, 55, 70, 71
Gregory of Nazianzus, St. 29
Grey, Lady Jane, 47–48, 52–53, 58, 60
Guazzo, Stefano, xx
Guillaume de Lorris, *Romance de la Rose,*
    xiii

Harff, Eva van, 4, 5, 87
Heidelberg Catechism, 79–80, 128n
Heloise, 127
heresy, 2, 11, 19, 31–32; women and,
    133–34
hermaphrodites, 106, 136n
history, study of, 11, 25, 27, 44, 46,
    47, 57–59, 80, 90, 92
Homer, 81
Honthorst, Gerard, 12, 83
Hortensia, 52
humanism, xv–xvi; women and,
    xx–xxi, xxv
humanistic education, 3–4, 10–11,
    25–27, 35–37, 47, 50, 81, 87; van-
    ity of, 78–79, 84–85, 90–93. *See also*
    arts, creative; education of women;
    history, study of; languages, study
    of; natural sciences; physics; poetry
humors, ix
Huygens, Constantijn, 5, 20, 86

Jean de Meun, *Romance of the Rose,* xiii,
    xviii
Jerome, xii, 18, 71, 110, 114, 134
Jews, 3, 82, 92, 134. *See also* Rabbinic
    interpretation
Joan of Arc, 125
Juan II, king of Castile, xxi

Juan Rodríguez de la Camera, *Triumph of Women*, xviii
Juan Rodríguez del Padron. *See* Juan Rodríguez de la Camera
Judaism, 19, 107

Knox, John, *First Blast of the Trumpet against the Monstrous Regiment of Women*, xxiii
Krämer, Heinrich, *The Hammer of Witches*, xix–xx

Labadie, Jean de, 8, 9, 17, 73, 74, 76
Labadism, 14–15, 73–77
Laelia, 52
languages, study of, 3–4, 5–6, 10–11, 13, 16, 25, 27, 41, 47–48, 50, 53–54, 68, 70–71, 81–82, 90–91; Greek, 5, 11, 13, 27, 68, 70, 81–82, 90–91, 127; Hebrew, 5, 7, 8, 11, 13, 27, 71, 90–91; Latin, 5, 13, 71, 81–82, 127
Lansberg, Maria, 127–28
Latin language, xvi, xvii, xxv
law: biblical or divine, 17, 44, 114, 118–19, 122–23, 128–29; natural, 101, 117–18, 122–23, 128–29; Roman, x–xi, 43, 118–19, 120–21; Islamic, 120; Salic, 123n; trial, 27
leisure, 43, 44, 51, 55
liberal arts. *See* humanistic education
Luna, Alvaro de, xvii, xxi
Luther, Martin, 4
Lyra, Nicholas of, 112

Makin, Bathsua, 13–14, 67, 68
Margaret, duchess of Austria, xxi
Marinella, Lucrezia, 10, 55
Mary, mother of Jesus, 98, 104
Mary, Queen of England, 80n, 123
Mathéolus, *Lamentations*, xiii–xiv, xvi
misogyny, vii; in Christian theology, xi–xii; in Greek philosophy, viii–x; in medieval literature, xii–xiii; in Roman Law, x–xi. *See also Querelle des Femmes*
Molitur, Ulrich, xx
Montreuil, Jean de, xviii

Moor, Lady Dorothy, 13, 60, 61
moral virtue, 10–11, 26, 30, 47, 77, 90
Morata, Olympia, xxi, 52–53
More, Thomas, 44
Moulin, Mlle du, 69
Mutia, 52

natural sciences, 26, 45, 59, 90, 127
Nogarola, Isotta, xx, xxiv

Paul, St. 18, 30, 50, 51, 61, 74, 75, 77, 85, 89, 92, 93, 98, 117, 131, 132, 135
Paula, 52
Pella, 52
Penn, William, 15
Petersen, Johann, 15
physics, 27, 59
Pietism, 14, 15, 17
Pizan, Christine de, xvi–xvii, xxii, xxv; and *Querelle des Femmes*, xviii; *Book of the City of Ladies*, xvi–xviii, xxi; *Treasure of the City of Ladies*, xxi
Plato, ix, 11, 33, 98, 107, 124n, 125
Pliny, 105, 124, 129
poetry, 6, 7, 11, 27, 81–82, 127, 128
Precisianism, 17, 118n
Proba Falconia, 52, 126–27
procreation, women's role in, 18, 100–101, 103–5
prolepsis, 113–15
public affairs, women and, 11, 18, 29, 34, 36, 43, 46, 50–51, 53, 84, 92, 122–23, 131, 134–35

Querelle des Femmes, xvii–xix, 19, 97–100, 137n

Rabbinic interpretation, 107, 110, 114
reason, use of, 11–12, 17, 27, 31, 33, 43, 47, 48, 77, 93, 94, 98, 101–2, 105, 110, 116
Reformation, 2, 76
regeneration, need for, 15, 88–89, 108
Remonstrants, 2, 16, 128
Rémy, Nicholas, xx
Renaissance, 2, 3, 18
rhetoric: and women, xxiv

Ribera, Pietro Paolo de, xvii
Rivet, André, 5, 6, 10–12, 25, 39–56,
    64, 65, 71, 87, 90, 93, 114, 115
Rohan, Anne de, 64–65

Sabbath, 17, 18, 115
scholasticism, 2, 12, 17–19, 27, 66–67,
    93–94, 97, 103, 104–5
Schurman, Anna Maria van, xxiv,
    4–21, 126; writings, 39–94
Schurman, Frederik van, 4, 5, 81, 87
Schurman, Hendrik Frederik, 4, 81
Schurman, Johan Godschalk, 4, 5, 8,
    61, 81
Schurman, Willem, 4, 83n
Schütz, Johann Jakob, 15
sectarianism, 8, 17
Sempronia, 52
Seneca, 30, 43, 51, 81, 85
Spanheim, Frederick, 12
Spener, Philipp Jakob, 15
Spenser, Edmund, *Faerie Queene*, xxiv
Sprenger, Jacob, *The Hammer of Witches*,
    xix–xx
superstition, women and, 132–33

Tertullian, xii
Thomas à Kempis, 85
Thomas Aquinas, ix–x, xii, 4, 94, 100,
    102, 103–5, 109

uterus (*hystera*), in Greek psychology,
    ix
Utrecht, 4, 5, 6, 16; guild of painters,
    6; university, 5

Valeria, 52
Virgil, 81, 124–25
Virgin Mary, xii
Visscher, Anna Roemer, 5
Vives, Juan Luis (Ludovico), xxi, xxiv,
    12, 51, 55
Voetius, Gisbertus (Gijsbert Voet), 4,
    5, 6–7, 8, 12, 16–21, 87; writings,
    97–141

war, women and, 49n, 53, 123–25
Weyer, Johann, xx
wife beating, 119–22
witchcraft, xix–xx
woman: whether a misbegotten male,
    100–103; whether created in image
    of God, 98, 107–9; whether created
    on sixth or seventh day, 109–17
women: catalogues of, 6, 16, 18, 20,
    126, 135–36; and chastity,
    xxi–xxiii; in Christian thought,
    xi–xii; and the church, xv; and
    dress, xxiv; in Greek thought,
    viii–x; and learning, xx–xxi,
    xxiv–xxv; in medieval literature,
    xii–xiv; notable, 52–53, 126–29;
    and power, xxiii–xxiv; in Roman
    law, x–xi; speech, xxiv; and virtue,
    xxi–xxii; and warfare, xxiii; and
    work, xiv–xv; as writers, xx–xxi.
    See also *Querelle des Femmes*

Yvon, Pierre, 7, 8, 9, 16, 20, 73

Zenobia, 52

DATE DUE
REMINDER

"/15/02		

Please do not remove
this date due slip.